LANGUAGE MATTERS

Language Matters

Laurie Bauer, Janet Holmes and Paul Warren

palgrave
macmillan

First published 2006 by
PALGRAVE MACMILLAN
Houndmills, Basingstoke, Hampshire RG21 6XS and
175 Fifth Avenue, New York, N.Y. 10010
Companies and representatives throughout the world

PALGRAVE MACMILLAN is the global academic imprint of the Palgrave Macmillan division of St. Martin's Press, LLC and of Palgrave Macmillan Ltd. Macmillan® is a registered trademark in the United States, United Kingdom and other countries. Palgrave is a reg..tered trademark in the European Union and other countries.

ISBN-13: 978–1–4039–3628–8
ISBN-10: 1–4039–3628–5

This book is printed on paper suitable for recycling and made from fully managed and sustained forest sources. Logging, pulping and manufacturing processes are expected to conform to the environmental regulations of the country of origin.

A catalogue record for this book is available from the British Library.

A catalog record for this book is available from the Library of Congress.

10 9 8 7 6 5 4
15 14 13 12 11 10 09 08

Printed and bound in Great Britain by Cromwell Press Ltd, Trowbridge, Wiltshire.

For our long-suffering families

Contents

List of Boxes   viii
List of Figures   ix
List of Tables   x
Preface   xi
Acknowledgements   xii

Introduction   1

Part I   Origin and Development of Language
  1   Where Does Language Come From?   7
  2   Why Don't We All Talk the Same?   18
  3   Things Ain't What They Used to Be   26
  4   Linguistic Relations   36
  5   Bee Talk and Monkey Chatter   49

Part II   Language Structures
  6   How Do You Spell *Accommodation*?   61
  7   How Many Words Do the Eskimos Use?   72
  8   Going On and On: the Never-ending Story   82
  9   Primitive Languages   92
 10   Who Needs Grammar?   102
 11   Mobile Messages   112

Part III   Language and Society
 12   How Do We Lose Languages and Does It Matter?   125
 13   What Shall I Call You?   135
 14   Do Women and Men Speak Differently?   146
 15   Sexist Language and Linguistic Sexism   157
 16   What Language Do You Use to Your Grandmother?   169
 17   Why Can't People in Birmingham Talk Right?   180

Part IV   Language, Brain and Mind
 18   Why My Feets Hurted?   193
 19   Does Bilingualism Rot the Brain?   203
 20   Building Another Tongue   213
 21   You've Tasted the Whole Worm   222
 22   Is Language a Strait-jacket?   231
 23   When Language Breaks Down   241

Conclusion: Who Cares about Language?   250

Language Index   259
General Index   262

List of Boxes

1.1	Word-classes	8
1.2	Ferdinand de Saussure	15
3.1	Glosses	28
3.2	Replacing one word by another	32
6.1	George Bernard Shaw	62
6.2	'Making the letter say its name'	66
6.3	'<i> before <e> except after <c>'	67
6.4	Pronoun	69
7.1	'Just plain snow'	74
7.2	'Word'	77
8.1	What do you produce from memory?	87
10.1	Noam Chomsky	103
10.2	Grammatical terms	105
12.1	Terms for language loss and revival	126
14.1	Deborah Tannen	146
14.2	Grammatical features that males use more than females	148
14.3	Folk reactions to women's speech	151
15.1	The sexist litmus test story	160
16.1	Some linguistic features of Patois or Jamaican Creole	174
17.1	Accent vs. dialect	180
17.2	Scouse accent kills Lisa's Dublin dream	188
18.1	Terminology of language acquisition	194
19.1	Parental strategies	206
19.2	Code-switching	209
19.3	Tangrams	210
22.1	Edward Sapir	233
22.2	Benjamin Lee Whorf	233

List of Figures

1.1	Schematic sagital section through the heads of 3 mammals	13
4.1	A fictitious family tree	37
4.2	A species tree	38
4.3	The Indo-European language family	42
4.4	The Polynesian language family	44
11.1	Word length (in letters) plotted against frequency of occurrence (per million words) for a set of 26 English words	114
11.2	Dvorak keyboard layout	118
13.1	The solidarity dimension	136
13.2	The status dimension	138
14.1	Percentage vernacular (n) pronunciation by women and men in a New Zealand speech community	147
17.1	Example of an accent evaluation scale	182
18.1	Vocabulary size over the first 36 months	198
20.1	Average grammar scores in English for US immigrants from Korea and China, by age of arrival	217
21.1	'They fired the caterpillar'	227
23.1	A sketch of the relationship between a dictionary entry and language skills	245
23.2	Sketch of the left hemisphere of the human brain	246
23.3	The 'Cookie Theft' picture from the Boston Diagnostic Aphasia Exam	247

List of Tables

4.1	Corresponding words in some European languages	36
4.2	The present subjunctive of the verb meaning 'give' in three languages	41
4.3	Words for numbers in several languages	43
4.4	Comparing Maori and Samoan	45
4.5	Comparing four varieties	47
7 1	Compounds from simpler words	76
7.2	The paradigm for the French verb *marcher* 'to walk'	76
7.3	West Greenlandic forms for frozen water	78
8.1	Examples of sentences cited from memory	87
9.1	What languages are called 'primitive'?	93
10.1	Basic word order in a selection of languages	106
10.2	Word order and word endings in German	106
11.1	Digit–letter correspondences on telephone keypads	115
11.2	Letter frequency rankings and Scrabble scores	119
13.1	Terms of insult	142
15.1	Non-parallel terms	162
18.1	Development of child vocabulary	197
18.2	Acquisition stages for English past tenses and plural	199
18.3	Acquisition stages for English wh-questions	200
20 1	Scales of difficulty in learning a second language, as developed in the Contrastive Analysis approach	219
20.2	Developmental sequence of L2 question formation	220
21.1	Example stimuli from spoonerism experiments	225
22.1	Berlin and Kay's hierarchy of colour terms	236
22.2	The numbers 1–20 in four languages	237

Preface

Although all three authors have worked closely together in creating this book, individuals have taken primary responsibility for the different chapters, usually in line with the lectures given in the course on which this work is based. These primary responsibilities are as follows:

Laurie Bauer	Chapters 1–9, the Introduction, the Conclusion
Janet Holmes	Chapters 12–17
Paul Warren	Chapters 10–11, 18–23

We should like to thank Helen Ainsworth for editorial assistance on the final draft of the typescript.

L.B.
J.H.
P.W.

Acknowledgements

The authors and publisher would like to thank the following for permission to reproduce copyright material:

AKG Images, London, for the photograph of Ferdinand de Saussure (on p. 15); the photograph of George Bernard Shaw (on p. 62);

CORBIS for the photograph of Noam Chomsky (on p. 103);

The Irish Post, for 'Scouse Accent Kills Lisa's Dublin Dream', *The Irish Post*, 17 March 2001 (on p. 188);

Pro-Ed, Inc., for 'The Cookie Theft' (on p. 247), from Goodglass, Kaplan and Barresi, *Boston Diagnostic Aphasis Examination*, 3rd edn (1983), Pro-Ed, Inc.; used with permission of Pro-Ed, Inc.

Dr. Seuss Enterprises, L.P., for the extract from *Fox in Sox* by Dr. Seuss (1965). © Fox in Sox™ and © Dr. Seuss Enterprises, L.P. 1965, renewed 1993. All rights reserved; reproduced by permission of Random House Children's Books, a division of Random House, Inc.;

Deborah Tannen for permission to reproduce the photograph on p. 146;

University of California Press, for Aoki, *Nez Perce Texts* (1979) on p. 97; © 1979 The Regents of the University of California; reproduced by permission of University of California Press;

Yale University Library, Manuscripts and Archives Dept., for the photograph of Benjamin Lee Whorf (on p. 233).

Introduction

What's the matter?

Language surrounds us from before we are born. Even in the womb you can hear the rhythms and intonation of your mother tongue, if not the detail of the individual consonants and vowels. By the time you are five, you are using language so complex that modern computers still can't cope with it, and the kind of machine language that Arthur C. Clarke predicted for HAL in *2001* still seems as far off now as it did when the book was written in 1968. Whether you work in a university or on a farm, in an office or down a mine, you use language all day long, and when you sleep, you dream in language. You find it virtually impossible to think without using language.

Yet most people know virtually nothing about language as a phenomenon or about the way in which their own language works. There are two aspects of this.

The first is that questions about the way languages work or what languages there are in the world are not seen as sexy topics for *Trivial Pursuit* or *Who Wants to Be a Millionaire?* They have not been taught in schools for some time, and most adults in the English-speaking world are extremely ignorant about them.

The second is that the way language functions is extremely complex. We have discovered a lot about the complexities in the last hundred years or so, but we certainly do not fully understand how language works. This makes language interesting for the researcher, but difficult for the lay person to discuss. There are many things which we still do not know about, and some of those will be mentioned in this book.

Unfortunately, some people think that they do know everything about the way in which language (or English) works. They are prepared to tell you that X is right and Y is wrong, apparently on the basis of having spoken English (well, according to their own perceptions) for a number of years. This is equivalent to thinking you know how the internal combustion engine works on the basis of having driven a car for several years. If your car needs to be checked, you see a mechanic, not a Sunday driver; if you want to know about language, you need to consult a linguist, not a journalist. Yet the people who claim to have the answers gain a large following, perhaps because they give clear right/wrong answers which everyone can understand (even if they are incorrect). We often find things stated with certainty in the pages of popular publications that are demonstrably wrong or where the real complexities of the issues are simply not recognized. We can call these things LANGUAGE MYTHS, things which competent members of our culture believe about language, but which language specialists either believe to be wrong or to be so oversimplified as to be laughable. These vary from such relatively simple things as, 'Double negatives are wrong', through statements like, 'Italians talk too fast' to statements such as, 'Italian is a beautiful language but German is an ugly one' (see Bauer and Trudgill 1998). We will try to bring some of these myths out into the open in this book.

In some cases, people are either aware that there might be some myths out there, or aware of their ignorance, and then they do ask. Linguists are always being asked questions about language by their students, colleagues and members of the public. In many cases, the best answer to the question is: 'Have you tried looking it up?' Most people aren't aware of the richness of the resources available, and certainly don't know which to use. One such question asked of one of the authors recently was when the word *scam* meaning 'fraud' came into English (according to the *Oxford English Dictionary* it is first recorded in 1964.) That was an unusual question. Many of the questions we are asked we hear frequently: How many languages are there? Why don't we all use a single language? and so on. We will try to answer some of those questions in this book.

But we also want to kindle in you something of the sense of wonder that we, as professional linguists, feel when faced with language. We are professional linguists, on the whole, because we find language fascinating not only on the level of finding statements like (1) and (2) interesting, but in being in awe of the human capacity to deal so quickly with the amount of complex material which language forces us to process.

(1)   There is no English word which really corresponds to German *gemütlich*.

(2)   There are some languages which have no words for *yes* and *no*.

For example, in order to speak at a normal rate you need to send some 1400 motor commands to the muscles which operate the organs of speech every second. This is a lot faster and more accurate than is required of a concert pianist (Laver 1994: 1). How do we ever manage to sort out the difference between *Time flies like an arrow* and *Fruit flies like a banana*, which have a similar superficial form, but which differ quite radically in their interpretation?

So it is our intention to take you on a tour of language as a phenomenon. We will have to be selective in what we show you, sticking to some of the highlights, and not giving you too much detail: in most cases we will give you a brief chapter on something that you could spend six weeks on without exhausting the material. We will provide signposts for you to go and find out more for yourselves, and we hope you will do that. This book is not the only source of information.

How this book works

We have arranged the material in the book in four main themes. Within the themes the chapters may be only loosely connected to each other, though you will find certain points repeated in different chapters as we consider them from different angles. Although the themes and the chapters are presented in a linear order which allows you to read straight through from beginning to end, the relative order of the sections is rarely of particular importance. You should not find yourself disadvantaged if you choose to read sections or chapters in a different order from the one in which they are presented. Feel free to dip in!

The chapters are loosely built round a standard format. First we set out the topic of the chapter. Then we discuss the various points that lie at the centre of the chapter. In such short chapters we can, of course, only be selective in what we discuss, and can do little more than provide a basic introduction to the topic under discussion. To show you how that topic might develop we have a section at the end of each chapter called 'Where next?' This may point you to related topics or talk about the kind of background in linguistics you would need to acquire if you wanted to go into the topic in great depth. At the end of this section we provide some points to ponder – questions for you to consider in the light of the exposition of the chapter or to discuss with classmates if you are using this as a textbook. Finally, we provide a section with a list of the works we have referred to in the course of the chapter and other reading which we recommend if you want to take matters further. Usually we have chosen fairly elementary materials for you to start on, but sometimes we direct you to more complex material as well, especially where that is readable without too much specialized knowledge.

Where next?

As you work through this book, whether on your own or with the help of a teacher and classmates, we keep challenging you to think about where the topics we are introducing might lead you. We have tried to make this book as user-friendly as possible by missing out much of the formalism which beginners frequently find daunting in introductory linguistics classes. In order to explore the questions we raise in greater depth, though, you will need to know much more about linguistics, including its formal and notational aspects. We hope that dealing with language study in this relatively humanistic context will inspire you to move on to more rigorous linguistic study and, perhaps, one day, to do your own bit in helping to answer some of the unanswered problems about language.

SOME POINTS TO PONDER

▶ If there is no English word which corresponds exactly to German *gemütlich*, how can we translate successfully from German to English? If we assume we can translate successfully between any pair of languages, what does this imply about different languages? (Incidentally, note that we italicize words and phrases which we are mentioning as examples, a standard piece of notation for linguistics.)

▶ Alan Turing suggested that a machine is intelligent if a human being can talk to it and not realize that they are not talking to another human. What kinds of things can you do which your computer cannot do when it comes to using language?

▶ If you are busy sending 1400 messages to your articulators every second while you speak, how do you manage to think while you speak? What does this tell us about language?

READING AND REFERENCES

Each chapter finishes with a reading and references section where we not only list the works to which we have made reference in the chapter concerned, but also suggest follow-up reading on the topic of the chapter. Here we recommend Bauer and Trudgill (1998) as a good companion volume to this book, and Fromkin and Rodman (1988 [1974]) as a suitable book for taking you further in your linguistic studies. For thoughts specifically on the translatability between unlike languages, see chapter 1 of Baker (2001).

Baker, Mark C. (2001) *The Atoms of Language* (New York: Basic Books).

Bauer, Laurie and Peter Trudgill (eds) (1998) *Language Myths* (Harmondsworth: Penguin).

Clarke, Arthur C. (1968) *2001: A Space Odyssey* (London: Hutchinson).

Fromkin, Victoria and Robert Rodman (1988 [1974]) *Introduction to Language*, 4th edn (New York: Holt, Rinehart & Winston).

Laver, John (1994) *Principles of Phonetics* (Cambridge: Cambridge University Press).

Part I

Origin and Development of Language

Where Does Language Come From?

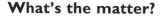

What's the matter?

The biblical account of the origin of language presents us with something of a quandary. In the King James version it goes as follows:

> **Genesis 2:19.** And out of the ground the LORD God formed every beast of the field, and every fowl of the air; and brought them to Adam to see what he would call them; and whatsoever Adam called every living creature, that was the name thereof.

There is nothing here to tell us where Adam got the names of the animals from, or how he was able to invent so many different names and keep them separate in his memory. Neither are we told how things other than the animals and birds got their names: were fish named by some other process, and what about plants? Were they left for Eve to name? Worse still, this gives us no way of knowing how abstract things like distance or hatred were named. And worst of all, it treats naming things as the crucial bit of language (and remains silent on the rest), so leaving us with a notion of language as a series of nouns but without adjectives, verbs or any other word-class (Box 1.1), or any rules for sticking these different kinds of words together into sentences.

Such gaps in explanations for the origin of language are not only characteristic of biblical or mythological accounts of the origin of language, they still cause problems for modern, more scientific, accounts of the origin of language. Perhaps the best we can say about the ultimate origin of language is that nobody knows how it arose.

Some nineteenth-century theories

In 1866 the Société Linguistique de Paris forbade discussion of the origins of language at its meetings, because it was taking up so much time with so little to show for it. The ban stifled speculation for about a century, and it is only recently that serious discussion of the topic has become academically respectable again. The problem then, as now, was a lack of evidence. We have no direct evidence of language until the invention of writing, and writing is

BOX 1.1   Word-classes

The moment we start talking about language, we need to discuss different kinds of word. The distinction between various WORD-CLASSES or PARTS OF SPEECH is absolutely fundamental to any linguistic discussion. Here, we will mention only the very basic word-classes, not a complete list (if any such thing is possible). You need to realize that the criteria for defining the various word-classes may differ from language to language.

Nouns are words which can fit into the gap in the following frame (choose any one of the elements enclosed in braces):

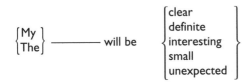

In languages such as French and German, nouns are words which have gender – masculine, feminine or neuter.

In English, verbs are words which can change their form when referring to the present time or referring to past time. For example, *They cook dinner at six o'clock* (every day, including today) versus *They cooked dinner at six o'clock yesterday*. Most English verbs also change their form when we say that *he*, *she* or *it* does the action of the verb as opposed to *I*, *you*, *we* or *they*. For instance {*I, you, we, they*} *arrive at noon*, but {*He, she, it*} *arrives at noon*. A small set of words called 'modal verbs' such

⇨

a very new skill. The earliest writing of which we have a record stems from some 5500 years ago (3500 BCE). Most scientists think that language is somewhere between 35,000 and 150,000 years old.

When we look at the theories of the origin of language which were current at the time of the Société Linguistique de Paris's banning such discussions, we can see why it might have seemed a good idea to avoid discussing them. Jespersen (1993 [1894]) provides a summary, using nicknames which had been used in the discussions of the period. The nicknames have the effect of trivializing the theories, but perhaps no more than they deserve.

The 'bow-wow' theory

The 'bow-wow' theory of the origin of language states that language is basically onomatopoeic; humans simply imitated sounds from their surroundings. We find some support for this notion in words like *cuckoo* and *kiwi* which are ordinary words whose origins lie in the imitation of the call of the birds denoted. But there is a major problem with this theory. It is that in any language, the number of onomatopoeic words is small, so onomatopoeia can be a motivation for only a very few of the words of any language. We as *can, could, may, might, shall, should, will, would* may not clearly fit either of these criteria. In languages like Russian, verbs are marked as perfective or imperfective.

Adjectives are words which fit into the gaps in the following frames (some adjectives fit all of these, all fit in at least one):

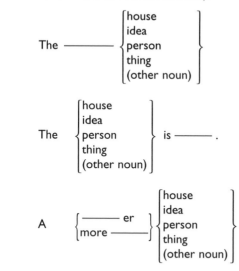

In languages like Spanish or Swahili, adjectives agree with the nouns they tell you about for number and gender/noun-class. While all languages have nouns and verbs, some languages are said not to have adjectives as a separate class of words. In such languages, the notions for which adjectives are used in English are usually covered by verbs, which accordingly mean things like 'be red', 'be enormous' and so on.

certainly cannot get at words for 'enmity' and 'knowledge' through onomatopoeia.

The 'pooh-pooh' theory

The 'pooh-pooh' theory of the origin of language suggests that the original words were formed from emotion-carrying grunts: sounds of exertion, relief, jubilation, and so on. Some of these may be universal, as Darwin (1989 [1890]: 97) suggests when he notes that

> under feelings of contempt or disgust, there is a tendency, from intelligible causes, to blow out of the mouth or nostrils, and this process sounds like *pooh* or *pish*.

This seems to suggest that all people will make similar sounds to express similar emotions, though it is not in every culture that people say *pish*, or shout *ow!* if they drop a rock on their toe. But even if we accept the basic principle here, it fails to explain how words went from being concomitants of physical action to naming objects and actions.

The 'ding-dong' theory

The precise claims of the 'ding-dong' theory are difficult to pin down. It depends on a 'faculty peculiar to man in his primitive state' (*sic*), which is always a dubious way of arguing. In this primitive state, humans had the ability to reflect in a 'vocal expression' any 'impression from without' (Max Müller, cited in Jespersen 1993 [1894]: 330). This might be no more than an extension of the 'bow-wow' theory, with the same objections applying to it, or it might imply more.

One possible extension is the use of SOUND SYMBOLISM, the use of sound to reflect in some direct way the meanings of words. The example of this most often cited is the use of vowels produced with the tongue very close to the roof of the mouth to indicate small things (as in the word *teeny*, for example) and vowels with the tongue a long way from the roof of the mouth to indicate large things (as in the word *large*, for example). Many examples can be given which seem to support this tendency, but *small* and *big* are the wrong way round.

Perhaps most fancifully, it is sometimes suggested that the reason that so many languages (though not Japanese) have words, especially nursery words, for 'mother' which have an [m]-sound in them, is because the production of an [m]-sound mimics closing the lips over the nipple in order to get milk. (Here as throughout the book, we enclose speech sounds in square brackets, so that [m] represents the sound of the first part of *mar*, for example.) Similarly, *ta-ta* as a nursery word for 'goodbye' might mimic in its tongue movement the movement of the hand in waving. It is unfortunate for this theory that *bye-bye* looks very much like *mama* rather than like *ta-ta*.

While this theory is said to be based on some facility which no longer exists (and which thus cannot be tested for), the fact that so few words can be used to provide support for it is a problem in itself.

The 'yo-he-ho' theory

The 'yo-he-ho' theory assumes that the major task facing primitive humans was that of cooperation. They had to work together to hunt and to haul things back to their place of shelter. Thus the first meaningful utterances derive from encouragement to pull or work together. Again, while we might agree that people do need to cooperate from time to time, this theory seems to disregard the large amount of time people spend working in parallel without active cooperation, working in isolation, minding their own business or being downright contrary.

The 'la-la' theory

The 'la-la' theory is the name that has been given to Jespersen's own ideas, which mirror, apparently coincidentally, those of Darwin as set forth in Darwin (1989 [1871]: Ch. 19). It is that language first developed from song, both as a means of sexual attraction and as an accompaniment to other physical activity. While we have plenty of other examples from the animal world of birds singing to find a mate or animals vocalizing in various ways for the same purpose, and while we find many examples from our own experience of people singing to make physical effort more rhythmical and thus easier (sea shanties, marching songs and the like), this theory assumes that these songs must have linguistic content. It is not clear why a song based on nonsense-syllables, like scat singing, should not be as effective for any purpose as one based on language. This theory appears to be arguing from the observed current state of events to purpose, rather than from purpose to a resolution of the problem.

Summarizing nineteenth-century theories

It seems quite possible that all of the factors raised in these various theories had something to do with the origin of language in some small way. The theories do not seem to be mutually incompatible. But they all suffer from major problems of one kind or another, in particular that they do not appear to get us past the one-word stage.

The discontinuity problem

The major problem facing those who try to speculate on the origin of language is the huge difference between naming individual objects and the grammatical complexity of human speech. On the one hand, we want to assume that language developed in small increments from non-language. The alternative is some kind of one-off unrepeatable event (often referred to in mathematical terms as a 'catastrophe'), which sees language emerging fully developed like Pallas Athene from her father's head. If the catastrophe is too big, it becomes indistinguishable from divine intervention – an argument which is no longer seen as good academic practice. There have been various attempts to show that the step from animal communication systems – which we do not count as language – to human language is smaller than we might think. We will consider some of these attempts in Chapter 5. But none of them can really explain how any communication system can develop by small stages from one which allows messages like, 'Look out, there's a snake around!' (which may just be made up of a single call which we might interpret as meaning 'snake') to one which allows messages like Jane Austen's 'It is a truth universally acknowledged, that a single man in possession of a good fortune must be in want of a wife.' The two systems appear to be of very different types, not just different degrees of the same type. This is the DISCONTINUITY PROBLEM which scholars face in attempting to explain the origin and development of human language.

Early attempts to find the original language

An alternative approach to finding the origin of language, one popular for as long as we have records, is to find out what the original language of humankind was. The Greek historian Herodotus tells the story of an experiment carried out by Psamtik I, an Egyptian king from the seventh century BCE. Psamtik had two young babies put into the care of a shepherd, who had strict instructions never to talk to them. After two years they used the word becos, which turned out to be the *Phrygian* word meaning 'bread', and so Psamtik decided that Phrygian must be the original language of humanity. Frederick II of Hohenstaufen (1194–1250) carried out a similar experiment, but with less happy results: the children died. James IV of Scotland (1473–1513) is also said to have carried out a similar experiment, putting two infants with a dumb woman on Inchkeith (an island in the Firth of Forth) to find out what language they would speak. It seems that propaganda worked just as well in the fifteenth century as it does today, because Robert Lindesay, who reported on the case, said, 'Some say they spoke good Hebrew, but as to myself I know not but by hearsay.' Evidence from 'wild children' or 'wolf children' – children who have survived infancy without any linguistic input from human carers – is not very supportive: most of them cannot speak, and those who learn to speak frequently do not make a good job of it. Mowgli emerging from the jungle to talk nicely to a new girlfriend might make a good ending to a Disney film, but it is scientific nonsense.

Note that both Psamtik and James IV clearly expected not only that there would be an original language, but also that this oldest/original language would be one they could recognize. Whatever we might or might not know about the earliest human language, we know that it is not recognizably the same as anything spoken by anyone today, because all languages change (see Chapter 2). Although most modern linguists believe that there was a single original human language, we do not even know this much: there may have been several languages, possibly originating in different places in the world. Certainly, experiments such as those undertaken by Psamtik or by James IV would not today be considered to show anything about the original human language (even if they could get past university ethics committees!).

Results from modern science

We might expect modern science to have rather more interesting things to say about the origin of language than was possible in the nineteenth century, if only because we know rather more about the evolution of hominids now than was known then. And it is certainly true that although the origin of language remains a mystery, there are some areas where we can see clear progress.

The palaeontological evidence

Perhaps the most interesting type of evidence concerns the construction of the vocal tract in different anthropoid species. Basically, most monkeys and apes have a flat tongue in a flat mouth. This is the general mammalian pattern (see Figure 1.1). This layout of the organs makes swallowing easier and choking harder, because it is difficult for most mammals to breathe in and swallow at the same time. Human new-born babies have the same pattern. Adult humans, on the other hand, have a domed tongue in an L-shaped oral cavity. One result of this is that humans are able to produce a wide range of sounds (especially vowel sounds) that are simply impossible for other apes, and which would have been impossible even for Neanderthals. Another result is that humans are much more likely than other apes to choke to death. The development of this peculiarly shaped tract arises in pre-humans concurrently with: (a) an increase in brain size, and (b) the change to bipedal locomotion. Bipedal

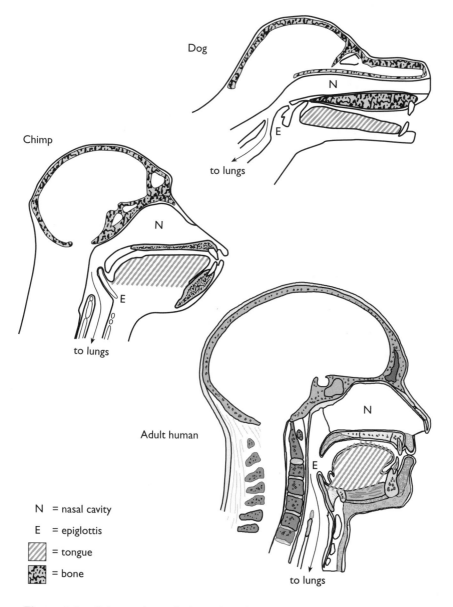

Dog

Chimp

to lungs

to lungs

Adult human

N = nasal cavity

E = epiglottis

= tongue

= bone

to lungs

Figure 1.1   Schematic sagital section through the heads of 3 mammals

locomotion may be the cause of the change of position of the larynx, which gives rise to the new L-shaped vocal tract. What is not clear is whether the increased brain size causes the rise of language, whether the development of language demands the increase in brain size, or whether the two are completely separate developments.

Genetic evidence

In the late twentieth century, a family was discovered in Britain in which a severe language deficit was found over three generations. The pattern of inheritance of the problem suggested that there was a genetic base to it, and eventually a gene was discovered which appeared to be the cause of the problem. This gene was first called SPCH1 (speech defect gene 1), but was subsequently rechristened the FOXP2 gene. People who inherit the defective gene have difficulty in giving lists of words which start with the same letter, difficulty in making some linguistic linkages (for example, they cannot tell you that a creature which goes round splozzing all the time must be a splozzer), and also cannot move their facial muscles in such a way as to produce fluent speech. Much was made in the media, rather misleadingly, of this 'first gene of speech': because when the gene is faulty in modern humans it causes speech defects, it would seem that speech cannot have arisen until this mutation of the gene was in place. The gene appears to have changed to its usual form in humans somewhere between 120,000 and 200,000 years ago, a time-depth which means that this change occurred after humans had become genetically distinct from chimpanzees.

This gene does not only affect things to do with speech. Its importance is that it causes the development of a number of different parts of the brain in ways which are compatible with the development of speech. Speech is such a complex phenomenon that we should not expect it to be connected to just one particular gene in any direct way, and the FOXP2 gene makes that clear. It has implications for specific motor abilities, but also affects the development of Broca's area (see Chapter 23), and affects the ability to understand and produce language.

The suggestion that there is an evolutionary catastrophe which makes humans more able to produce speech than the other great apes is of considerable importance in discussions of the origin of language. It should be noted, however, that this gene does not make us talk; it provides some of the ability that allows speech to develop. Further investigation will let us see precisely what it does, and what other genes are also involved.

L'arbitraire du signe

It is not until the start of the twentieth century, with the work of the celebrated Swiss linguist Ferdinand de Saussure (Box 1.2), that it became generally accepted among linguists that the norm is for the meaning of a word not to be related to its form in any direct way. The position was argued for by the anomalists in ancient Greece, but remained contentious until as recently as

BOX 1.2   Ferdinand de Saussure

Saussure (1857–1913) was best known in his life-time for his thesis, published in 1879, in which he postulated the existence of an unknown sound in Proto-Indo-European (the parent language of many of the modern European languages, see Chapter 4) in order to explain the sound-patterns in the languages derived from Proto-Indo-European. His thesis was subsequently proved beyond doubt when Hittite was deciphered, shown to be an Indo-European language, and shown to have a sound in precisely the places predicted by Saussure. Subsequently, Saussure became better known for his *Cours de Linguistique Générale* (Course in General Linguistics), which was put together after Saussure's death by his students on the basis of their lecture notes. This must be a good reason for being sure to take good notes in all your linguistics classes! Saussure's *Cours*, first published in 1916, ushered in the era of structuralism, not only for Linguistics and Semiotics (the study of signs), but also for other social sciences such as anthropology and sociology.

this. If this were not so, it is hard to see how English *dog,* French *chien,* German *Hund,* Japanese *inu,* Kambera *ahu,* Maori *kurii,* Russian *sobáka,* Spanish *perro,* Swahili *mbwa,* West Greenlandic *qimmiq* and Yimas *yura* could all mean the same thing. Saussure talked about 'the arbitrary nature of the sign' (*l'arbitraire du signe*). Acceptance of this single fact makes many of the nineteenth-century theories about the origin of language look less solid.

The discontinuity problem again

Even if *Homo sapiens* is able to utter more different sounds than any other anthropoid, how would this give rise to the kind of human language which regularly distinguishes between sentences such as *Animals kill people* and *People kill animals?* We might argue that the ability to make a larger number of distinguishable sounds would mean that humans had less need for grammar rather than more.

Much ground has been covered in the speculation concerning the origin of human language. For example, there is a recurrent suggestion that human language developed on the basis of mechanisms that were already in place to permit the use and interpretation of gestural systems (Corballis 2002). But the discontinuity problem does not go away. One serious attempt to bridge the discontinuity gap is that by Carstairs-McCarthy (1999). He argues that the mental structures used to cope with complex syllables were put to extra use to cope with grammatical structure. The proposal is controversial, and may not be entirely convincing; it does, however, show that the discontinuity gap is something which contemporary scholars are attempting to bridge.

Where next?

Just to understand about the development of the ability to produce speech sounds, you need to understand quite a lot about physiology, physical anthropology and the way in which the modern human physiology is exploited in the production of speech. Only this last point is generally accepted as part of Linguistics, coming under the heading of PHONETICS. To understand other aspects of linguistic evolution, other specialities are needed. One of the reasons that so little is known about this field may be that phoneticians and linguists do not, in general, know about the other necessary fields of study, and specialists in those fields do not know enough about phonetics and linguistics. Recently there seems to have been some cooperation between the two sides, and we may perhaps look forward to some discussion which is rather more enlightening than that which caused the Société Linguistique de Paris to close down discussion of the topic.

SOME POINTS TO PONDER

▶ What arguments might there be for a single source of all human language rather than multiple sources of human language?

▶ We have seen that changes to the physiology of the vocal tract mean that humans can produce more sounds than other apes, and that the FOXP2 gene means that humans can articulate more rapidly than other apes. What other things are needed for language or speech to develop? You might like to think about matters of meaning, matters concerning the ways in which words are strung together, or ways in which words are built up from sounds and smaller meaningful units. Which of these things do you think chimpanzees might be capable of?

▶ How much can you communicate with your class mates using only onomatopoeic words? Be careful to distinguish between using such words and using them in a particular order.

▶ Can you see any evidence that being able to sing well increases your chances of reproducing? Are the words of your songs important in any such advantage? What about your ability to speak well? Are the words of your utterances important in any such advantage?

READING AND REFERENCES

For general discussion on the origin of language see articles on 'Origin and evolution of language', 'Origin of language debate' and 'Origins of language' in Asher (1994). Crystal (1987) gives a very clear abbreviated discussion, with reference to Jespersen's various theories. Aitchison (1996) gives a summary of more modern research. Curtiss

(1977) gives a discussion of a child who grew up without language. Originally a thesis, this book is an academic discussion of 'Genie's problems'. Genie is still alive as far as we know, but for her own privacy is no longer studied. On the story told by skull anatomy, see various works by Philip Lieberman. Lieberman (1998) puts that discussion in a wider perspective. Corballis (2002) is an immensely entertaining discussion of the gesture-first hypothesis, while Carstairs-McCarthy (1999) is a controversial approach to the discontinuity problem, wide-ranging and closely argued. Some of this material is reviewed in a different context in chapter 8 of Jackendoff (2002). For a more technical discussion of the FOXP2 gene, see Marcus and Fisher (2003).

Aitchison, Jean (1996) *The Seeds of Speech* (Cambridge: Cambridge University Press).

Asher, R. E. (ed.) (1994) *The Encyclopedia of Language and Linguistics* (Oxford: Pergamon).

Carstairs-McCarthy, Andrew (1999) *The Origins of Complex Language: An Inquiry into the Evolutionary Beginnings of Sentences, Syllables, and Truth* (Oxford: Oxford University Press).

Corballis, Michael C. (2002) *From Hand to Mouth* (Princeton and Oxford: Princeton University Press).

Crystal, David (1987) *The Cambridge Encyclopedia of Language* (Cambridge: Cambridge University Press).

Curtiss, Susan (1977) *Genie: A Psycholinguistic Study of a Modern-day "Wild child"* (New York: Academic Press).

Darwin, Charles (1989 [1871]) *The Descent of Man and Selection in Relation to Sex, Part Two*, in Paul H. Barrett and R. B. Freedman (eds), *The Works of Charles Darwin*, vol. 22 (London: Pickering).

Darwin, Charles (1989 [1890]) *Expression of the Emotions*, in Paul H. Barrett and R. B. Freedman (eds), *The Works of Charles Darwin*, vol. 23 (London: Pickering).

Jackendoff, Ray (2002) *Foundations of Language* (Oxford: Oxford University Press).

Jespersen, Otto (1993 [1894]) *Progress in Language with Special Reference to English*, new edition with an introduction by James D. McCawley (Amsterdam and Philadelphia: Benjamins).

Lieberman, Philip (1998) *Eve Spoke: Human Language and Human Evolution* (New York: W. W. Norton).

Marcus, Gary F. and Simon E. Fisher (2003) '*FOXP2* in Focus: What Can Genes Tell Us about Speech and Language?' *Trends in Cognitive Sciences*, 7: 257–62.

Why Don't We All Talk the Same?

What's the matter?

Why don't you talk just the same way as your parents talk? Why do we have so much prejudice based on the way people talk? Wouldn't it be simpler, and perhaps more friendly, if we all talked the same way? On a larger scale, why are there so many languages in the world? Surely international cooperation would work better if we all spoke a single language instead of having several thousand languages in the world. A report on-line from the BBC (http://news.bbc.co.uk/2/hi/europe/3604069.stm, accessed 8 July 2004) points out that with 20 languages in the European Union alone, there are 190 possible pairs of languages to translate between, and the expected cost of the exercise is over €800m per annum. While there are those who point out that this cost amounts to approximately €2 per citizen per annum, it still involves a lot of money which might otherwise be spent on something else, and produces a mountain of paper each year. When we think of the number of international organizations which are faced with similar problems, albeit on a smaller scale, the cost of translation to the world can be seen to be enormous. All of this is before we start looking at personal costs, such as the case of trained doctors who cannot get jobs outside their homeland because they cannot be understood, even though the area where they want to work needs doctors; or the number of refugees who can only find jobs that pay minimal wages in their adoptive countries because they do not speak the local language well enough.

The answer seems to be that, despite all these apparent benefits of having a single language for all of humanity, that ideal would not meet our needs as social animals.

An alternative view

Some readers may have attended secondary school in places influenced by the British system (whether in Britain itself or in some of the former colonies), where school uniforms are worn. A school uniform is called a *uniform* for a good reason. The tenth edition of the *Concise Oxford Dictionary* (Oxford University Press, 2002) defines the adjective *uniform* as meaning 'the same in all cases and at all times'. It is clearly the case that school uniforms should make all students look the same, not simply so that they are easy for outsiders to identify (as might be the case with nurses' uniforms, for example), but so that each is seen as being the equal of all the others. However, those with an experience of such a school will know that this is not how uniforms are used in school.

School uniforms are not 'the same in all cases' because:

(a) individuals differ physically, and the uniform looks different on different people;

(b) there are sanctioned differences, e.g. between junior students and senior students or between prefects and non-prefects; some of these may be minor (such as the wearing of a badge), others may be major (e.g. colour of shirt or blouse);

(c) there are unsanctioned differences, whereby groups of friends tend to dress the same way, possibly by wearing shirts or blouses not tucked in or by wearing trousers or skirts on the hips rather than at the waist, or by wearing different accessories (such as piercings, or dyeing their hair).

Neither are they 'the same . . . at all times' because:

(d) individuals change as they grow up, and grow into or out of their uniforms;

(e) the uniforms become more worn with the passing of time;

(f) the uniforms are changed to be rather more in tune with current norms of clothing: most girls' schools these days do not insist on full-length skirts as would have been the case in 1906.

What has all this to do with language? The point is that if we assume that everyone once started out trying to speak precisely the same language, variation would have crept into that language in the way that variation creeps into the use of school uniforms. Moreover, the reasons would be much the same:

(a) Individuals differ physically and thus have different voices caused by different-sized larynges (or voice boxes) and different-sized vocal tracts, etc. This is not enough to prevent anyone from learning any particular language, but it is enough to ensure that we all sound like ourselves.

(b) People in different functions speak rather differently, if only because they use the technical terms and expressions associated with their position. Lawyers talk about *goods and chattels*, linguists don't mean the same by *subject* as secondary school pupils, news readers are expected to speak very clearly.

(c) People mark who they are by the way they speak (see further, Chapter 17). We all want to sound like our friends and the people we admire; we don't want to sound like people who are socially very different from us. This is such an important reason that we will return to it below.

(d) Our language changes as we grow up, partly because we change and partly because we change our language to fit in with new norms as we grow older. When you were three you might have said *I goed to Nana's,* but you probably wouldn't now. A recent study considered the way in which Her Majesty Queen Elizabeth II has pronounced her various Christmas messages to the Commonwealth during her reign, and discovered that her accent has changed in the same direction as the southern English accent over that period (Harrington et al. 2000).

(e) We can think of bits of language getting worn out with repeated use, and falling into disuse (see Chapter 3).

(f) Language changes in very much the same way as fashions change, sometimes predictably and sometimes not (see further, Chapter 3). Nobody talked about SMSs before 1990 because the expression did not exist; British speakers used to say *I have forgot,* but now it is only regional in Britain.

From a linguistic point of view, perhaps the most important point here is (c). This is the reason why a language without variation would not be of any use to us. We all use language as a way of marking in-group and out-group. We even (inaccurately) talk about people who 'have an accent' and people who 'don't have an accent', where what we mean by the latter group is 'people who have an accent which I cannot hear because it is just like mine'. As a child you have the capacity to change your accent to fit in with the group around you – which is why after moving to a new area young children sound like their school friends rather than like their parents. This facility reduces once we reach puberty, though we may still try to change our accent when we go to university, or if we are hoping for promotion from a blue-collar job to a management position. This feature of language works with amazing subtlety. Our children tell us that we don't sound 'cool' because we don't pronounce the word *cool* properly. An Australian can usually recognize a Pommie (a person of English origin) before they have heard a complete sentence from them. And Protestants and Catholics in Belfast may be able to recognize each other from the way in which they pronounce the words *pull* and *push* (McCafferty 2001: 48). In each case, this facility allows us to hear people who are not like us. It does not necessarily allow us to hear how others are different from each other, as the many Australians who have visited the USA and been mistaken for Pommies can attest. What is more, we want to talk differently from others. Teenagers do not want to talk just like their parents, bishops do not want to sound like bookmakers, Smith does not want to sound like Jones.

This goes some way to explaining why it would not only not suit us but also not be possible for us all to talk exactly the same way. However, it does not tell us anything about why or how this variation could lead to change in whole languages. We go on to consider that point.

Variability and change

Let us return to the uniform analogy and undertake a thought experiment. If two groups of people wearing ostensibly the same uniform were moved to separate towns and never saw each other, would the uniforms of the two groups look the same after 30 years or so? If you think they would, it's probably because you imagine the external definition of the uniform regulating what might happen. In the case of language, there is no such external definition, and until very recently there was never anyone to regulate what was or was not possible (the idea that there is just one correct way of using language is probably an eighteenth-century invention). The result is that where languages are concerned (and possibly also uniforms), the outcome from a lot of variation is that a certain amount of it leads to change. Change is added to change, until the two versions of the original language may be noticeably different. After a large period of time, the two versions may not even be mutually comprehensible.

There is a theory to explain this gradual change where language is concerned. This theory states that a lot of the differences between the language of one generation and the language of the next arise because of inaccurate learning on the part of the new generation. Young people heard their elders saying *That begs the question*, but while their elders meant 'that seems to answer the question by assuming the answer that you wanted', the young people didn't understand this properly, and thought it meant the same as 'that raises the question [of . . .]'. The result is that while the first edition of the *Concise Oxford Dictionary* in 1911 defined *beg the question* as 'assume the truth of matter in dispute', the tenth edition (2002) gives the core sense as 'invite a question . . . that has not been dealt with'. At one stage in the history of Spanish, speakers thought they were trying to say a [b] sound in a word like *habla* 's/he speaks', though they often got it not quite right and said it without closing their lips properly. In a subsequent generation, people believed that the pronunciation without fully closed lips was what people were trying to say, and they copied that (giving the modern pronunciation).

One of the interesting corollaries of this is that variation is often a sign that change is taking place in a community. It need not be a sign of change – there are some known examples of variation staying pretty much the same from generation to generation (how much you 'drop your aitches' might be such an example – but it is certainly the case that when the language of the community or some part of the community changes, one of the signs of change is variation. There is, when we look at it, a vast amount of our language which shows variation. In New Zealand, the following questions typically give rise to different answers within any group of 50 or more undergraduates. You might like to try these questions for yourself, either to see what your answer is or to see how your friends answer, or you might like to think of similar questions which would give rise to split answers in your classroom.

(a) Do you say 'assyoom' or 'asoom' or 'ashoom' for *assume*?
(b) Where is the main stress on the words *anchovy, comparable*?

(c) What forms of the words *strive* and *stride* would you use in the following sentences:
  (i) We have ____ to make this area as safe as possible.
  (ii) She had ____ out of the room before anyone had got over her announcement.

(d) At primary school, if you were playing tick/tig/tigs/tag/tiggy and your shoelace came undone, what did you say (perhaps while crossing your fingers) to indicate that you had temporary immunity from the rules of the game?

(e) Which of the following would you say to your friends?
  (i) He hasn't a car.
  (ii) He hasn't got a car.
  (iii) He doesn't have a car.
  (iv) He's not got a car.

Each of these examples, where there is some variation in a speech community, indicates a position where there is the potential for language change. When languages, over long periods and often because the speakers of different dialects are separated physically from each other, do change at a large number of points, we say that we end up with different languages. For example, the Latin that was once spoken over a large part of Southern Europe has today given way to French, Italian, Spanish, Portuguese and so on. The surprising thing, from this point of view, is not so much the changes we can see in language, but that so much stays the same for so long and that language remains relatively stable over periods of over a century at a time (you can understand a lot of material that was written in the nineteenth century, even if you would not write like that yourself). There are good reasons why it should not change too quickly, three of which we take up immediately below.

Language is a social phenomenon

Not only do we want to be different from other social groups, but we want to be like our own social group; so we try to speak like our own social group. In other words, we don't want to change what our own group does. We may nevertheless make changes, but they will be relatively minor.

Also we have to communicate with our own families. If language changed so fast that grandparents could no longer understand grandchildren (far beyond the usual complaint of 'young people today don't speak as clearly as they did in my day'!) it would not be effective in allowing cohesion within the family, let alone any wider social grouping. So language has to change relatively slowly to allow speakers time to get used to the changes, otherwise it could not fulfil its task of allowing communication.

Language is often influenced by a standard

These days, in Western societies, we often meet a variety of language in the formal broadcasts on television and on the radio and in the newspapers which does not really correspond to the way in which most of us speak our language. This form of language is given a certain amount of prestige: it is the kind of language we expect foreigners to learn, and we often think of it as being – in some often undefined sense – better than the language of our everyday interaction. While there are some people who always speak or write in this way, they are usually in a minority of speakers/writers. This variety of the language is called a STANDARD form of the language. In earlier times the standard might have been what you heard from the pulpit, or what the mayor spoke when a messenger came from the monarch.

To a certain extent, what is perceived as a standard variety may be haphazard. People who speak mutually comprehensible dialects close to the German–Dutch border may nevertheless go home and watch television or read newspapers in different (not mutually comprehensible) languages. They may gain education in different languages, have to fill out forms in different languages. In this sense, we can see language as a tool of governments, giving rise to the relatively modern idea of a single standard language for each nation state (marking the in-group on a larger scale). It is also true that what variety of the language is taken to be the standard is a matter of historical accident. If the Normans had been conquered in 1066 and the capital of England had been set in York rather than London, the standard English spoken in England (and in much of the rest of the world) today would be considerably different.

Nevertheless, when a standard is accepted it has an effect on the language of the people for whom it is a standard. In particular, the standard variety tends to allow less variation than non-standard varieties (Milroy 1992: 129). One of the results of this is that the pull of the standard variety is towards a reduction in variation, and hence towards a slowing of linguistic change. This is a second reason why linguistic change is usually not particularly fast.

Language is a system of systems

As well as having a social dimension, language has a structural one. Some people have viewed language as a 'system where everything is connected' or a 'system of systems', where the relevant systems are usually taken to be the structural ones. These systems seem by themselves to constrain what is a possible or a likely change in a language: we might say that they act as another force acting against some changes. For example, many languages force their speakers to distinguish between one item and many items (in other words, between SINGULAR and PLURAL) and also between first, second and third persons. English is one such language: we have to decide whether we are speaking about a cow or several cows; our language does not allow us the possibility of allowing the number of beasts to be determined by the context in the way that it does allow the sex of somebody called simply a *friend* to be determined by the context. English also demands that we specify whether I or you or he or she or it carries out the action of the verb (or similarly in the plural). We cannot leave this to be deduced. Under such circumstances, we expect English to force us to distinguish between singular second persons and plural second persons. It fits with what has been called 'the genius of the language'. Failing to distinguish between categories which are otherwise general in the language is something which is unexpected. English thus did something unexpected when it lost the distinction between second singular and second plural (at least standard English – *thou* is maintained in some British regional dialects as a singular form, and *youse* or *y'all* or *you guys* has been introduced in other varieties as a second person plural pronoun). However, by the time this happened, English had stopped marking singular and plural obligatorily on verbs (in the first person, in the past tense, etc.), so there is a sense in which we can see this as part of a general movement, and balance is maintained. Some things are so well woven into the tapestry of a particular language that there are limits on how far they can change. The patterns in language themselves limit some of the things that can happen to that language.

Where next?

To discuss variation and change in languages, you need to be able to describe those languages clearly and in detail. This involves a study of their phonetic structure and their grammatical structure (MORPHOLOGY and SYNTAX if we are to use more technical terms, i.e. both the differences in the shapes of words and differences in the ways words are strung together). Ways in which words change are usually studied under the label of LEXICOLOGY, which deals with the structure of vocabulary, a subject which is often not given a great deal of weight within linguistics because it is so closely related to external social changes in any community and because it is so resistant to linguistic generalization.

Variation in a given community at any one particular time is studied under the title of Sociolinguistics, either as a matter of DIALECTOLOGY (when rural dialects are usually considered) or as a matter of VARIATIONIST SOCIOLINGUISTICS (when urban dialects are usually considered). These areas also require you to have some understanding of sound structure and grammatical structure.

The study of the way in which languages change over time is the domain of historical or diachronic linguistics. Again, the serious study of these areas requires knowledge of phonetics, grammar and even SEMANTICS (the study of meaning), but also requires knowledge of some of the languages you wish to consider. If you want to look at the way Latin has changed to become Portuguese and Romanian, you need to know something about both of these modern languages at least, and preferably something about Latin as well. To some extent, the ability to use the languages will be sufficient, but the ability to analyse them carefully is a requirement for advanced work.

The more general question we have been considering here – namely, why do speakers behave in this way? – can only be answered against a background of considering variation in language communities and looking at discussions of what goes on there and the examples the different communities provide. The 'why?' questions are often the hardest, but the most interesting; they frequently demand the most study before you can start on a coherent analysis.

SOME POINTS TO PONDER

▶ Why do you think the equation of a language with a nation state is such a modern idea?

▶ In what way might the language of broadcast news be better than the kind of language you speak to your friends? In what way might it be worse? Take care not to fall into the common trap of assuming that what you speak is somehow not adequate or not aesthetically pleasing: to accept that is to accept the propaganda of a minority.

▶ Does English as it is used in different countries provide evidence to support the idea that standards change when users of the language are not in direct contact?

▶ Consider the example of Dutch and German given above. What does this tell you about standard languages?

▶ What would happen if you started talking to your friends like a member of the Royal family? Why?

READING AND REFERENCES

As a general work on why and how languages change, you can consult Aitchison (1981), which is eminently readable. The quotation about language being a system where everything is connected, is usually attributed to Meillet (1903: 407), 'chaque langue forme un système où tout se tient'. For a study of the history of English which takes account of the social pressures on language, see Leith (1983) or Knowles (1997). For cases like the Dutch–German one, see chapter 1 of Chambers and Trudgill (1980). For more details (which also means that it is harder for the beginner to read), see chapter 19 of Bloomfield (1935), which is a classic linguistics text.

Aitchison, Jean (1981) *Language Change: Progress or Decay?* (London: Fontana). (There is also a second [1991] and a third [2001] edition of this book published by Cambridge University Press. The relevant chapters are 'The reason why' and 'Doing what comes naturally', but you might find others interesting as well.)

Bloomfield, Leonard (1935) *Language* (London: George Allen & Unwin).

Chambers, J. K. and Peter Trudgill (1980). *Dialectology* (Cambridge: Cambridge University Press).

Harrington, Jonathan, Sallyanne Palethorpe and Catherine Watson (2000) 'Does the Queen Speak the Queen's English?' *Nature* 407: 927–8.

Knowles, Gerry (1997) *A Cultural History of the English Language* (London: Edward Arnold).

Leith, Dick (1983) *A Social History of English* (London: Routledge & Kegan Paul).

McCafferty, Kevin (2001) *Ethnicity and Language Change* (Amsterdam and Philadelphia: Benjamins).

Meillet, Antoine (1903) *Introduction à l'étude comparative des langues indo-européennes* (Paris: Hachette).

Milroy, James (1992) *Linguistic Variation and Change* (Oxford: Blackwell).

Things Ain't What They Used to Be

What's the matter?

All living languages change. We have known this for centuries. Chaucer noted that 'in form of speche is chaunge' in the fourteenth century, and the observation has been repeated many times since then. But while many people seem willing to accept this truism, they are nonetheless worried about the direction of the change. 'Tongues, like governments, have a natural tendency to degeneration', according to the eighteenth-century lexicographer Samuel Johnson, and it is easy enough to find statements from more recent times which echo the sentiment. The dedication in Jean Aitchison's (1981) book on language change reads: 'To those of my friends, and particularly Tony, who think that language change should be stopped.' Attempting to stop language change, as Aitchison is well aware, is akin to attempting to stop the tide from coming in – something which got Canute a very bad press. As to whether language change is degeneration, we should note the continuation of the passage from Chaucer cited above, where he notes that although people used different words a thousand years earlier from those they used in his period, yet they 'spedde [fared] as wel in love as men now do'. If language has been degenerating for all those hundreds of years, surely it must have reached the totally degenerate state by now? Yet it is only the latest changes that people object to, not the older ones: people have on the whole stopped complaining about the use of *aggravate* to mean 'annoy', although this was a common complaint in the mid-twentieth century.

Just occasionally we find someone who believes the opposite, that language is changing for the better. For example, Otto Jespersen (1993 [1894]: 14) says that

> the analytic structure of modern European languages is so far from being a drawback to them that it gives them an unimpeachable superiority over the earlier stages of the same languages.

Jespersen's line of argumentation is not the same as that of people like Johnson: Jespersen is arguing about overall language structure, Johnson about the use of words. We should also recall that Jespersen is specifically arguing against earlier nineteenth-century scholars who did see in the structure of languages like modern English an instance of decay from the structures of older Germanic languages. Nevertheless, there is clearly room for differing opinion in this area.

Most modern linguists would probably want to argue that change in itself is neutral and that, as Hamlet puts it, 'there is nothing either good or bad but thinking makes it so'. Language rarely changes so as to become dysfunctional – or if it does, some other change comes along so that the language functions well again. At the same time, while for some kinds of change we may be able to see that the value of a change is all in the eye of the beholder, in some instances we can see why the notion of decay arises.

Roundabouts and swings: a view of grammatical change

If we look at things which have happened to the Germanic and Romance languages, and the ways in which they have changed over the period for which we have documentation, we find remarkably consistent patterns of change. Rather than try to illustrate this in several languages, we shall take a single example here – Latin and modern Italian, but you could find similar changes in the shift from Old English to modern English, from Common Scandinavian to modern Danish, and so on. (See Box 3.1 for an explanation of glosses.)

In (1) we find a couplet from the Latin poet Martial, and in (2) there is a translation of the same thing into modern Italian.

(1) Latin:

Exigis	ut	nostros	donem	tibi,	Tucca,	libellos.
Require.2SG	that	our.ACC.PL	give.SUBJ.1SG	you.DAT.SG,	Tucca,	book.DIMIN.ACC.PL.

'You require that I should give our little books to you, Tucca.'

Non	faciam:	nam	vis	vendere	non	legere.
Not	do.FUT.1SG:	for	want.2SG	sell.INF	not	read.INF

'I won't do it, because you want to sell them, not read them.'

(2) Italian:

Esigi	che	io	ti	doni	i nostri	libretti,	Tucca.
Require.2SG	that	I	you.SG	give.SUBJ.1SG	the our.PL	book.DIMIN.PL,	Tucca

Non	lo	farò:	poiché	vuoi	vendere	non	leggere.
Not	it	do.FUT.1SG:	because	want.2SG	sell.INF	not	read.INF

You can easily see some differences between the Latin and the Italian that show how the language has changed through time: there are spelling differences, reflecting differences in pronunciation (*exigis::esigi; legere::leggere*),

BOX 3.1   Glosses: how do you tell someone about the structure of another language?

In order to explain the structure of another language, linguists provide INTER-LINEAR GLOSSES as well as translations of foreign language data. A gloss is a literal translation of each of the words in the sentence, and an indication of the GRAMMATICAL CATEGORIES which are marked on those words. Grammatical categories are things like TENSE (present, past or future), GENDER (masculine, feminine or neuter in Indo-European languages), NUMBER (singular or plural), and CASE (the role the marked element plays in the sentence). Each word in the gloss corresponds to a word of the original. The marking of these grammatical categories uses quasi-standardized abbreviations, and to show that they are the names of grammatical categories, puts them in small capitals. So ACC stands for 'accusative', DAT for 'dative', DIMIN for 'diminutive', FUT for 'future', INF for 'infinitive', PL for 'plural', SG for 'singular', SUBJ for 'subjunctive' and so on. You may know some of these labels already, but we are not going to insist on them all here: the important points here are similarities and differences rather than the precise meanings of all of these labels.

there are new words either replacing old ones (*nam::poiché*) or where there were none before (*io; i; lo*), some words have changed their shape, while apparently continuing to show the same meanings (*donem::doni; faciam::farò*). All this is the standard material of studies of language change. There are also other grammatical differences. In the Latin the words *nostros* and *libellos*, which are closely related, do not come together in the sentence, while in the Italian they do. Linked with this is the fact that the Italian has no markers of accusative and dative – cases telling us what role the nouns marked with these cases play in the sentence. If these functions need to be marked in the Latin, why are they not marked in the Italian? The answer is that the order of the words has the function in Italian that the case-marking had in Latin (see further, Chapter 11). Because *nostros* and *libellos* are the only accusative plurals in (1), we know they go together, but in (2) we have to put them together to show that they belong together.

So in the passage from Latin to Italian, this language has lost some of the variation in the shape of the word and instead given extra weight to the order in which the words appear. Similar things have happened in the history of English – rather more so, in fact. If this is a recurrent process, we might ask, is it also an inevitable one? Do languages always go from more complex words to simpler words and more importance for order?

The answer is 'no'. We also have examples of language gaining more complex words, and paying less attention to word order. An interesting example comes from modern French.

If you have learnt school French or French from written texts, you will be familiar with sentences like (3), which is a perfectly normal sentence of written French (albeit, like most linguistic examples, rather strange out of context).

(3)   Marie a donné la bicyclette à Paul
      Marie has given the bicycle to Paul

However, if you were to go to France and listen to spoken French, you would be more likely to hear things like (4) with the same meaning.

(4)   La bicyclette, elle la lui a donnée Marie à Paul
      The bicycle she it to.him has given Marie to Paul

      Marie, elle la lui a donnée la bicyclette à Paul
      Marie she it to him has given the bicycle to Paul

Now, French writes *elle la lui a donnée* as a sequence of five words, but these are not fully independent words: they can no more stand alone than the *'ll* on the end of *she'll* in English. It would probably be more linguistically helpful to see all that as a single word made up of a root and a series of prefixes, rather like the Swahili words in (5). And if we accept that, we can see that French has built a very complex word where it used not to have them. Moreover the order of the bicycle and Marie has become less important as a result.

(5)   a·ta·wa·penda
      he·will·them·like
      'he will like them'

      ni·ta·ku·penda
      I·will·you·like
      'I will like you'

      (NB: the decimal point is used here to separate the meaningful elements of words which are usually written together.)

One-way streets: some uni-directional changes

The examples above make it look as if language change might be a process like chasing one's own tail – you keep coming back to a situation very like the one you have already left. But that is not true in all cases. Some things seem to change only in one direction.

The first example of this carries on from the French example given just above. The elements, which it was suggested are like the prefixes in a Swahili word, all derive from ordinary words. If we look over a wide enough time span, we find many examples of words changing into prefixes or suffixes.

The *-ly* which appears on the end of a word like *manly* is derived from a Germanic form *-liko* meaning 'appearance, form, body', so that in the very distant past, the forerunner of *manly* must have meant 'having a man's body or appearance'.

The *-dom* which shows up at the end of *kingdom* is related to an Old English form *dōm* (related to modern English *doom*), meaning 'judgement or jurisdiction', so a *kingdom* was what was within the jurisdiction of a king.

The *-hood* which we find in *childhood* was originally a separate word meaning 'condition, quality or rank' so that *childhood* was the condition or rank of being a child, a meaning which makes sense in many contexts today.

The *en-* which we find at the beginning of words like *enslave* goes back to the Latin preposition *in* (and in some cases we can still spell the word either way in English: *enclose* or *inclose*).

These are just a few of many examples which show the same trend. If we move away from English to other languages, we find similar things happening. For example, in the French word *donnera* 'he/she/it will give' the final *-a* derives ultimately from the word meaning 'has'. The Zulu word *isihlalwana* 'little chair' (from *isihlalo* 'chair') contains an element which derives from a word which originally meant 'child'. In Karelian *velleŋke* 'with the brother' the final *-ke*, which means 'with', derives from a word which originally meant 'at a turn' (Karelia is a Russian republic, bordering Finland). The *-b-* in the Hungarian *világba* 'into the world' is all that remains of a word which once meant 'belly' (so, literally, 'into the belly or interior of the world'). The pattern is widespread. The technical term for this kind of change is GRAMMATICALIZATION.

But what about changes in the other direction? Do we find bits of words branching off and becoming words in their own right? The answer is: not really.

There are a few instances where we appear to have a prefix or suffix standing in isolation, but either it is chance that the form resembles a prefix or suffix, or it is still felt to be a prefix or suffix. There are, for example, books and websites devoted to isms and ologies. Usually, but not always, these are written with a hyphen: *-isms* and *-ologies*. The hyphen seems to indicate that these are still felt to be suffixes. *Super* can be used to mean, among other things, 'superintendent'. But *Websters Third New International Dictionary* (Merriam-Webster, 1966) lists *supe* with the same meaning. Both arise from shortening *superintendent*. It can thus be seen to be chance that the more general form *super* happens to coincide with the form of the prefix we find in words like *supersonic*. Neither of these examples really shows prefixes or suffixes turning into full words, and this is typically the case.

So we regularly find instances where words turn into more or less meaningful elements in larger words, but we rarely find instances where meaningful elements in words turn into fully fledged words by themselves. This is a change which seems to work in one direction only.

A very different case is found in the way meanings of certain words change. As words that denote women change their meaning, they tend to become more pejorative. This example is developed in Chapter 15, and we do not need to repeat that material here. To the extent that such words do not change to denote high prestige or more positive implications, this is another one-way-street change.

If we look at changing sounds, it seems obvious that once sounds have completely disappeared, we cannot reconstruct them. There are occasional examples where people have tried, with rather strange results. Here (and in the rest of this chapter) we can illustrate most easily from English, though parallel examples can be found in other languages. So given the word *lord*, there is no way that we can discover that it came from something which might have been the forerunner of *loaf-ward* (or 'bread-guardian'). The sounds have gone, and we cannot get them back. There is nothing in the way the language is pronounced to tell us that *night* and *knight* used to be pronounced differently, or that *site* and *sight* at one stage in the history of English did not sound the same. In the same way, it ought to be the case that once *waistcoat* is pronounced [weskɪt] (as it used to be by nearly everyone, and still is by a very few) we can no longer discover that it contains the vowel [əʊ] from *coat*. Strictly speaking, that is true. What has happened is that once *waistcoat* was pronounced [weskɪt] a new pronunciation was introduced based on the spelling: the spelling allowed us to go backwards, not the pronunciation itself. This creation of new pronunciations based on the spelling is called SPELLING PRONUNCIATION, and they are a relatively recent phenomenon in language change, since widespread literacy is a relatively recent phenomenon.

Change for change's sake

Except for the spelling pronunciation example, it might seem that the changes mentioned above are, indeed, changes for the worse, though we might equally argue that they are changes in favour of greater economy. But there are many other changes which are neither clearly erosions nor clearly improvements: they are just changes.

Consider, for example, the replacement of the older English form *coney* (which rhymed with *honey* and *money*) by the modern form *rabbit*. It is generally accepted that *coney* met its demise because it sounded too much like the word for female genitalia, and so people were embarrassed to say it. Where *coney* did survive (in the fur trade and in New York's Coney Island), the pronunciation changed so that it rhymes with *bony* and *phoney* as an alternative way out of the impasse. During the change there was no doubt a certain amount of awkwardness involved here. But before the change there was an English word meaning 'rabbit' and after the change there was an English word meaning 'rabbit'; both were two syllables long. It seems very unlikely that there is any great disadvantage to the new system over the old or that the new system is much of an advantage either. The two are just different. There are many such instances (see Box 3.2).

A similar case is changes which affect the past tense and past participle forms of verbs in English. While we now say things like (6), that was not always so.

(6a) I help my parents with the shopping every week.
(6b) I helped my parents with the shopping last Tuesday. (past tense *helped*)

ILLUSTRATION

BOX 3.2   Replacing one word by another

Here are some examples of instances where one word has replaced another in the history of English. In some cases, replacements do not occur in all varieties of English. In New Zealand, *train station* is in the process of replacing *railway station*, for example, but that may not be happening everywhere. In each instance, though, the language appears to function in very much the same way after the change as before the change.

What we now call	used to be called
badger	brock
city	burg
dog	hound
donkey	ass
newt	eft
radio	wireless
river	ea
spider	attercop (literally: 'poison head')
take	nim

Some of the examples here are modern, the change having occurred within living memory; others go back to the dawn of a language we can call 'English' or beyond.

(6c)   I have helped my parents with the shopping for years. (past participle *helped*)

There is an older form where we would have had *holp* in (6b) and *holpen* in (6c). *He rang the bell* would, in earlier forms of English, have been *He ringed the bell*. Some of these examples leave traces in local regional dialects, which stick to the original form. Some examples of this type are still in the process of change. More and more speakers of English appear to be adopting *dove* as the past tense of *dive*, *snuck* as the past tense of *sneak*, and even *drug* as the past tense of *drag*. What you use as the past participle of *spit* will depend on where you come from: some people say *He had spat at me*, others say *He had spit at me*. People generally seem to avoid the past participles of *tread* and *stride* and *strive* if they can. And you might find many potential past tenses and past participles of *cleave*.

We may have feelings about some of these which are not due to the actual form that is being used. For instance, our reaction to *drug* for *dragged* is likely to be related to the kind of people we think will use the form. On the other hand, people who use *dove* for *dived* say that *dived* sounds like baby talk – just like *bringed* for *brought*. It is clear that before or after the change, English still permits a present, past tense and past participle form, and that as long as you can find one if you need it, there is no problem (the past participle of *stride* may be a problem here, but you need it so infrequently that it is not a great problem). The only way we could really judge improvement or degeneration would be by looking at the overall pattern of simplification or complication over a period of thousands of years. That is not easily assessed.

Languages also lose and gain words. Few people today can distinguish a *barouche* from a *brougham* – the words are found only in a historical context. And people of 50 years ago would have looked blankly at expressions such as *DVD, superbug, tough love* and so on. We can easily see why. The terms were not in use then. It may be less clear why individual words have dropped out of use or come into use at different periods of history, or why some words have apparently changed direction and started meaning something quite different (occasionally leaving behind a fixed expression with the old meaning). For example, if you consult an etymological dictionary for the emphasized word in each of the following expressions, you may get a surprise to discover what it originally meant: *One man's **meat** is another man's poison; His finger-nails were chewed down to the **quick**; That is a **nice** distinction; My **kith** and kin.* But even if we do not always understand why this has happened, and cannot reliably predict when it will happen, words get lost because people stop using them, and words arrive because people find a need for them, and so it is hard to argue that we are really much worse off or much better off after the event than we were before it. Both before and after a change the language system allows us to communicate successfully: during the change there may be some slight disruption to communication for a few speakers, but that disruption is removed once the change is complete.

Where next?

We have seen that all aspects of language change: words, sounds, sentence structure, meaning. Some features may change very rapidly, others may change very slowly. But change is always occurring. Change may be the result of social forces such as embarrassment or political change, or come from within the language system itself. We have also seen that change itself is inherently neutral: it neither 'improves' a language nor 'harms' a language (it may solve a local problem or cause a temporary ambiguity, but in the great scheme of things, these things even out). Of course, changes may occur because of external things that are happening to a language (such as if speakers of the language are punished for speaking it), but even then it is the external factors that harm the language, not change itself.

To develop our ideas about change in language, we might wish to go on to discover how our language has changed, or whether all languages follow similar patterns when they change. To answer either of these questions we need a fuller understanding of how languages are structured, so that we can describe changes with precision. This means we need to have a way of describing sounds (which we get though the study of phonetics), a way of describing grammatical structures (which we gain through a study of morphology and syntax), a way of describing lexical relationships (something which might influence our understanding of dictionaries, thesauruses and the like). On top of that, we need good data on how individual languages have changed, whether our own or other people's. This implies not only good descriptions, but a multiplicity of good descriptions, in comparable terms, of a range of languages and of the same language at different periods. This, in turn, implies that we have some record of languages at different periods, and that we can interpret that record in a linguistically reliable way. None of this is trivial, and it is all interdependent. To see what happened in one language we might need to be informed of the way things are generally assumed to happen across languages; to see what the general rule is, we certainly need detailed descriptions of individual changes in individual languages. It is no wonder that the serious study of language change requires considerable scholarship.

SOME POINTS TO PONDER

▶ The word *ass*, which is used in the King James version of the bible, has generally yielded to *donkey* in modern English. The reasons are probably similar to those that gave rise to the demise of *coney* and the rise of *rabbit*. Can you see how a problem arises? Look in an etymological dictionary for the source of the word *donkey*, which is rather surprising.

▶ The following are words listed in a dictionary of new words which arose in the period 1963–72 (Barnhart et al. 1973). Which of these are still in use? What conclusions can you draw about dictionaries and about the speed of change from these examples? You may need to check some of these words in a number of dictionaries or by looking on the web.

    bird strike, Indian hay, kinky boot, mariculture, metrication, provo, visagiste, washeteria

▶ Consider the word *mini* meaning 'a small car'. Is it an exception to the rule that affixes cannot turn into words or not? Defend your answer.

▶ Look up either the word *nice* or the word *silly* in a dictionary which provides etymological information. What have these words meant in the past? How many of these meanings are still in use? Of those still in use, do some of them occur only in specific expressions or in specific subject areas, or can they be used freely?

▶ A passage from Chapter 27 of Jane Austen's *Emma* (first published in 1816) is presented below. On the basis of this passage, what ways can you find in which English has changed over the last two centuries?

> *Emma did not regret her condescension in going to the Coles. The visit afforded her many pleasant recollections the next day, and all that she might have been supposed to have lost on the side of dignified seclusion must be amply repaid in the splendour of popularity . . .*
>
> *[T]here were two points on which she was not quite easy. She doubted whether she had not transgressed the duty of woman by woman in betraying her suspicions of Jane Fairfax's feelings to Frank Churchill . . .*
>
> *The other circumstance of regret related also to Jane Fairfax, and there she had no doubt. She did unfeignedly and unequivocally regret the inferiority of her own playing and singing.*

READING AND REFERENCES

For any serious study of the way English has developed, *The Oxford English Dictionary* is a fundamental work. There are also specialized dictionaries of etymology. On *ladies* and *whores*, and on *rabbits* and other fascinating insights into changing language, see Burridge (2002). Aitchison (1981) provides an extremely accessible view of language change in general, as does Trask (1994). For a more technical discussion of this area, see Crowley (1997). There are a great many books which deal with the development of English, of which Strang (1970) is recommended as neither too advanced nor too simple. Hogg (2002) and Horobin and Smith (2002) provide approachable introductions to particular periods in the history of English. There are similar works covering the histories of many well-studied languages – consult a library catalogue.

Aitchison, Jean (1981) *Language Change: Progress or Decay* (London: Fontana). Later editions are published by Cambridge University Press.

Austen, Jane (1816) *Emma* (London).

Barnhart, Clarence L., Sol Steinmetz and Robert K. Barnhart (1973) *The Barnhart Dictionary of New English, 1963–1972* (London: Longman).

Burridge, Kate (2002) *Blooming English* (Sydney: ABC Books).

Crowley, Terry (1997) *An Introduction to Historical Linguistics*, 3rd edn (Auckland: Oxford University Press).

Hogg, Richard (2002) *An Introduction to Old English* (Edinburgh: Edinburgh University Press).

Horobin, Simon and Jeremy Smith (2002) *An Introduction to Middle English* (Edinburgh: Edinburgh University Press).

Jespersen, Otto (1993 [1894]) *Progress in Language* (London: Swan Sonnenschein; New York: Macmillan). Reprinted with an introduction by James D. McCawley (Amsterdam and Philadelphia: Benjamins).

Strang, Barbara M. H. (1970) *A History of English* (London: Methuen).

Trask, R. L. (1994) *Language Change* (London: Routledge).

Linguistic Relations

What's the matter?

Learning a foreign language is always a difficult thing for an adult to do. In Denmark one of us was told 'In French a horse is called a *cheval*, and the rest is like that too'. But some languages seem easier than others simply because the difference is not always as great as that between *horse* and *cheval*. Consider what would happen if a Dane considered learning German instead of French (Table 4.1).

Table 4.1 **Corresponding words in some European languages**

English gloss	Danish word	German word	French word
arm	arm	Arm	bras
customs (and excise)	told	Zoll	douane
house	hus	Haus	maison
man	mand	Mann	homme
mouse	mus	Maus	souris
rain	regn	Regen	pluie
tongue	tunge	Zunge	langue

The examples have, of course, been carefully chosen to make the point, and the fact that the English word looks like the Danish and German in most of these cases is also the result of careful choice. Nevertheless, the commonalities we can see in this list between Danish and German are not coincidental, they are real, and arise because Danish and German are RELATED languages, much more closely related than Danish and French are. So what does it mean for languages to be related? Are languages related in the same way that you are related to your grandfather and aunt? And what does the family tree of a language look like? Those are the questions that we go on to consider in this chapter.

Natural families

You are probably used to two kinds of family tree. The first is the kind illustrated in Figure 4.1, which shows just a bit from the family tree of a fictitious John Smith marrying an equally fictitious Mary Jones. A family tree of this type can be interpreted in terms of shared genetics, assuming that the genes of the offspring come from both parents (that is, that no child is adopted or born as a result of adultery, artificial insemination, etc.).

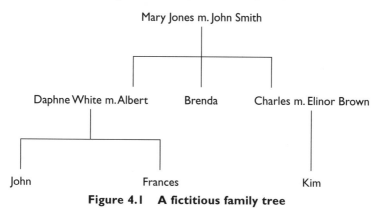

Figure 4.1   A fictitious family tree

The other kind of family tree you are likely to be familiar with is that in Figure 4.2. Here we are not concerned with the source of incoming genes, but with mutations through time, and the way in which what was originally one species divides into two or more species, so that we end up with a series of 'related' species, 'related' in terms of sharing a common ancestor.

The metaphor which talks about languages being 'related' to each other is based on the kind of tree shown in Figure 4.2, and languages are to be understood as being related in the same way that the species in Figure 4.2 are related. That is, they share a common ancestor, and they derive from that common ancestor by a number of mutations. In this parallel, languages are seen as being equivalent to discrete species, and the changes which affect languages over time are seen as being equivalent to the genetic changes which distinguish one biological species from another. The fact that neither parallel is particularly exact should not detract from the usefulness of the analogy, although we will go on to show some of the problems with this picture of linguistic relatedness.

The nature of linguistic mutations

Perhaps the most obvious linguistic match for the genes which might mutate are the words of a language. Sometimes the descendant languages (or some of them) lose the normal word from the original language, and in some of those instances that word is replaced with a different one. What kinds of situations would give rise to this outcome?

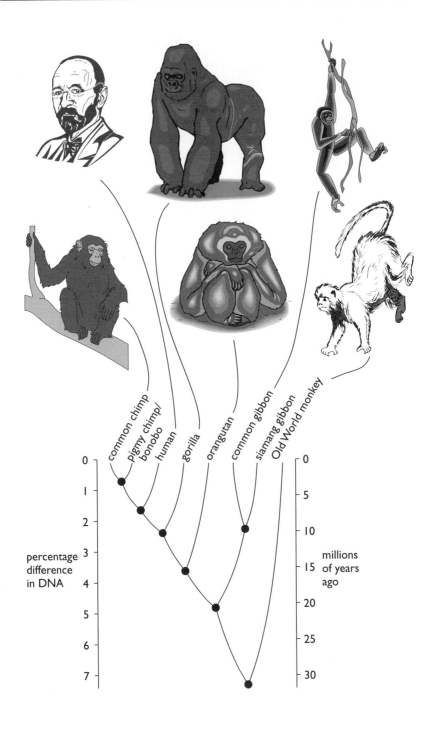

Figure 4.2   A species tree

In some cases, the new word will arise from the slang of the original language. We can illustrate this quite easily with the change of Latin to the modern Romance languages. This is a useful field for showing the various relationships, since we have texts surviving in Latin as well as in what are usually termed the DAUGHTER LANGUAGES, French, Italian, Spanish and so on. (The label 'daughter language' is common enough to be worth using, though it seems to imply the wrong kind of family tree – one like Figure 4.1 rather than one like Figure 4.2.). We therefore do not have to guess about what the original language looked like nearly as much as we usually do. For example, we have no texts written in the language that was the forerunner of English, Dutch, German and Swedish in the way that we have texts in Latin, so we have to RECONSTRUCT the original language based on the knowledge we have of the daughter languages. While the Latin of Virgil and Cicero is not quite what we can reconstruct on the basis of modern French, Italian, etc., it provides us with a good picture of the source language. And in this original language, the word for 'horse' was *equus*. This has given the modern English word, *equine*, based on the Classical Latin. However, if we look at the modern Romance languages (the languages derived from Latin), we find that the French word is *cheval*, the Italian is *cavallo* and the Spanish is *caballo*. These words are not derived from *equus* at all, but from a word *caballus* meaning 'nag, broken-down horse'. This was presumably the normal word in spoken every-day Latin, the Latin of the common or the vulgar people (hence 'Vulgar Latin') at some period, and got handed down to the modern languages. Similarly, the word for 'head' in Latin was *caput* (which we can still recognize in our word *capital* – whether applied to punishment or cities). While traces of *caput* remain in Spanish *cabeza* 'head', and the French word for the head of an organization, *chef*, the French word for 'head' as a body part is *tête* and the Italian is *testa*, deriving from a Vulgar Latin word *testa* meaning a 'pot'.

After the fall of Rome, various parts of the Roman Empire were invaded by non-Latin speakers who brought their own words with them. Sometimes they added their words, words which had not existed in Classical Latin (*naranja* 'orange', *albérchigo* 'peach' and *limón* 'lemon' are Arabic words still found in modern Spanish). At other times, one of the invaders' words took over from an earlier word with the same meaning. This has happened with French *blanc* 'white', Italian *bianco* 'white', Spanish *blanco* 'white'. This word, related to our word *blank*, was brought in by Germanic invaders and replaced the Latin word *albus*, which gives rise to the modern French word *aube* 'dawn' and the English words *albino* and *albumen* 'egg white'. The words for 'north', 'south', 'east' and 'west' were also borrowed into French (and from there into Italian and Spanish) from Germanic languages; English still keeps some remnants of the Latin names in learned vocabulary items like *Australia, meridional, occidental, oriental*. The word for 'beech', *fagus* in Latin, survives in Italian as *faggio*, and less obviously as *haya* in Spanish. In French, however, the word is *hêtre*, again from a Germanic language. We can recognize in it *heester*, the Dutch word for 'shrub'.

Some attempts have been made to add to the observation that words are replaced in languages with a statement on rates at which this happens.

Theories about this process are usually discussed under the heading of GLOT-TOCHRONOLOGY or LEXICOSTATISTICS (although the two terms are not synonymous for all writers, they are for some, and the difference is irrelevant here). The figure most often cited is that we expect about 80 per cent of the core vocabulary to be retained after a thousand years. There are two things to note here. The first is the idea of core vocabulary, which turns out to be difficult to define. In practice, it is usually measured on a list of 100 words which are expected to recur in most languages (words like *ash, black, cold, knee, woman*), though they certainly do not in occur in all languages; for example, not every language has a word for 'green'. The second thing to note is that we are talking here about some kind of average, and languages do not always change at the expected rate; there may be periods of rapid change and periods of very little change. Modern Icelandic and Modern Norwegian both derive from the language variously called Old Icelandic or Old Norse: but if you look at a piece of Old Icelandic and compare it with Modern Icelandic and Modern Norwegian, the Modern Icelandic will look much more like the Old Icelandic than the modern Norwegian will (see (1) below). Icelandic is a language which is generally considered to have changed relatively little in the last thousand years. The result is that we cannot really add a time scale to linguistic change to parallel the one in Figure 4.2.

(1) Old Icelandic   Kerlingin mætti trǫllinu á fjallinu
                          woman·the met troll·the on mountain·the
                          'The woman met the troll on the mountain'
     Modern Icelandic   Kerlingin mætti tröllinu á fjallinu
     Modern New   Kjerringa møtte trollet på fjellet
     Norwegian

Alongside changes such as losing or gaining words, languages change in other ways as well. They change, for example, in their pronunciation and in their grammar (see Chapter 3). In the time that it has taken Latin *caballus* to become Spanish *caballo*, Latin *caput* has changed into Spanish *cabeza*. One pair looks much more similar than the other, because of the ways the sounds have changed in different parts of the system. While we would say that we are left with the same word in these two cases, we might not be able to recognize 'the same word' without considerable linguistic training.

Again with grammar, we have already seen (in Chapter 3) that the Latin subjunctive form *donem* corresponds to the Italian *doni*. We can provide slightly more data for a comparison in Table 4.2.

Note that in Italian all three persons have the same form in the singular (as they do in spoken French, where the final <s> of *donnes* is not pronounced). (When we enclose an item in angle brackets, as <s>, we refer specifically to the spelling.) Note also that while Italian and French still have the appropriate categories (at least in formal styles), they have changed the grammar in subtly different ways: Italian has acquired a consistent *doni*- before the endings; in French, where final <-nt> is not pronounced, the third person singular and plural sound alike. There are more subtle changes in that the

Table 4.2   The present subjunctive of the verb meaning 'give' in three languages

Present, subjunctive, of 'give'	Latin	Italian	French
1st person singular ('I')	donem	doni	donne
2nd person singular ('you')	donēs	doni	donnes
3rd person singular ('he, she, it')	donet	doni	donne
1st person plural ('we')	donēmus	doniamo	donnions
2nd person plural ('you [all]')	donētis	doniate	donniez
3rd person plural ('they')	donent	donino	donnent

subjunctive is indistinguishable from the indicative for many persons in French, but rather more distinct in Italian.

Cumulation of changes

Eventually, there will be so much difference between the two varieties of what was once the same language that its speakers will start thinking of the two as being separate languages. It might be expected that linguists would have a very good idea about when two varieties belonged to the 'same language' and when they belonged to 'different languages', but they do not. Linguists certainly know that it is not simply a matter of mutual comprehension: with some good will (and some practice as well) speakers of Italian can understand speakers of Spanish and speakers of Danish can understand speakers of Swedish, while it is easy enough to find two speakers of English who cannot understand each other. Whether two varieties count as the 'same language' or not is often more a political decision than a linguistic one. It is sometimes said that a language is a dialect with an army and a navy. That makes the point very succinctly.

Results of changes

The result of all this is that we can see languages as related to each other in terms of the number of changes which distinguish them from their earlier forms (their ancestor languages). This allows us to draw family trees like the one in Figure 4.3 for a 'family' of languages now usually known as the Indo-European language family (because languages belonging in this family spread from India through to Europe). A partial tree for another language family, the Austronesian language family, is given in Figure 4.4.

We can also see language families in the words different languages use. In Table 4.3 the words for the numbers one, two, three, four and five are given from a number of different languages. By careful study of the table, you should be able to answer the questions given below, and convince yourself of the reality of language families.

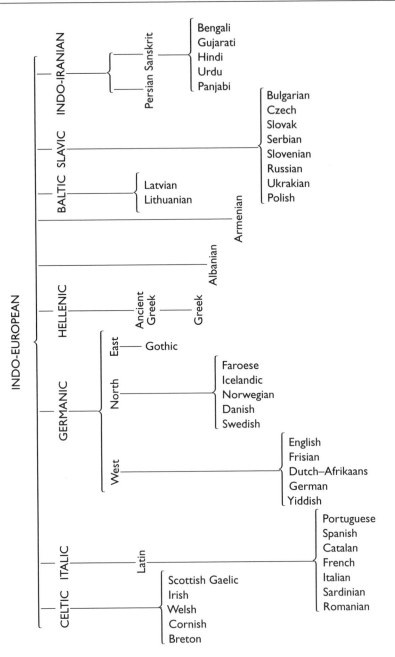

Figure 4.3   The Indo-European language family

Questions to answer in regard of Table 4.3:
(a) If there is a language in the table related to Maltese, what is it?
(b) What is the most closely related language to Breton?

Table 4.3 Words for numbers in several languages

Language	1	2	3	4	5
Albanian	një	dy	tre	katër	pesë
Basque	bat	bi	hirur	laur	bortz
Breton	unan	daou	tri	pevar	pemp
Catalan	un	dos	tres	quatre	cinc
Cornish	onen	dew	try	pager	pemp
Danish	en	to	tre	fire	fem
Dutch	een	twee	drie	vier	vijf
English	one	two	three	four	five
Fijian	dua	rua	tolu	vaa	lima
Finnish	yksi	kaksi	kolme	neljä	viisi
French	un	deux	trois	quatre	cinq
Frisian	ien	twa	trije	fjouwer	fiif
Gaelic	haon	dà	trì	ceithir	cóig
Gallego	un	dous	tres	catro	cinco
German	ein	zwei	drei	vier	fünf
Hebrew	eHad	shnayim	shlosha	arba'a	Hamisha
Icelandic	einn	tveir	þrír	fjórir	fimm
Irish	aon	dó	trí	ceathar	cuig
Italian	uno	due	tre	quattro	cinque
Latin	unus	duo	tres	quattuor	quinque
Maltese	wieħed	tnejn	tlieta	erbgħa	ħamsa
Maori	tahi	rua	toru	whaa	rima
Portuguese	um	dois	três	quatro	cinco
Romanian	unu	doi	trei	patru	cînci
Russian	odin	dva	tri	chetyr'e	p'at'
Samoan	tasi	lua	tolu	fa	lima
Spanish	uno	dos	tres	cuatro	cinco
Swahili	moja	mbili	tatu	nne	tano
Swedish	en	två	tre	fyra	fem
Tongan	taha	ua	tolu	faa	nima
Turkish	bir	iki	üç	dört	beş
Welsh	un	dau	tri	pedwar	pump
West Greenlandic	ataasiq	marluk	urpik	sisamat	tallimat

(c) What is the most closely related language to English?
(d) What languages here are closely related to Maori?
(e) What set of languages does Catalan belong with?
(f) Are German, Russian, Albanian and Italian related?
(g) Which listed languages have no other related languages listed?

How far can we go?

A question which is currently causing a great deal of discussion among linguists is how far this notion of a family tree of languages can be pushed, and, specifically, what counts as evidence for the relatedness of members of a family.

For most linguists, the evidence that permits us to build up family trees like those in Figures 4.3 and 4.4 is very restricted. We must find regular patterns of correspondence in whole sets of words. For example, if we look at the word for 'one' in Maori and Samoan we see that Maori <h> corresponds with Samoan <s>. We can find corresponding differences in a number of other words (see Table 4.4).

It is the consistent pattern of regularly related forms in related words which allows us to postulate the existence of a family relationship. Another example was presented at the beginning of this chapter, when we saw that Danish *told* is related to (we would normally say IS COGNATE WITH, meaning that they derive from a single common earlier form) German *Zoll* and Danish *tunge* is related to German *Zunge*. The change between initial Danish <t> and initial German <Z> is a regular one.

Some linguists, though, are prepared to be rather less thorough in their matching of forms between languages, as long as there are enough points of comparison to suggest that similarities are greater than chance. This method-

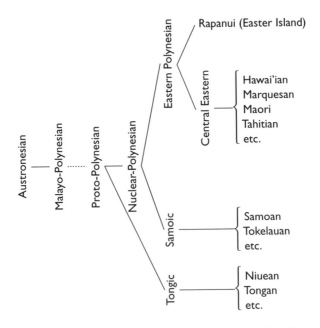

Figure 4.4 The Polynesian language family

The dotted lines indicate that there are several more branches in this family. The wider Austronesian family includes languages from Taiwan, and the Malayo-Polynesian group includes Malagasy, Indonesian, Tagalog (Pilipino) and many languages of Papua New Guinea and Micronesia.

Table 4.4   **Comparing Maori and Samoan**

Maori	Samoan	Gloss
hako	sa'o	'straight'
hina	sina	'grey (of hair)'
ihu	isu	'nose'
tuhi 'write'	tusi 'something written'	

ology has been strongly condemned by more conservative linguists, who point out just how much can happen by chance. However, application of the new methodology has allowed some spectacular claims to be made. First of all, it is suggested that we can trace languages further back in time than we show in the Indo-European family tree (Figure 4.3), and that Indo-European is linked to Afro-Asiatic languages like Hausa (spoken in Nigeria), Uralic languages like Finnish, and Altaic languages like Turkish. This super-language family is called NOSTRATIC. Some scholars want to push things even further back, and see all human languages linked as descending from what is called PROTO-WORLD. This hypothesis is not given much credence by most linguists at the moment. Whether or not it is true that there is a single language underlying all human language, we cannot prove convincingly that this is the case by comparing the modern languages.

Some warnings

Although the family tree picture of language development is well entrenched in the way in which we view language, it has a number of problems associated with it.

The first point is that a family tree like Figure 4.2 shows relations between species which arise by mutation, but does not expect genetic interference from outside in the way the family tree in Figure 4.1 does. But languages are frequently influenced from outside. This influence is often most clearly seen in the words used. For example, English is, in its fundamental patterns, related to Dutch and German (see Figure 4.3), but much of its vocabulary – especially its less basic vocabulary such as *chastise, hotel, priest, treasure* – comes from French. Contact phenomena such as this are very common, but cannot readily be put into the family tree picture. In the case of pidgin languages (see Chapter 9) it is often true that most of the words come from one language while most of the grammatical structures come from another, and this resembles the kind of picture given by the tree in Figure 4.1 more than that given in Figure 4.2.

Languages which develop from the same language are very often spoken in neighbouring areas, so that speakers of one may have an influence in the area of the other. Thus the picture that is given in the tree that the two languages simply split apart at some point is usually false: splitting can take a very long time. Occasionally the clean split is found, usually aided by geography, but it is rare.

Even where two languages have split, they may come to look more similar because of some external development. For example, both Dutch and English have been strongly influenced by French at different points in their history, so the fact that Dutch has a word *liberaal* corresponding to English *liberal* is nothing to do with how close Dutch and English are on the family tree: they have independently borrowed that word from an external prestigious source.

Where next?

In order to work out the ways in which languages can diverge from a common ancestor, you need to understand a lot about the structure of languages and how that is described. That is, you need to know about phonetics and phonology, and also about grammar. One point that has not been discussed here is that the 'same word' can end up meaning different things in related languages (see *tuhi* and *tusi* in Maori and Samoan as illustrated in Table 4.4 for a simple example). To look at the notion of possible change in meaning (something which has not been discussed in this chapter, but which is clearly important), you also have to know something about semantic description. Apart from an understanding of the basic descriptive methodology, you need experience in the analysis of what happens to related languages. Certain patterns of change turn out to be common and expected, while others are rare and unexpected. Most linguists would be unhappy about setting up a derivation which depended upon extremely unlikely things happening all the time. Finally, most of the linguists who work in this area have a good first-hand knowledge of a range of related languages: dictionaries are very difficult to work with if you do not speak the languages they describe. So working out just how two languages have diverged from a common ancestor is a very difficult task, and one which cannot easily be undertaken by beginning students. Students may, nevertheless, get some idea of the intellectual puzzle by doing some of the exercises in textbooks on historical and comparative linguistics.

SOME POINTS TO PONDER

▶ With the examples of the word for a pot being used to mean 'head' or the word for a nag being used for any horse, we can clearly see how the meaning has changed. In some other cases it is far less obvious. Consider the word *spam* 'unsolicited electronic communications sent to multiple addresses'. Look in a modern dictionary to find out how it got its new meaning.

▶ There is a German word *Laune* which has a Danish cognate *lune*, but there is no corresponding cognate form in English (the English translation is 'humour, spirits'). Why would this be?

▶ There is a German word *Laus*. On the basis of the data given in Table 4.1, what would you expect the Danish cognate to be? What might the word mean? Similarly, what would you expect the cognates of the German word *Lunge* to be?

▶ Would you expect to find cognates of the English word *priest* in German and Danish following the same set of rules as governs the cognates in Table 4.1? Why (not)?

▶ Consider the data given in Table 4.5. What does this tell you about the different varieties of language illustrated in columns 1–4? Are they different dialects of the same language or not?

Table 4.5   Comparing four varieties

1	2	3	4
base	base	base	base
bench	banc	banco	banco
tide	marée	marea	marea
fierce	féroce	feroce	feroz
death	mort	morte	muerte

Does it make any difference if you know that the four columns are English, French, Italian and Spanish respectively?

READING AND REFERENCES

The line about a language being a dialect with an army and a navy is usually attributed to Max Weinreich, in an article written in Yiddish in 1945 (you may see it erroneously attributed to his son, Uriel, who was also a linguist). The quotation is better known than its author. The example from Icelandic and New Norwegian is from Arne Torp (personal communication). For a good introduction to the topics of this chapter, see Trask (1994). For more detail, see the relevant chapters of Crowley (1997) or Trask (1996). For a journalistic view of Nostratic and Proto-World, see Wright (1991). For most of the other topics mentioned, including glottochronology, see Crystal (1987). For further exploration of Indo-European, see the website listed below. For a detailed investigation of linguistic reconstruction see Fox (1995).

The answers to the questions relating to Table 4.3 are:

(a)   Hebrew
(b)   Cornish
(c)   Frisian
(d)   Fijian, Samoan, Tongan
(e)   French, Gallego, Italian, Latin, Portuguese, Romanian and Spanish.
(f)   Yes, but they are not the most closely related of languages (see Figure 4.3)
(g)   Basque, Finnish, Swahili and Turkish – but see the later discussion of Nostratic.

Crowley, Terry (1997) *An Introduction to Historical Linguistics*, 3rd edn (Auckland: Oxford University Press).

Crystal, David (1987) *The Cambridge Encyclopedia of Language* (Cambridge: Cambridge University Press).

Fox, Anthony (1995) *Linguistic Reconstruction* (Oxford: Oxford University Press).
Trask, R. L. (1994) *Language Change* (London: Routledge).
Trask, R. L. (1996) *Historical Linguistics* (London: Edward Arnold).
Wright, Robert (1991) 'Quest for the Mother Tongue', *Atlantic Monthly*, April, 39–68.

http://www.cofah.utsa.edu/drinka/pie/pie.html <== Proto Indo European Language
   demonstration and explanation.

Bee Talk and Monkey Chatter

What's the matter?

What can your dog communicate to you? At the very least it can communicate alertness, anger, depression/sadness, excitement, fear, friendliness, frustration, happiness, hunger/thirst, immediate need, interest, playfulness, warning/threat, and can presumably also communicate things to other dogs via the sense of smell. You may be able to think of a few more. Most animal communication systems allow for up to 30 or 35 different messages, though some of these messages can, of course, show differences of degree, such as mild or extreme depression. But as Bertrand Russell famously remarked, 'No matter how eloquently [a dog] may bark, he cannot tell you that his parents were honest though poor.' Human communication systems not only allow for far more than 35 different messages (see Chapter 8), they can include messages on topics which simply are not possible in the dog communication system given above.

The difference between animal communication systems and human language reflects the difference between the way in which the ancestors of humans must have communicated and the way in which we communicate now. In particular, we made reference in Chapter 1 to the DISCONTINUITY PROBLEM: the question of how we changed from something which is not language-like to our current linguistic proficiency. One strategy that has been invoked both by people who wish to show the distinctiveness of human language and by people who wish to show that human language might well have evolved out of other kinds of communication system has been to look in detail at the ways in which animals communicate. If human language is completely different in type from animal communication systems, and we can show in what ways it is different, we can illustrate the problem of discontinuity in greater detail. If human language evolves gradually from animal communication systems, we might expect to find some animals whose communication system is very similar to human language, and perhaps animals which can be taught to communicate in some analogue of human language.

Design features: defining human language

Those linguists who have been concerned with establishing what it is that makes human language distinct from other communication systems have set up a number of criteria which are called DESIGN FEATURES of human language. We do not need to look at all the design features that have been proposed, but we can consider some of the more important ones, and see how they show human language to differ from other methods of communication.

Let us begin with what is sometimes called 'the language of flowers'. 'Say it with flowers' is the advertisers' slogan, but most of us can say very little with flowers: perhaps 'I love you' on St Valentine's day and 'I'm sorry you are dead' at a funeral (or, more accurately, 'I want you to believe that I love you' and 'I want to convince someone that I'm sorry you are dead' at the funeral). Some people can communicate rather more than this: Leopold in the movie *Kate and Leopold* found a bunch of flowers presented by a less knowledgeable admirer of Kate's to be sending very inappropriate messages, and Ophelia in Shakespeare's *Hamlet* shows her knowledge of the symbolism of flowers in some detail.

> OPHELIA: There's rosemary, that's for remembrance; pray you, love, remember; and there's pansies,[1] that's for thoughts. . . . There's fennel[2] for you, and columbines;[3] there's rue[4] for you; and here's some for me; we may call it herb of grace o' Sundays; oh, you must wear your rue with a difference. There's a daisy;[5] I would give you some violets,[6] but they withered all when my father died . . . (*Hamlet*, IV.v)

Even Ophelia, while she may be able to communicate a large number of messages to someone who recognizes rue and is as familiar as she is with the code, cannot communicate, 'Meet me at our favourite restaurant for dinner on the 15th' in this way. Nevertheless, she is able to communicate some definite and fixed messages. This is better than can be managed with music, despite the fact that we sometimes find music talked about as a language. You may have seen Disney's *Fantasia* where images are put to famous pieces of music. Some of these images are quite abstract; some, like Mickey Mouse getting into trouble with magic buckets, are very concrete. But while a particular piece of music clearly communicated something to the Disney animators, there is no guarantee that anyone else listening to the same piece of music will get the same image (unless they watch the movie, of course). The difference here brings up one of the design features (DF):

> DF1:   **semanticity**: in human language the elements of the message have specific and fixed relation to real-world situations.

The flower communication system and the dog communication system show other things about human language. First, both of these communication systems can only tell you about what is happening here and now. The dog cannot signal, 'I'll be angry next Thursday', the flowers cannot signal, 'I loved you last week, but now I've found somebody new'. Even less can they signal such things as, 'if you let me out I'll be playful' or 'there is no intruder in the room'. This is covered by another two design features.

DF2: **displacement/freedom from stimulus**: in human language it is possible to talk about events remote in time and place.

DF3: **productivity**: in human language new messages can be produced from the elements of familiar messages; there is no fixed set of possible messages.

Some animal communication systems seem to meet these criteria. In the 1920s Karl von Frisch described the communication system of honey bees. As he described it, their communication system seemed to meet the criteria of displacement and productivity. It now seems that von Frisch's description missed out some very important features of the communication system (in particular, the role played by odour), but there is sufficient truth in the system as he described it to make it worth considering. When honey bees find a source of nectar, they return to the hive and they tell the other bees about the source of the nectar, including how good a source it is (how much nectar), how close it is to the hive, and what direction to fly in to find it. If the source is close to the hive, the communicator bee does what is called a 'round dance'. This doesn't tell the recipient bees where in relation to the hive the source of nectar is, only that there is one. If the source is further than about 50 m from the hive, then the communicator bee does a tail-wagging dance. The tail-wagging dance shows the angle in relation to the sun at which the recipient bees have to fly (the sun is represented by the vertical in the dance). The length of time spent travelling up the vertical line in the dance is proportional to the amount of time the bees have to fly to reach the source. The number of times the dance is repeated tells the recipients about the value of the source (its sweetness). So the communicator bee can use elements to provide new messages about source quality, direction and distance, and recipients understand the message, because they go and look for a source of nectar in an appropriate place. This is arguably displacement (the nectar isn't here, it's somewhere else – though note that the bee could also be argued to communicate its current excitement level) and productivity (it can tell you anywhere within 360 degrees and at distances up to several kilometres). So is it just like language?

Scientists who work with animals other than humans keep saying that every time they come up with something that looks like a language, linguists go all coy on them and say that it can't be a language because … In this case, the bees' communication system can't be language because it fails to show the next two design features.

DF4: **dual articulation/duality of patterning**: in human language sounds can go together to make up words, words can go together to make up sentences. (There are gestural equivalents of these two levels in sign languages, where hand shapes and positions go together to make up different signs which combine to make sentences.)

DF5: **discreteness**: human language uses a small set of discrete contrastive elements.

What this last design feature means can most easily be illustrated with speech sounds or the letters which represent them. If we consider the word *pat*, we can turn it into a different word by replacing the initial [p] with a [b] (to give *bat*) or by replacing the vowel with an [e] (to give *pet*), or by replacing the final [t] with an [n] (to give *pan*). In each case we have taken a different item from the small set of distinctive sounds (or letters if we view this as written language) to create a different word. *Pat* contrasts with *bat*, *pet* and *pan* because [p] contrasts with [b], [æ] (the symbol used for the vowel sound in *pat*) contrasts with [e], and [t] contrasts with [n]. We can't have a word for something which is half-way between a sip and a sup by having a vowel which is half-way between the vowels in the words *sip* and *sup*. This notion of CONTRAST and discrete elements is a fundamental notion in linguistics. By a continuation of the same logic, *cat* contrasts with *dog* because *The cat bit me* and *The dog bit me* are different sentences, the present tense contrasts with the past tense because *I walk to work every day* is a different message from *I walked to work every day*, and so on.

The bees' dance is a matter of more or less of the same thing, or the same thing at a different angle, not a matter of contrasting units in this way. Nor do we find two levels involved in building up the bees' messages: there is nothing corresponding to words in their system.

What, then, about parrots? It might seem that parrots use dual articulation and discreteness when they mimic human language. It is certainly the case that there are some very intelligent parrots which have been taught to speak words and phrases of human language on appropriate occasions, and which manage to replace words in sentences with an appropriate item: for example, they can change the message from *I want a nut* to *I want a grape*. This shows discreteness. Yet despite the fact that at least one of these parrots can use the words *grey* and *grape*, there is little evidence that the words are any more than (more or less similar) unitary calls rather than made up of independently manipulable consonants and vowels (as in the *pat* example above). That being the case, dual articulation is not a feature of such parrots' communication system.

Our closest relatives: the great apes

The question about apes and languages was originally raised to see how far language behaviour is a specifically human phenomenon and how far similar behaviours are shared by other animals (in which case it may be more developed in humans, but we know where it comes from).

In an early experiment, a chimp was brought up along with humans in a human family. The human baby learned to talk; the chimp did not. In retrospect, this is no surprise. We now know something that was not generally appreciated at the time, namely that chimps do not have the correct physiology for speech (see Chapter 1). They cannot talk. They cannot even easily vocalize on demand. However, chimps do have the manual dexterity required to sign. So it seemed likely that if chimps could be taught a human language, it would be a sign language. Accordingly, a chimp called Washoe was taught American Sign Language (ASL). She was brought up in a signing community, and she was also deliberately and consciously taught ASL (something that would not be necessary for human children). At the age of four Washoe could produce some 85 different signs, and was said to be able to combine them meaningfully into two-word 'utterances' such as 'more fruit', 'hug hurry'. This has dual articulation, it has discreteness, it has semanticity and (limited) productivity. It is not clear whether it shows displacement. To put Washoe's achievement in some kind of perspective, a more recent report (Kaminsky et al. 2004) indicates that an intelligent dog can understand over 200 verbal commands from a human.

Then a chimpanzee called Sarah was taught to use plastic symbols backed with metal and stuck onto a magnetic board vertically to produce sentences. The symbols were different shapes and colours, but the shapes and colours were not related iconically to the object they denoted – the plastic token for the word *Sarah* was an exception in that it was shaped like a chimp, but the token meaning 'banana' was a small red square. The experimenters claim that Sarah's communication showed productivity. A command such as *Sarah insert banana pail apple dish* ('Sarah put the banana in the pail and the apple in the dish') was obeyed at the same level (about 80 per cent) as the simple sentences. The argument is that Sarah has real syntax.

A gorilla called Koko was also taught ASL. When asked in ASL what she wanted for her birthday, Koko signed 'Cereal there. Good there drink.' When asked about her kitten, she signed 'soft, good cat cat'. How far such utterances show productivity and displacement may be a matter of dispute. In August 2004, when Koko was 33 years old and reported to know 1000 signs, she made the sign for 'pain' and 'pointed to her tooth' to indicate to the researchers that she had toothache. Interestingly, while pointing to her tooth may just have been the ASL for 'tooth', she doesn't appear to have had a way of saying 'very great pain', because the researchers had to construct a scale of pain for her to respond to.

Another chimp, Nim Chimpsky (named ironically for the linguist Noam Chomsky whose theories of the specialization of the human language faculty it was hoped he would disprove – see Chapter 18) was also taught ASL. He learned 125 signs, but (a) he never used more than a three-word utterance, except things like 'give orange me give eat orange give me eat orange give me you'; (b) he only signed when he was signed to, he did not initiate conversation; (c) he mostly repeated what his trainers signed at him; (d) his utterances didn't get longer or more complex with time; and (e) he was not creative in his language use. All of this is very unlike what happens when human children learn language.

The most promising of all the ape studies, and the one for which most has been claimed, is the study of a pygmy chimpanzee or BONOBO called Kanzi. Kanzi began by using symbols on a keyboard to communicate. These are abstract symbols, rather like the ones Sarah used, but there are more of them. Kanzi's production, moreover, shows a certain amount of productivity and perhaps displacement: while many of the apes taught to communicate had learnt to ask to be tickled (a game they much enjoy), only Kanzi asked the experimenters to tickle each other while he sat back and watched! When it suits him, Kanzi also appears capable of understanding *if . . . then . . .* sentence structures. Kanzi also learnt to understand English words, alongside the signs he generally used. He even learnt to vocalize, although his 'vocabulary' of spoken words seems to be very small. While there is probably no dual articulation in Kanzi's communication system, this is as much a feature of the communication system used as it is a feature of Kanzi's abilities.

So far, despite the fictional accounts by authors such as Michael Crichton (1980), we know of no apes that have successfully taught their offspring to sign or use such languages to talk to other apes. In this, apes have failed to show another design feature:

DF6:   **cultural transmission**: human children learn language from the surrounding cultural group, it is not innate.

But even cultural transmission is not necessarily unique to humans: it has been noted in parrots.

The animal communication specialists are no doubt right that as linguists have become more precise about what makes human language unique, so they have pushed back our understanding of what other animals, and in particular other apes, are capable of. It is even claimed for Kanzi's communication that it shows syntactic structure. If this is so, some linguists will still not want to call what Kanzi produces language in the same sense that you produce 'language'. But the gap between the two is becoming narrower. We may not entirely have crossed the discontinuity, but the gap between the two sides no longer looks as big as it once did.

Where next?

There are two sides to the ape-language debate that seem worthy of consideration. The first is the question of syntactic structure in the language of the apes. We are told that Kanzi (at least sporadically) can comprehend *if . . . then . . .* structures, but does he ever produce them? At a more fundamental level, what kind of evidence of structure is there in his language. To appreciate this, you not only need to know more about Kanzi's production than has been provided here, you need to know something about syntactic structure in human language, the kinds of phenomena that you find there, and that you might expect to find in the production of apes if their production is to be deemed worthy of the title of 'language'. For some of the kinds of structure that are found in human languages, see Chapter 8. The second point is that the production of apes is often compared with the production of literate adult human beings. This seems an unfair comparison. A fairer comparison is with the production of young children. What structures do they use, and how do those structures compare with the structures used by the apes? This involves knowing something about the way in which syntax develops in humans, as well as about the communication skills of apes.

It is sometimes said that the production of apes (in general, rather than say that of Kanzi in particular) looks like the production of two-year-old children, and that this level of production is also found in pidgin languages before they gain native speakers and turn into creoles (see Chapter 9). Under this view, apes, human children and human adults under certain circumstances use a PROTOLANGUAGE which will develop into a real language only under the most auspicious of circumstances. To evaluate this view on language development, it is helpful to know something about pidgin languages (languages spoken where people who do not share a common language come together and have to communicate). (See Chapter 9.) In particular, the structure of pidgin languages is important in this context. This view brings us back to the discontinuity problem which the researchers in the Kanzi experiments are trying to play down. A serious evaluation of their stance cannot be made without a clear understanding of what goes on in a number of different kinds of communication.

SOME POINTS TO PONDER

▶ The seventeenth-century playwright Thomas Shadwell wrote that 'Sighs are the natural language of the heart'. To what extent could sighs of lovers be said to form a language if this statement were taken literally? Consider which of the design features they might fulfil.

▶ There are both advantages and disadvantages to attempting to define language in terms of a set of criteria such as the design features listed here. One of the disadvantages is that there is a tendency to lose sight of the overall nature of language by concentrating on the details. What advantages might there be to this approach?

▶ One of the apes being taught a language saw some swans and described them as *water birds*. What features of human language does this show?

▶ It is said that the chimpanzee Sarah responds appropriately to commands about 80 per cent of the time. Is this a high or low figure? How would you decide? How often do you think the average three-year-old responds appropriately to commands? How often do you?

READING AND REFERENCES

The quotation from Russell is from Russell (1948: 74). As so often, Crystal (1987) provides a good summary of much of this material. The classic work on design features is chapter 64 of Hockett (1958). An updated view of these is given by Lyons (1977:

§3.4) and again by Anderson (2004). The original work on honey bees is von Frisch (1954 [1927]). References to later work on the topic, and some hints as to the development of thought in this area can be gleaned from Kak (1991), which is, however, largely concerned with the topic as a piece of history of science. On parrots, see especially Pepperberg (1999), and other publications by the same author, or go on-line (see references below). Premack and Premack (1972) provides a readable survey of one of the early ape studies, while Savage-Rumbaugh and Lewin (1994) is the main reference on Kanzi. Wilson (1972) provides a (now rather dated) overview of animal communication systems, and Hövelmann (1989) provides a good counterbalance for those easily swayed by the propaganda that is broadcast in this area of study. For an excellent (though at times quite advanced) discussion of the whole area, see Anderson (2004).

Anderson, Stephen R. (2004) *Doctor Dolittle's Delusion* (New Haven, CT and London: Yale University Press).

Crichton, Michael (1980) *Congo* (New York: Alfred A. Knopf).

Crystal, David (1987) *The Cambridge Encyclopedia of Language* (Cambridge: Cambridge University Press).

Frisch, Karl von (1954 [1927]) *The Dancing Bees*, tr. Dora Isle and Norman Walker (London: Methuen).

Hockett, Charles F. (1958) *A Course in Modern Linguistics* (New York: Macmillan).

Hövelmann, Gerd H. (1989) 'Animal "language" Research: the Perpetuation of Some Old Mistakes', *Semiotica*, 73: 199–217.

Kak, Subhash C. (1991) 'The Honey-bee Dance Language Controversy', *Mankind Quarterly*, 31: 357–65.

Kaminsky, Juliane, Josep Call and Julia Fischer (2004) 'Word Learning in a Domestic Dog: Evidence for "Fast Mapping"', *Science*, 304 (11 June 2004): 1682–83.

Lyons, John (1977) *Semantics*, 2 vols (Cambridge: Cambridge University Press).

Pepperberg, Irene Maxine (1999) *The Alex Studies* (Cambridge, MA and London: Harvard University Press).

Premack, Ann James and David Premack (1972) 'Teaching Language to an Ape', *Scientific American*, 227 (October): 92–9.

Russell, Bertrand (1948) *Human Knowledge: Its Scope and Limits* (London: Allen & Unwin).

Savage-Rumbaugh, Sue and Roger Lewin (1994) *Kanzi: The Ape at the Brink of the Human Mind* (New York: John Wiley).

Wilson, Edward O. (1972) 'Animal Communication', *Scientific American*, 227 (September): 53–60.

<http://ftp.brown.edu/Departments/Anthropology/apelang.html> <== provides link to other pages about primates.

<http://www.alexfoundation.org/> <== material about the grey parrot, Alex.

NOTES

1 Cf. French *pensée* 'thought' from which the name derives.
2 A symbol of flattery, sometimes of lust.
3 Variously a useless flower, ingratitude, forsaken lovers, cuckoldom.
4 Rue, also known as herb of grace or herb-grace, was used in exorcism to expel devils. Symbol of repentence, compunction or compassion because of a pun with *to rue*, etymologically unrelated.
5 The 'dissembling' daisy warns girls not to trust promises made by amorous bachelors.
6 For faithfulness.

Part II

Language Structures

How Do You Spell *Accommodation?*

What's the matter?

English spelling is notorious for being difficult and inconsistent. Very few people can manage to write out the sentence in (1) without any spelling mistakes, and sentence (2) makes its own point about the inconsistent link between pronunciation and the spelling *-ough*.

(1) A harassed pedlar met an embarrassed saddler in a cemetery in order to gauge the symmetry of a lady's ankle.
(2) I thought I saw a dough-faced ploughboy coughing and hiccoughing his rough way through Scarborough.

George Bernard Shaw (Box 6.1) suggested that English spelling was so stupid that you could spell the word *fish* as <ghoti> (here, as elsewhere, we enclose spellings in angle brackets <. . .> and pronunciations in square brackets [. . .] to distinguish between them): <gh> spells [f] in *enough*, <o> spells the vowel sound in *fish* in the word *women* (at least in Shaw's dialect), and <ti> spells the final sound in *fish* in the word *nation*.

The bad reputation is only partly deserved. There are several things that we have to remember about English spelling if we are going to criticize it. Among these points are:

(a) English spelling has been relatively fixed for a very long time, and the way we pronounce English has changed, sometimes drastically, over that period; our spelling thus often reflects an older pronunciation.
(b) English spelling is doing more than just representing the sounds we make when we say individual words, so that criticizing it for failing to represent sounds is often to disregard its other virtues.
(c) When we criticize English spelling we tend to focus on a few extreme examples (such as that illustrated in (2)). We ignore the large proportion of English spelling which makes perfectly good sense and is regular. Whatever Shaw said, there is only one way in which *fish* could be spelt in English, and that is <fish>.

We could consider our spelling system from a number of different angles, but this chapter is too short to allow us to deal with all of them. So here we will concentrate on just two facets of the spelling system: How do children learn to spell, and what goes wrong? Why does our spelling system so frequently cause problems for adult (and supposedly competent) writers?

BOX 6.1   George Bernard Shaw

Although best known as a playwright, George Bernard Shaw (1856–1950) was an astute commentator on language and a strong supporter of spelling reform for the English language. His interest in the sounds of speech can be seen in the way he tried to manipulate English spelling in his play scripts to allow the accents of his characters to emerge. In this he was not always successful, and it is sometimes said that it is difficult to see (as opposed to hear) the difference between his upper-class characters and his lower-class characters in his re-spellings. His most famous linguistic play is *Pygmalion*, later turned into a musical under the title of *My Fair Lady*. The main character, Henry Higgins, is supposedly based on two outstanding phoneticians of Shaw's period: Henry Sweet and Daniel Jones. In the play, a Cockney flower-girl becomes socially upwardly mobile when she is taught to use the speech patterns of the upper classes, thus illustrating the importance we give to accents. Shaw left money in his will to the cause of spelling reform, though little was achieved with the money.

Learning to write

Most children learning to write treat writing as a way of putting down on paper the sounds they say. This was the original idea of an alphabetic system, but given that some of the most common words of English are also irregularly spelt, it is perhaps surprising that they should pick up this principle so well. Under a 'look and say' teaching system, we might also expect children to refuse to write anything unless they can spell the whole word. If that were the case, the main source of wrong spellings would be imperfectly recalled standard spellings. While this does remain a cause of spelling mistakes into adulthood, it is not the most important one for children. Some children's spellings are remarkably perceptive, as the genuine examples in (3) show (these are not all from speakers of the same variety of English, so some of the spellings may make better sense in the varieties spoken by the children who wrote them than they would in your variety).

(3) dongkee 'donkey' nachr 'nature' sed 'said'
    B cwiyit 'be quiet' bkos 'because' litl 'little'
    lafft 'laughed' cold 'called' addid 'added'

The spelling *<dongkee> (the asterisk indicates that this is not a possible spelling in the adult version of the written language), shows that the child is aware that they have the same sound in the middle of *donkey* and at the end of *song*. We find that most undergraduate students need to have this overtly pointed out to them before they notice what is happening. Similarly, many students refuse to believe that they put the same sound in the middle of *nature* as they have at the beginning of *chance*. The spelling *<sed> shows that *said* rhymes perfectly with *bed*. If <c> is what you find at the beginning of *cat*, and <w> is what you find at the beginning of *wild*, then it makes perfectly good sense to believe that the beginning of *quiet* should have both of these letters in it. Bob Dylan (in 'Farewell, Angelina') rhymes *deny it* with *quiet*, and the spelling here puts a clear *it* at the end of *quiet*. Many speakers have a very short vowel or no vowel sound at all between the [b] and the [k] in a rapid pronunciation of *because*, and there are many varieties of English where the tongue stays in contact with the roof of the mouth all the way from the [t] to the [l] in *little*, so that there can be no vowel sound there. For a child who has a short vowel in *laugh* (e.g. a child from North America, Scotland or the North of England), it makes good sense to put two <f>s after the <a>, just as we would in a word like *gaff*. The child has then quite correctly noticed that you add a [t] sound to make the verb past tense. The spelling *<cold> for *called* looks odd to us, because we know that it spells a different word; but any speaker who pronounces the <r> in *horse* and has the same vowel in *called* and *horse* will be able see the sense of the spelling. And finally *<addid> makes it clear that the second syllable of this word is just like *did* – something which is not true in all varieties of English, but is in many. So each of these spellings provides insights to prove that the children producing them are very much on the right track and thinking sensibly about the task that confronts them (even if, in these instances, they have ended up with something that is not correct by adult norms).

Some evidence of how children deal with hard words comes from an experiment in which 988 ten-year-olds were asked to spell *saucer*. The answers are given in (4).

(4) Ten-year-olds' spellings of *saucer* (from Peters 1970)
    saucer   462
    sauser   67
    sorser   23
    suacer   23
    sacer   20

sorcer	18
sosa	1
sari	1
no answer	21
all others	352
Total	**988**

It is noteworthy that even with a difficult word like this, the most common spelling was the one which is correct according to adult norms. The main 'error' combines some memory of how the word is spelt in books with some notion of writing down the sounds, and writing down the sounds and mis-remembering how the word is spelt give the next most common errors. Even at the lower end, a spelling like *sosa* is clearly based on the sounds; *sari* and a number of the 'other' spellings remain totally incomprehensible, and could have any one of a number of sources. Nevertheless, despite the large number of 'wrong' spellings, there are signs here that a great deal has been learned, and that some imperfect control over the system has been acquired.

Since, as we have already noted, English spelling is not just about writing down the sounds we speak, any child who relies upon that as the basis for spelling is bound to come to grief sooner or later. We will look at some such features below. More interesting, because they show the way in which progress is made in spelling, are those errors which are typical for young learners but which tend not to persist.

Making the letter 'say its name'

'Making a letter say its name' refers to the tendency to suppose that any letter is to be read in a word the same way as it would be read in isolation. We have already seen an example of this in (3) with B *cwiyt*, where the <B> 'says its name' and is pronounced just like *be*. While the example shows what happens when the principle is used with a consonant, this is a partic-ular problem with vowels. Children need to be taught that <I> does not 'say its name' but is pronounced [ɪ], that <A> says [æ] and so on. This is always something of an unnatural exercise, since [æ] (along with most of the other relevant vowel sounds) never occurs finally in any English word, but this does not seem to cause too many problems. In the basic words of English, if you want to make a single vowel letter say its name, it has to be followed by no more than one consonant and then another vowel. So we can see the difference in pronunciation of the vowel letters in the pairs of words in (5).

(5)	mat	mating
	pet	Peter
	sit	sited
	pot	potent
	cut	cuticle

To prevent this happening, we have to double the consonant letter, and the preceding single vowel letter will then be pronounced short, as shown in (6).

(6) mat   matting
     pet   petted
     sit   sitter
     pot   potter
     cut   cutting

These are the basic rules for consonant-doubling, although this ignores a lot of exceptions (the rules do not always apply in words taken from Greek and Latin; the rules apply consistently only when the vowel letter is in a stressed syllable; some letters, such as <v>, rarely double; and so on). But the patterns shown in (5) and (6) do not allow us to write a long vowel sound in a mono-syllabic word which ends in a consonant. To do this, we have to add what the schoolteachers call 'magic <e>', an <e> which is not pronounced itself, but which alters the pronunciation of the stressed vowel in the same way as is illustrated in (5).

(7) mat   mate
     met   mete
     sit   site
     not   note
     cut   cute

'Magic <e>' is thus the English spelling system's way of making a letter say its name.

Despite the great deal of regularity that is provided in the English spelling system by consonant-doubling and magic <e>, many people seem to manage to get through the education system without becoming aware that there are rules governing these phenomena, and are thus incapable of recognizing the inherent regularity of the <mm> in the middle of *accommodation* or the fact that *occurrence* must have <rr> in the middle.

Children are often in the situation of not being in control of the principle of what allows a letter to say its name. Misuse of the principle gives spellings like those in (8).

(8) sticke 'sticky'   tip   'type'   stad   'stayed'
     likt   'liked'   opn   'open'   brefcas   'briefcase'

Again, spellings like those in (8) do not show incompetence: rather they show a stage in development which needs to be (and usually is) passed. This childish use of making a letter say its name resurfaces in adult spellings only in jokes, games, text messaging and personalized car number plates (Box 6.2).

BOX 6.2 'Making the letter say its name'

You may recall from your childhood being asked how to spell 'hungry horse' in four letters. The answer was *MTGG* ('empty gee-gee'), and relies on saying the name of each letter and then reinterpreting it to provide the required message. The same kind of rebus principle is used in a number of the abbreviations used in e-mail, text-messaging and the like. A brief search of the World Wide Web provided, among others, the following list: *CUL8R* 'see you later', *BCNU* 'Be seeing you', *IC* 'I see', *NEI* 'anyone', *QT* 'Cutie', *RUOK* 'Are you okay?', *thanq* 'thank you', *XLNT* 'excellent'.

In New Zealand, car owners may purchase personalized number plates, which may make use of any unassigned sequence of up to six letters and digits. The following examples also involve the use of making a letter say its name: *B MINE* 'be mine', *MYLFA* 'my Alfa [Romeo]' (*Al* and *Elle* sound the same in New Zealand English), *NVTHIS* 'envy this', *RKITX* 'architects', *RUISTE* 'are you thirsty' (seen on a soft-drink delivery truck).

Simplifying consonant sequences

Many languages have no consonant clusters at all, and it is clear that it is harder to say sequences of consonants than it is to say sequences of consonant and vowel. The same seems to be true when learning to write. While children will often miss out the vowels in a word and leave only the consonants (so *tp* for *tip, top* or *type*), where there is a sequence of consonant sounds in the original, they have difficulty in getting that right. The worst case is where there is a nasal consonant (<m> or <n>) immediately before another consonant, especially [p, t, k, b, d, g]. Children seem not to hear the nasal as a separate consonant sound, with the result that we find spellings such as those in (9), with the <m> or the <n> omitted.

(9) staps 'stamps'   ad   'and'   nooigland 'New England'
     pesl 'pencil'   wotid 'wanted'   plat   'plant'

Again, this seems to represent a stage in the development of spelling which children eventually get over, but it is a recurrent source of spelling mistakes while it lasts.

Confusing the more established user

While we have seen some of the features of English spelling that clearly confuse the beginning writer, and have argued that there are many places where English spelling is less bad than is often supposed, nevertheless there are also places where English spelling regularly confuses adults who are supposedly competent in its use. There are basically a handful of problems which cause most of the difficulties for adults, and we can look at them here.

BOX 6.3   '<i> before <e> except after <c>'

If we remember any of the rules of English spelling, it is likely to be this one. It is a rule which really needs a whole lot more explanation than it usually gets. For example, although we might think that *friend* fits the rule, forms like *heifer* (and *leisure* for non-American speakers), and also *foreign* and *surfeit*, *feint* and *vein*, show that it really applies only when the vowel sound is [iː] (the vowel sound in *meet*). So it tells us which way round to write the letters <e> and <i> in *relief* and *receipt*. But if we look further, we find that there are quite a few apparent exceptions, such as *caffeine, Keith, Neil, protein, Reith, seize, weir, weird* (and derivatives) and, in some varieties of English, *either, neither, leisure*. The rule is most useful after <c>, where we do not find *<cie> except in diminutives and a few other exceptional word-final combinations (*specie, prima facie*). Unfortunately, there are not many words where the rule really works: *ceiling; conceive, deceive, perceive, receive; conceit, deceit, receipt*. Apart from *ceiling*, these all derive from a single Latin verb stem. We might ask how valuable the rule really is under these circumstances.

Unstressed vowels

The vowel sound that is found in the first syllable of *about* and *contain*, the second syllable of *absentee* and *preferential* and the last syllable of *data* and *verandah* is called 'schwa' by phoneticians. They use the phonetic symbol '[ə]' to write it. It is the most common vowel sound in spoken English. Just how frequently it occurs depends on the kind of English you speak. For example, some people who pronounce the letter <r> in a word like *letter* may feel that they do have a schwa before it, others may not; for speakers for whom *added* sounds like *did* at the end, there is no schwa in the second syllable, while for other speakers (e.g. Australians), there is. For some speakers, all of the words in (10) have the underlined vowels pronounced [ə], and most speakers will accept most of these as containing the same vowel. (Note: if you say these words too slowly, you may get different vowel sounds; try to speak them as naturally as possible at as normal a speed as possible when judging them for yourself.)

(10) burgl<u>ar</u>, moth<u>er</u>, doct<u>or</u>, V<u>ir</u>ginia, flav<u>our</u>, fig<u>ure</u>; <u>a</u>bout, want<u>ed</u>, poss<u>i</u>ble, sec<u>o</u>nd, s<u>u</u>ppose

Since precisely the same vowel sound can be spelt with every single one of the vowel letters in English, when you hear this vowel sound, you cannot necessarily tell how to spell it. This is why *grammar* is so often misspelt as *<grammer>. The sequence <er> is a more common representation of this vowel sound at the end of words than <ar> is, and people choose the most likely option. Sometimes the strategy is bound to backfire. Not knowing which vowel letter to spell [ə] with is one of the most common sources of adult spelling mistakes.

Homophones

Homophones are words which are written differently, mean different things, but sound alike. Some examples are presented in (11). These may not all be homophones in the kind of English you speak, though most of them will be, and they are all homophones in some varieties of English. You can probably think of other similar examples. Some of these cause the most frequent spelling mistakes for English writers.

(11) brake   break
     buy   by
     hoarse   horse
     howl   owl
     one   won
     principal   principle
     stationary   stationery
     their   there   they're
     to   too   two
     wood   would
     your   you're   yore

Homophones like these are sometimes mentioned as being a strength of English spelling, because English spelling allows us to make distinctions we don't even say. You may not agree with this assessment, because it can be difficult to remember which member of the set is spelt which way. There is certainly conflict between the two possible ideals of allowing homophones to be distinguished in writing and always writing down a word precisely as it is pronounced.

The apostrophe

We could write a whole chapter about the use of the apostrophe, and at the end of it all the reader would still be confused. The main problems are apostrophes in plurals, and the difference between *it's* and *its*. Where plurals are concerned, the rule which will give the fewest errors is: if you just want to indicate 'more than one' never use an apostrophe. Using an apostrophe will mean 'belonging to one' (if the apostrophe is before the <s>) or 'belonging to more than one' (if the apostrophe is after the <s>). This is an oversimplification, takes no account of allowable alternatives, and fails to deal with many of the situations in which you might need apostrophes, but is a reasonable place to begin from. We will not worry any more about apostrophes in plurals.

The difference between *its* and *it's* is linguistically rather more interesting, since there is a rule. Consider the forms in (12). How many of them require an apostrophe?

(12) my   mine   our   ours
     your   yours   your   yours

his	his		
her	hers	their	theirs
its	its		

The expected answer is 'none'. The forms in (12) ending in *-s* all have something in common: they are all PRONOUNS (Box 6.4). And they all behave in the same way: there is no apostrophe in the pronoun *its* in the same way that there is no apostrophe in the pronoun *his*. When [its] is not a pronoun, it means 'it is' or 'it has' (as in (13)). Here [its] is not just a pronoun, but a reduction of two words, a pronoun and a verb. In these cases, and only in these cases, do we need the apostrophe.

(13) It's a pity that she couldn't come. [*It's* = it is]
It's made me think, I can tell you. [*It's* = it has]

TERMINOLOGY

BOX 6.4 Pronoun

A pronoun is a word which usually stands for (hence 'pro') a noun or a whole phrase based on a noun. This is illustrated in (i)–(iv), where the underlined noun or noun phrase in the (a) sentence can be replaced by a single word pronoun, as shown in the (b) sentence.

(i) a. Knowledge is difficult to acquire.
   b. It is difficult to acquire.

(ii) a. A tiger is not a pet.
   b. It is not a pet.

(iii) a. The man in the moon came tumbling down.
   b. He came tumbling down

(iv) a. I saw a very tall woman with grey hair who was wearing spectacles.
   b. I saw her.

The pronouns illustrated in (i)–(iv) and those in the same series are called personal pronouns; those in (12) (the forms with a final <s>) are called possessive pronouns; we also have reflexive pronouns (*myself, yourself, . . . themselves*).

Getting the syllables right

Because of a very natural tendency to drop unstressed syllables, we sometimes find that there is a discrepancy between the number of syllables that are written and the number of syllables that are pronounced. The name *Margaret* is written with three vowels, but often pronounced [mɑːgrɪt] with two. *February* is often pronounced [febjəri]; *secretary* may be pronounced [sekətri]. People very often make spelling mistakes when they represent in the spelling precisely what they say.

Ignorance of the rules

English spelling has many irregularities (*build, does, you, doubt*, etc. and *proceed, intercede, supersede*), but not as many as some people would have us believe. Spelling mistakes arise because people treat the spelling system either as something totally irregular, or as simply a representation of sounds (when it does other things, too). There are some rules, and spelling is easier if you are aware of them. The rules will stop you writing *mating* for *matting* or vice versa, and *<hopless> for *hopeless*. It should be added that, despite the problems, there are also problems with spelling reform. We're stuck with what we've got: learn to manipulate it!

Where next?

We have looked here at some of the problems that native speakers of English may have with their spelling system at different stages of their development. In order to consider the relationship between the sound system and the spelling system in more detail, it would be necessary to learn a lot more about the pronunciation of English, which is the realm of phonetics and phonology. For example, although we are used to thinking in terms of five vowel letters in English (possibly six, if we include <y>), it may come as a shock to realize that you may have as many as 20 different vowel sounds, depending on the variety of English you speak. Or you may like to consider how many different ways you can spell the sound [ʃ] (the sound you make for getting someone to be quiet, or at the beginning of a word like *ship*): keep going until you have at least ten!

   The problems associated with the notion of spelling reform are very interesting, but if you want to look at them in detail you will need a knowledge of the ways in which different accents of English may vary. Equally, if you want to know about the things that English spelling is trying to tell you (apart from what sounds to say), you will need to know about etymology – the origins of words, to see the differences between words which have come into English from Latin, Greek and French, for example. Then to understand spellings like the <wh> in *where*, the <kn> in *knot*, the <ight> in *knight* and so on, you would need to know something about the history of English, and the way in which the sounds of English have changed over the last half-millennium. Such knowledge would also tell you about the <ea> spelling in *head*, the <oa> spelling in *broad* and the <oo> spelling in *blood*, and why two of these represent short vowel sounds, while the other represents a long vowel sound. The English spelling system carries with it many remnants of things which were once useful, even if they are no longer so.

   You might then want to ask about the advantages of a spelling system like the English one (which does not just represent the sounds of the language directly) as opposed to a system like the one in Spanish or Finnish which is much closer to a direct representation of the sounds. Which is better for advanced readers and writers? Which is better for beginning readers and writers? Is having capitals and small letters useful or a hindrance? To answer such questions you would need to get involved in the psychology of writing systems, an area which tends to be dealt with by educational psychologists as much as by psycholinguists.

SOME POINTS TO PONDER

▶ American and British spellings differ in that consonant-doubling is used less often following an unstressed vowel in American spellings, while in British English it is used slightly more after unstressed vowels. This accounts for differences such as <kidnapping> versus <kidnaping> and <travelled> versus <traveled>. Can you find any other similar pairs? Note that <fulfil> and similar British spellings seem very illogical by this rule.

▶ How do you spell the plural of the noun *MP?* Are you consistent with similar words such as *BA, CD, GI, SMS*, and so on? What about foreign words like *aroma, pizza, visa, yucca; daiquiri, rabbi, taxi; folio, salvo, sombrero?* Is there a standard rule about the use of apostrophes in all these cases?

▶ Some of our students have produced spelling mistakes such as *<calender>, *<definate>, *<elimentary>, *<intrest>, *<summerises> and <there> for <their>. What difficulties with the English spelling system lie behind these errors? Collect some spelling mistakes from your own group and see whether the same problems are relevant.

▶ Text messaging involves the use of a number of homophones (e.g. *4* instead of *for*). Make a list of such cases. How far are the words used real homophones when they occur in a sentence (as opposed to when they are said in isolation)?

READING AND REFERENCES

For a user-friendly introduction to English spelling, see Carney (1998). A full discussion of English spelling is provided in Carney (1994), with a simplified, textbook presentation in Carney (1997). Of the many available discussions of the apostrophe, Little (1986) and the presentation in McArthur (1992) are recommended. Many of the examples of children's spellings in this chapter are taken from Barr (1985) and Read (1986).

Barr, Jennifer E. (1985) *Understanding Children Spelling* (Edinburgh: Scottish Council for Research in Education).

Carney, Edward (1994) *A Survey of English Spelling* (London and New York: Routledge).

Carney, Edward (1997) *English Spelling* (London: Routledge).

Carney, Edward (1998) 'Myth 5: English Spelling Is Kattastroffik', in Laurie Bauer and Peter Trudgill (eds), *Language Myths* (Harmondsworth: Penguin) pp. 32–40.

Little, Greta D. (1986) 'The Ambivalent Apostrophe', *English Today*, 8 (October–December): 15–17.

McArthur, Tom (ed.) (1992) *The Oxford Companion to the English Language* (Oxford: Oxford University Press).

Peters, Margaret L. (1970) *Success in Spelling* (Cambridge: Cambridge Institute of Education).

Read, Charles (1986) *Children's Creative Spelling* (London: Routledge & Kegan Paul).

How Many Words Do the Eskimos Use?

What's the matter?

> The Eskimos, as is well known, have fifty words for types of snow – though curiously no word for just plain snow.   (Bryson 1990: 4)

In the film *Being John Malkovich*, the number of Eskimo words for snow was given as 49. The number has been cited, in apparently reputable publications, as being anywhere between three and 200 (Pullum 1991: 164). So there are a number of things we might want to ask about Bryson's 'well-known' fact: Why is this fact so surprising? Is it curious that there is 'no word for just plain snow'? Is the statement true? What does it mean, anyway? (Incidentally, we should note that in Canada the Eskimos now prefer to be called *Inuit*, using a word from their own language.[1] However, we can retain *Eskimo* here as the more general term.)

The surprisingness of multiplicity

Would we be surprised to learn that dog-breeders have 50 different words for dog (*Afghan, Alsatian, Basset, . . .*), that geologists have 50 different words for rock or that interior decorators have 50 names for colours? Probably not. It is therefore a bit perplexing that we should find the notion that there might be fifty different words for snow so interesting. Perhaps this is the point: it ought to be true, whether it is or not. Even if we look away from technical terms of the types mentioned here, there are plenty of instances where we have many words which are closely related in meaning. For example, here are more than 50 English expressions meaning 'drunk', culled from the pages of various thesauruses:

> **drunk**, inebriated, intoxicated, inebriate, drunken, tipsy, in one's cups, under the influence, the worse for liquor, mellow, merry, jolly, happy, screwed, full, fou, besotted, drunk as a lord, drunk as a fiddler/piper, crapulent, crapulous, plastered, pickled, soused, canned, tanked, oiled, high (as a kite), hopped up, loaded, stinko, pie-eyed, half-seas over, three

sheets in the wind, one over the eight, bacchic, bevvied, blotto, Brahms and Liszt, elephant's (trunk), legless, tight, zonked, tiddly, pissed, sloshed, steaming, rat-arsed, paralytic.

There is a Danish proverb *Kært barn har mange navne* 'a well-loved child has many names'. In the spirit of the proverb we might decide that drunkenness is a well-loved and familiar state for English speakers, but we should probably not be surprised that any language can operate with large numbers of synonyms or near-synonyms.

The lack of a generalization

Bryson also finds it surprising that the Eskimos have no word for 'just plain snow'. Given the examples used in the last section, this might indeed seem odd: even dog-breeders have the word *dog* as a general term for all those breeds. A little further thought, and a different example, though, should make it clear that this is not all that surprising.

English has a whole series of words for fruit of plants of the gourd family: *marrow; courgette, zucchini; pumpkin, butternut; kumikumi; squash*. Danish has a single word for all of these, *græskar*. Now put yourself in the place of a Danish speaker learning English. They might say 'English has lots of words for *græskar* – though curiously no word for just plain græskar', which would be true for those speakers of English for whom *squash* is a kind of such plant rather than a cover-term for all of them. But this would be to misunderstand the English situation: there is no word for 'just plain græskar' because as far as many English speakers are concerned there is no commonality here. Marrows and pumpkins are different enough to require different words. It is only when we look at them in a more scientific way that we might want to refer, as we just did above, to 'fruit of plants of the gourd family', but that is not the sort of classification that is of any use to a cook. If you are sent to the market for a pumpkin and return with a marrow you have definitely done the wrong thing from the cook's point of view. So in this example, and many like it, it is really not at all surprising that there is no word for 'just plain græskar'. Similarly English does not have a word that covers all of *baking dish, double-boiler, kettle, pot, roasting dish, saucepan* and the like, nor one that covers all of *black, blue, green, red, white, yellow*, etc. (*coloured* so often excludes *white*). If we have a term that covers all of *walk, run, crawl, hobble, stride, sprint* it is probably the rather learned term *locomote*. While we cannot predict a priori whether the Eskimos will think *snow* is like *græskar* or like *dog*, neither result should strike us as being particularly odd (see Box 7.1).

What are words anyway?

In order to find out whether the claims made about the Eskimo languages are true or not, we will have to consider what it means for a language to have a

---

BOX 7.1   'Just plain snow'

Afghans, Alsatians and Bassets are all kinds of dog; dogs, along with cats, horses, and so on are all kinds of animal. But while marrow, kumikumi and pumpkin are all kinds of vegetable, they do not appear to have a term at the same level as dog to mark them off from other vegetables. We can diagram the difference as:

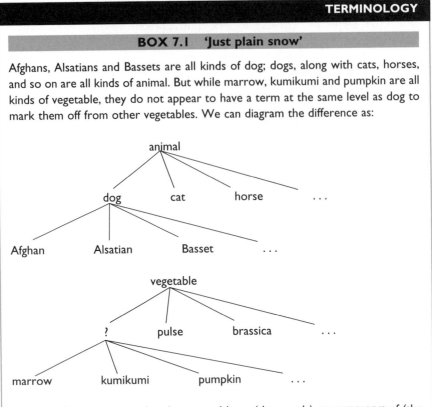

In technical terms we say that *dog*, *cat* and *horse* (the words) are HYPONYMS of (the word) *animal*, and that *animal* is a SUPERORDINATE for *dog*, *cat* and *horse*. *Dog* and *cat* can be called CO-HYPONYMS. The relationship between *animal* and *dog* is a relationship of HYPONYMY. While *Alsatian* and *Basset* have a superordinate term below the most general term *animal*, *marrow* and *pumpkin* do not, for many English speakers, have a superordinate below the most general term *vegetable*. (Note that terms like *pulse* and *brassica* are learned terms, not everyday ones; it seems English speakers do not group their vegetables, but treat them all as equal.)

---

word. That is, we need to gain a better understanding of the term 'word'. This turns out to be less simple than we might think.

Let us begin not with Eskimo words at all, but with English. Consider the paragraph in (1).

(1) When I was a boy, I went to school. And as a schoolboy I learned to speak French in the way a schoolboy does.

If you were asked to count up the number of different words in (1), would you, having already seen *school* and *boy*, add *schoolboy* as a new word? The obvious reason for answering 'yes' is that the word *schoolboy* is surrounded by space, just like *school* and *boy* were earlier in the paragraph. This method of counting is thus using the spelling or ORTHOGRAPHY as a guide to what a word is. But there are languages where this will not be sufficient. There are many languages that have never been written, for example, and among those that have, not all have spaces between words: modern Thai and Classical Greek are examples of this. In any case, consider (2) in the same light.

(2) When I was a student, I went to university. And as a university student I learned to speak French in the way a university student does.

It is not clear why English orthography should treat *schoolboy* as one word and *university student* as two; it seems to be something to do with the length of the individual elements. There is no other obvious difference between *schoolboy* and *university student* to make us want to say that (1) contains fewer words than (2), and if you are familiar with languages such as Dutch or German, you will know that they would both readily be written as single words in those languages.

Words like *schoolboy* and *university student*, which are made up of two (or more) smaller words, are called COMPOUNDS. Here it is the compounds which are causing the problems. There are many other compound words which cause problems in similar ways. There is simply no agreed way of spelling them. Consider *setscrew, set-screw* or *set screw*, for example, which are the spellings listed respectively in *Merriam Webster's Collegiate Dictionary* (10th edition, 1996), *Chambers English Dictionary* (1988 edition), and the *New Oxford Dictionary of English* (1998). In case it should be thought that the first spelling is only American, the same spelling is given in *Collins English Dictionary* (3rd edition, 1991). We also find *seafront, sea-front* and *sea front* in the same dictionaries, but, keeping the dictionaries in the same order, *sea grass, sea-grass* or *seagrass*.

Does any of this matter? Does it have any practical outcomes? One place where it might is when you ask how many words a person knows. Suppose we found a strange person who said they knew three words of English, perhaps *boat, fly* and *house*, or *box, wall* and *window*. Do we want to say that they know only three words of English, or do we want to say they might know nine, as shown in Table 7.1?

The words in the first column are mostly words that can be found in printed dictionaries (except for *flyhouse* which has been invented, but clearly refers to the place in the zoo where flies of different species live); the words in the third column are mostly not found in dictionaries, yet they are perfectly interpretable (as shown). Since the more simple words we know the more possible compounds we know, we magnify our apparent vocabulary size tremendously if we include compounds in the total number of words known. While we might wish to exploit this for propaganda purposes, it is clear that we could end up with very different counts depending on our assumptions.

There is another problem in determining what a word is (Box 7.2). Any regular English verb can occur in any of four different forms, as with *walk, walks, walked, walking*. Some irregular verbs have more forms, as with *see,*

Table 7.1   Compounds from simpler words

Word	Meaning	Word	Meaning
boatfly	'type of water bug'	boxwall	'wall made of boxes'
boathouse		boxwindow	'window shaped like a box'
flyboat	'small swift boat'	wallbox	'box fastened to a wall'
flyhouse	invented!	wall window	'a window which fills a whole wall'
houseboat		windowbox	
housefly		window wall	'a wall in which there is a window'

sees, saw, seen, seeing or, the most irregular English verb of all, *be, am, is, are, was, were, been, being.* English is a language that doesn't have very many forms for each of its verbs. If we consider French, we get the PARADIGM set out in Table 7.2 (actually, for those who know French, the subjunctive forms have been missed out, so the full paradigm is larger than that shown).

Now, if you learn the word *walk*, do we want to say that you learn a different word when you learn *walks* or *walking*? In one sense, of course, this is so: *walk* has different letters between the spaces on the page from *walking*. But in another sense it is very misleading, because when you learn *walk* you also learn that it can fit into the regular paradigm or pattern, and the other three forms come automatically. In English, we might not think it makes much difference whether we claim to know four words *walk, walks, walked* and *walking* or whether we think we know only one. But in French we have to decide whether we know one word or 33. In Finnish we have to decide whether each verb is one word or 850. In Erromangan, a language of

Table 7.2   The paradigm for the French verb *marcher* 'to walk'

present	imperfect	simple past	future	conditional
je marche	je marchais	je marchai	je marcherai	je marcherais
tu marches	tu marchais	tu marchas	tu marcheras	tu marcherais
il marche	il marchait	il marcha	il marchera	il marcherait
nous marchons	nous marchions	nous marchâmes	nous marcherons	nous marcherions
vous marchez	vous marchiez	vous marchâtes	vous marcherez	vous marcheriez
ils marchent	ils marchaient	ils marchèrent	ils marcheront	ils marcheraient
marchant		marché		

Vanuatu, we have to decide whether we are talking about one word or about 6000. And Archi, a language spoken in the Caucusus, is reported to have one and a half million forms in every verb paradigm. So we really do have to make a decision about which kind of word we are talking about.

TERMINOLOGY

BOX 7.2 'Word'

We can distinguish between various types of 'word' using a more precise terminology than is needed in everyday English. We can say that *walk* and *walked* are two different WORD-FORMS of the LEXEME 'walk'. Many linguists write lexemes in small capitals to make it clear whether they are discussing the lexeme WALK or the word-form *walk*. Compounds are usually classed as lexemes, although there is some controversy in this area. But when it comes to things like *kick the bucket* meaning 'die', which are made up of several lexemes but still have a unitary meaning that does not derive from the meanings of those lexemes, we talk of LISTEMES or LEXICAL ITEMS. Lexical items include idioms, phrasal verbs like *put up* 'lodge', compounds and non-compound lexemes.

Despite the potential for greater clarity that this terminology provides, there are many instances where 'word' remains a perfectly good term, since the precise meaning either is totally predictable from the context or is irrelevant to the discussion.

Is it true what they say about Eskimo?

The Eskimo languages do not have compounds in the same way that English does, but they do have a related phenomenon called INCORPORATION. In incorporation, you take a verb-word, and build into it (in much the same way as you do in compounding in English) a noun-word (usually the direct object of the verb) to create a new verb. So given a verb like *watch*, for instance, in these languages you can freely create new verbs like *sealwatch, peoplewatch, skywatch* and, of course, *snowwatch*. What is more, you can do this with virtually any semantically appropriate verb. So we could have not only *sealwatch*, but *seal-admire, sealfollow, sealkill*, and so on, but also *snowadmire, snowavoid, snoweat*, and so on. While this may not create words for snow in Eskimo, it certainly creates a lot of words of Eskimo that have something to do with snow.

The Eskimo languages are also POLYSYNTHETIC LANGUAGES. While this term is difficult to define technically, we can say loosely that it means that Inuit speakers regularly put into a single word things which we would need a whole sentence to say. One of the Eskimo languages is West Greenlandic, and in West Greenlandic we find words such as those in (3).

(3) *annuraaliaraa*   'she made it into an anorak'
　　tusanngitsuusaartuaannarsinnaanngivipputit 'you simply cannot pretend not to be hearing all the time'

aliikkusirsuillamassuaanirassagukku 'if I should say that he's a really good entertainer'
allattuivvissaaliqisarsimaqaanga 'I was really short of note-books'

There are plenty of reasons for believing that these things are words (for example, there can be several forms of these constructions, so that we can set up paradigms like that in Table 7.2), but they are very different from the words we are used to in English. Again, if we include such constructions, we would surely want to say that there are many more words which have something to do with snow in West Greenlandic than the 50 attributed to the language by Bryson and others. However, what about words which actually mean 'snow' in some way?

Pullum (1991: 167) suggests that next time you hear someone holding forth on this subject you should not

> be a coward like me. Stand up and tell the speaker this: C.W. Schultz-Lorenzen's *Dictionary of the West Greenlandic Eskimo Language* (1927) gives just two possibly relevant roots: *qanik*, meaning 'snow in the air' or 'snowflake', and *aput*, meaning 'snow on the ground'. Then add that you would be interested to know if the speaker can cite any more.

Pullum does add that saying this is not likely to make you popular. Will it make you right? In one sense, yes; but it still depends on what you mean by a 'word for snow', because, like English, West Greenlandic has a number of words denoting frozen water in various configurations. So we find at least the forms in Table 7.3.

Woodbury (1991) lists 15 different words for snow and related phenomena in Alaskan Yup'ik (a non-Inuit Eskimoan language), and points out some other problems in deciding the truth of the matter (Are all of these words for snow? How do you count synonyms?). He also points out that English has at least the following terms in the same area: *avalanche, blizzard, blowing snow, dusting, flurry, frost, hail, hardpack, ice lens, igloo, pingo, powder, sleet, slush, snow, snow bank, snow cornice, snow fort, snow house, snow man, snowflake,*

Table 7.3   West Greenlandic forms for frozen water

Word	Meaning	Word	Meaning
tuaq	'lump of old ice frozen into new ice'	imalik	'wet snow falling'
siku	'sea ice'	aput	'snow on the ground'
nilak	'fresh water ice'	qanik	'snowflake'
sirmiq	'glacier; ice forming on objects'	pukak	'snow crust'
sullarniq	'snow blown in'	kusugaq	'icicle'

snowstorm, to which we can add *(snow)drift, frazil, hailstone, icicle, serac* and others. This raises the interesting question of whether English might not have as many words for snow as Eskimo languages!

So how many do we know?

People have tried to work out how many words Shakespeare knew. And they've done it by typing the complete works into a computer, and printing out from that a list of all the different words the computer finds. And the answer is 29,066. But that includes all the different forms in each paradigm separately. If we say that *marcher* in French is one word rather than 33, then Shakespeare used in his works under 20,000 words (some of which he made up, as far as we know).

Unfortunately, it is not clear what this means. A computer count would count *ear* (to hear with) and *ear* (of corn) as the same word. Do we feel this is fair? It would also count *dry* as the same word in *dry wit* and *dry clothes.* The computer count would count *Henry* as a word, whether it was Henry IV, Henry V, Henry VI or Henry VIII (but *Hal* would be a different word). How should such things be counted as words? A computer count would certainly take *schoolboy* as one word and *university student* as two. And perhaps most important of all, there is a big difference for everyone between the number of words they use and the number of words they recognize (ACTIVE and PASSIVE vocabularies, respectively). So suggestions in the media that people with a tertiary education know about 30,000 words (or, according to some sources, twice that) are really no more than wild guesses, making a lot of assumptions (which are rarely spelt out).

We do not even know how many words there are in English. *Chambers English Dictionary* claims 265,000 definitions, but does not say how many words that covers. *The New Oxford English Dictionary* claims 350,000 'words, phrases and definitions' but not only is it not clear whether each word and each definition has been counted to give that large number, we need to note that this figure includes 12,000 encyclopaedic entries. But these are fairly general words. We can guess that the technical terms used by account-ants, burglars, chemists, cricketers, economists, philatelists, train-spotters or linguists – to name just a tiny proportion of the interest groups which tend to have their own vocabularies – have been left out of the list. We do not even know how many such interest groups there might be. When people suggest a total vocabulary of a million words for English, they recognize the difficulty in deciding what is a plausible answer, but really provide no more than guesstimates.

If we look at things the other way round, we can possibly be rather more accurate. A speaker who knows only the most common 1000 words of English will be able to understand somewhere between 71 per cent and 84 per cent of a passage written in English, depending upon the topic and style-level of the passage. The most common 2000 words will give a coverage of between 75 per cent and 90 per cent of most texts. With a vocabulary of

6000 words you can read over 90 per cent of most texts (see Nation 2001: Ch. 1). Beyond that level, the words you need will be determined to quite a large extent by the subject matter being written about. If 30,000 words is a good representation of a vocabulary size, it provides plenty of room for understanding the things we need to read.

Where next?

The material in this chapter should make you a little cautious about accepting bland statistics about the number of words that are used for anything: so much depends on how 'word' has been defined that the statistics are probably fairly meaningless without further elaboration. Some of the types of elaboration you might seek have been raised here.

The more general questions that arise are whether words are comparable from one language to another; how many different kinds of things there are which we could reasonably call 'words'; and how different languages can be in the way in which they use words. If Archi has one and a half million forms in each verb paradigm, are there other things it does not do to compensate? Can we meaningfully compare languages as different as Archi and English in terms of complexity or 'difficulty' when they treat words so differently? All these questions lead into the study of linguistic universals and the details of the structures of words.

SOME POINTS TO PONDER

▶ How might you design an experiment to find out how many words of English or some other language a given speaker knows? Take care: the question is a difficult one, and you have to take into account at least all the points raised in this chapter.

▶ There are several areas where you will know many words with the same or very similar meaning. How many words can you find meaning 'really good' or 'stupid person', for instance? Would you use all of these? Would you use all of them with the same audience (say, talking to your friends at lunchtime, or speaking to an authority figure)? Which of them would you use in writing rather than in talking to someone?

▶ If we expect speakers of Eskimoan languages to know a lot of words for snow, might we not, on the same basis, expect English speakers to know a lot of words for clouds and rain? How many can you find? How many are everyday words? On the other hand, English does seem to have rather a lot of words for horses. Why should there be a difference?

▶ Where we do find a lot of nearly synonymous words (like words for drunkenness or stupidity or excellence), are they related by hyponymy or are they all co-hyponyms? Is this a necessary truth about such sets, or could some work in a different way?

READING AND REFERENCES

For a discussion about the words for snow in one Eskimoan language, see Woodbury (1991). The examples in (3) and in Table 7.3 are from Fortescue (1984). On vocabulary size, see Crystal (1984) and the works he refers to. For more details on words, see Coates (1999) or Bauer (2003). For the oddities of marrows, pumpkins and squash, see Hargraves (2004).

Bauer, Laurie (2003) *Introducing Linguistic Morphology*, 2nd edn (Edinburgh: Edinburgh University Press).

Bryson, Bill (1990) *Mother Tongue* (London: Penguin).

Coates, Richard (1999) *Word Structure* (London: Routledge).

Crystal, David (1984) *The Cambridge Encyclopedia of Language* (Cambridge: Cambridge University Press).

Fortescue, Michael (1984) *West Greenlandic* (London: Croom Helm).

Hargraves, Orin (2004) 'Cucurbits', *English Today*, 20 (4): 50–64.

Nation, I. S. P. (2001) *Learning Vocabulary in Another Language* (Cambridge: Cambridge University Press).

Pullum, Geoffrey K. (1991) *The Great Eskimo Vocabulary Hoax and Other Irreverent Essays on the Study of Language* (Chicago, IL and London: University of Chicago Press).

Woodbury, Anthony C. (1991) 'Counting Eskimo Words for Snow: a Citizen's Guide'. Reproduced at <http://www.ling.ed.ac.uk/linguist/issues/5/5-1239.html>

NOTE

1 The etymology of the word *Eskimo* is of interest in its own right. It comes to us either from the French plural *esquimaux* or from the Danish interpretation of that as a singular in the form *eskimo*. The French took the word from some Algonquian language where it apparently meant 'eaters of raw flesh'. We can see why they might prefer to be called *Inuit* (meaning 'people').

Going On and On: the Never-ending Story

What's the matter?

While it may or may not be the case that certain languages make certain things easier to say than others (see Chapter 22), we rarely seem to find ourselves unable to say what we want to say unless we are talking in a foreign language. We may occasionally be lost for words, or have a word on the tips of our tongues (wherever that may mean!), but we generally have a fairly good idea of the general way we want to go about saying something, and even if we momentarily cannot think of the correct word, we know that there is one and what it means. It is hard to imagine ourselves in the position of knowing that we want to express something, having, say, a visual image of what it is we want to express, but being unable even to start a sentence which will explain this idea to some other person. This might happen in pathological cases (see Chapter 23), but not in everyday interaction. The interesting thing about this is that it appears to be true even when we have never said anything similar before. People feel perfectly at ease discussing the nature of unicorns, dragons and mermaids that they have never seen. And if we ask the question in (1), which we feel certain you have not been asked before, you nevertheless know what we mean and can voice an opinion on the subject.

(1) Do you suppose that the gold at the foot of the rainbow is so rare because the leprechauns have to make it all before they can let anyone find it?

In itself this is a non-trivial task. Your dog would not be able to understand (1), and it would not be translatable into growls and woofs and tail-position. It seems unlikely that even bonobos, supposedly the most human-like of the non-human animals, would be able to make anything of (1), even if they can understand quite a lot of sign language (see Chapter 5). What is it about human language that makes this possible? And what else does this allow us to do?

What we cannot say

Let us begin, though, at the other end of the scale. Are there things which our language prevents us from saying, which we quite literally cannot say? The answer is 'yes and no'. 'No' in the sense that if there is something we want to say, we can almost certainly find a way of expressing it. 'Yes' in that some languages are more restrictive than others in what patterns they let us use to say what we want to say.

Consider something which is quite easy to say in English. If we find a stone, we can say any of the sentences in (2), depending on how precise we want to be.

(2a) I found a stone.
(2b) I found a big stone.
(2c) I found a big, heavy stone
(2d) I found a big, heavy, rough stone.

However, while we could say the equivalent of (2b) in Maori, we could not use a literal equivalent of (2c). Rather we would say something like the example in (3) (from W. Bauer 1997: 304).

(3) Ka   kite·a   he   koowhatu   nui,   he   mea   taimaha.
     Tense   find·PASS   a   stone   big   a   thing heavy
     '*A big, heavy stone was found.*'

(The noun meaning 'stone' could have been repeated, but is not here. PASS means 'passive', which is translated as 'was found'.) Speakers of Maori can say something which means much the same as (2c), but they cannot say it in precisely that way.

If the sentences in (2) were to be translated into Japanese, the word for 'heavy' would have an ending in the past tense different from the one it would have in the present tense. So speakers of Japanese are obliged to give some information which speakers of English just do not see as relevant in this context.

If the same sentences were translated into Hixkaryana (a language of the Amazon basin), we would find that although there are words which we might translate as 'big' and 'heavy', they are not basic words as they are in English, but words derived from others, perhaps better glossed as 'having size' and 'having weight'. And while it might be possible to construct a sentence which would not look too much unlike (2b), it would not be possible to construct a sentence like (4) (Derbyshire 1979).

(4) I saw a stone which was big.

So speakers of different languages have to use different patterns to say the same thing, and sometimes they are restricted in how much they can do, even then. To illustrate this last point from a more familiar language, let us consider something we can do – just not too much – in English.

You are probably familiar with the nursery rhyme in (5).

(5) This is the priest all shaven and shorn
That married the man all tattered and torn
That kissed the maiden all forlorn
That milked the cow with the crumpled horn
That tossed the dog
That worried the cat
That chased the rat
That ate the malt
That lay in the house that Jack built.

We could imagine another version of this story, in which we introduced the things at the end of the line, and then said what had happened to them. For instance, we might introduce the cat, and then answer 'Which cat?' by saying *This is the cat that the dog worried*, just as we might say *This is the hat that I wore last Thursday*. The construction is quite complex, so let us consider it in terms of what we have done with what. Let us start from the easiest way of expressing this: *This is the cat and, by the way, the dog worried the cat* (or *This is the hat, and, by the way, I wore the hat last Thursday*). *By the way* is just a marker of less immediate relevance. If we ignore that, we get *This is the cat and the dog worried the cat* (*This is the hat and I wore the hat last Thursday*). Now, *the cat* appears twice, which is not really necessary, because we know we are talking about the cat, so we get rid of the words *the cat*, but change *and* to *that* to remind us that it is the cat we are discussing: *This is the cat THAT the dog worried* (*This is the hat THAT I wore last Thursday*). We do not really go through anything like this thought process (even unconsciously), but the result is much the same as if we had. The amazing thing is that we can carry out this process without conscious thought even though it is so difficult to describe the relationships between the words in the way it has just been done here. So far, so good. *This is the cat that the dog worried* is a perfectly normal sentence of English (as long as you are familiar with the idea of dogs 'worrying' cats in this sense). But what if we do the same thing all over again? Which dog? *This is the dog that the cow tossed.* Fine. But if we put the two together, we end up with

(6) This is the cat that the dog that the cow tossed worried.

And if we keep going, we get (7).

(7) This is the cat that the dog that the cow that the maiden milked tossed worried

(7) is totally incomprehensible without paper and pencil. Some people feel happy saying (6), and can say it so that it can be understood. With (7), nobody can manage it convincingly.

In this case we might argue about what is going on. We might say that the grammar allows us to produce sentences like (7), but memory restrictions of some type prevent them from occurring in actual use, or we might just say that we can do this sort of thing once, we might get away with it twice, but we cannot do it three times, and that (7) is not a grammatical sentence of English at all. Syntacticians tend to prefer the first of these alternatives, but in either case we discover that there are some things which speakers are unable to cope with.

What we can do

On the other hand, there are plenty of things we can do quite easily. We have already seen in (5) that there are some sentences which can continue for a long time without becoming impossible to understand. One version of this poem from 1820 has

(8) This is Sir John Barley-corn,
   That treated the boy that every morn,
   Swept the stable snug and warm,
   That was made for the horse of a beautiful form,
   That carried Jack with his hound and horn,
   That caught the fox that lived under the thorn,
   That stole the cock that crowed in the morn,
   That waked the priest all shaven and shorn . . .

There seems to be no grammatical reason why the sentence might not be longer still. For a simpler example, consider the sequence in (9).

(9) Algernon said that Belinda was clever.
   Algernon said that Charles believed that Belinda was clever.
   Algernon said that Diane had heard that Charles believed that Belinda was clever.
   Algernon said that Edward reported that Diane had heard that Charles believed that Belinda was clever.

Again, it seems that we might keep going until we got to Zoe and beyond, without the sentence becoming incomprehensible. It would become boring; by the time we got to the end of it, we might have lost track of who said or believed or reported what; but we could not say that adding the last *Zoe had been told that* suddenly turned this into an impossible sentence of English.

The same is true of the extendable sentence in (10).

(10) Anne arrived on time.
   Anne and Bill arrived on time.
   Anne and Bill and Claire arrived on time.
   Anne and Bill and Claire and Derek arrived on time.

Anne and Bill and Claire and Derek and Edwina arrived on time.

Again we will quickly get bored with this, but however long we make the list, if someone produces the same list but adds *Amaryllis and* to the start of it, we cannot thereby say that the whole sentence has collapsed.

It seems that our language (and the same is true of any human language) allows us to add bits to sentences as much as we want, and still be understood. And if this seems a very unlikely thing to want to do, consider that there is only one full stop in chapter 18 of James Joyce's *Ulysses,* and that's right at the end. And while that is something of a poor definition of a sentence (given that paragraphs *are* marked in the same chapter) it is relatively easy to find sentences that are a couple of hundred words long if you look in the right kinds of text. If there is no longest sentence, then we must conclude that the number of possible sentences in English is infinite.

If the number of sentences in the language you speak is infinite, how can you possibly learn them all in order to use them appropriately? The answer is that you cannot. It is impossible. Unless you operate with a very few of the possible sentences, then you cannot have learnt to parrot off all the sentences you need; therefore you must be able to deal with them 'on line' (as it were), both producing them and understanding them as the need arises. This is what allows you to deal with sentences you have never heard before (like sentence (1) and most of the other sentences in this book), and what allows you to produce sentences like (1) whenever you need them (see Box 8.1).

What is the situation with words? Is there a longest word in a given language, or are words also infinite? Consider first the situation with suffixes in English. We can find a word ending in *-ize*, and add *-ation* to it, as in *hospitalization*; we can find a word ending in *-ation* and add *-al* to it, as in *transformational*; we can find a word ending in *-al* and add *-ize* to it, as in *digitalize*. It might therefore seem that we have a potentially infinite loop. But we soon find that we cannot exploit this loop. Consider the words in (11).

(11a) department
(11b) departmental
(11c) departmentalize
(11d) departmentalization
(11e) departmentalizational
(11f) departmentalizationalize
(11g) departmentalizationalization
(11h) departmentalizationalizational

Words (11a–d) can be found listed in many dictionaries. The spelling checker on the computer on which this was composed is quite happy with them. But the same spelling checker will not accept (11e–h). This does not of itself show that they are not perfectly good words: the spelling checker does not like *syntacticians,* either. So we have to ask whether (11e–h) are words which speakers would be likely to use; whether they are easily comprehensible and usable; whether they would mean something different from the

BOX 8.1   What do you produce from memory?

We comment above that you can produce new sentences that nobody has ever said before. But that does not mean that you never produce a sentence which is familiar to your interlocutor. On the contrary, you produce a large number of them. If you can prevent your eyes from straying down the page to the examples below, you might like to think about the kinds of things which you recite from memory rather than making up. If you do, you will probably find that the ready-made phrases fit into a very few categories, as shown in Table 8.1.

Table 8.1   Examples of sentences cited from memory

Idioms	*Good as gold, Right as rain, So long.* Depending on your definition of idiom there may be anything from a few hundred of these to several thousand.
Proverbs	*All's well that ends well, A stitch in time saves nine, The early bird catches the worm.* These do not occur randomly in conversation, but tend to be used as summaries of what has gone before.
Greetings and farewells	*How are you? How do you do? Catch you later!* Many of these do not have full sentential form (as is also true of some of the examples above).
Citations	This is a varied category and may include tongue-twisters, prayers, poems, songs, literary quotations (possibly for some actors, the whole text of some plays would constitute a possible citation).
Repetitive, routine transactions	*Can I help you? Would you like fries with that?*

More subtly, there are chunks of sentences which may come prefabricated although they may need to be made to fit into the syntax of the sentence in which they occur. These include things like *PRONOUN HAVEn't seen PRONOUN/NAME in ages!* (e.g. *I haven't seen Kim in ages!*), *It BE about time (that)* (e.g. *It was about time that we heard from Kim*), *PRONOUN/NAME BE just off to the LOCATION* (e.g. *I'm just off to the pub*), and so on. The existence of such prefabricated chunks is not in doubt, but the proportion of ordinary discourse that is filled by such elements is currently in dispute, as is the implication of these for the ways in which children learn the syntax of their native language.

earlier words on the list. If we were betting people, we would be willing to put money on the majority of readers giving up somewhere in the range of (11e–h) and saying that they can no longer cope, and that this could not be a word of English. Of course, this may not be the end of the question. As we say with reference to (7), it might be that certain things are allowed by the grammar but not by our memory systems. So perhaps some extra evidence would be useful.

According to the *Guinness Book of Records*, the longest non-technical word of English found in print is that in (12).

(12) praetertranssubstantiationalistically

Depending on how you count, this has about six suffixes. That seems to be about the most we can cope with. Whether because our grammar does not allow for longer words, or whether because our brains cannot cope with longer words, that seems to be about as long as suffixed words get in English. The three prefixes in (12) also seem to form a maximal string.

But we have also seen that English has compound words, and that while short compounds like *schoolboy* get written as a single unit, longer ones like *university student* do not, even though there is no obvious difference in behaviour between the two. So what is the story with compounds? Well here we have some nice evidence from none other than Dr Seuss (1965), reproduced in (13).

(13) What do you know about tweetle beetles? Well . . .
When tweetle beetles fight it's called a tweetle beetle battle.
And when they battle in a puddle it's a tweetle beetle puddle battle.
AND when tweetle beetles battle with paddles in a puddle, they call it
a tweetle beetle puddle paddle battle.
AND . . . When beetles battle beetles in a puddle paddle battle and the
beetle battle puddle is a puddle in a bottle they call this a tweetle
beetle bottle puddle paddle battle muddle . . .

Here, in play, we have a compound which gets longer and longer without any apparent limits. Even the tweetle beetles are beaten by the German technical compound in (14a) (cited in Fleischer 1975: 82), and the German joke compound in (14b).

(14a) Über ·see ·reich ·weiten ·fern ·seh ·funk ·verbindung
over ·sea ·reach ·distance ·distant ·see ·radio ·connection

'overseas-range television broadcast connection'

(14b) Vier ·wald ·stätter ·see· dampf ·schiff ·fahrts
four ·wood ·places ·lake ·steam ·ship ·trip

gesellschafts ·kapitäns ·uniform·mütze
company ·captain ·uniform·cap

'Lake Lucerne steam-ship company skipper's uniform's cap'

In examples like those in (14), it again seems that whatever word we come up with, someone can add something to it without suddenly creating a totally impossible construction. Again therefore we have some evidence for saying that there is an infinite number of words in languages which allow constructions like these. That is, of course, not all languages. In some languages (like French, for example), you would have to create syntactic structures to say things like those in (14). We saw in Chapter 7 that there are other ways of making long words in the Eskimo languages.

What does this say about me?

From a very young age, children have the ability to cope with the kinds of construction we have been discussing here. In fact, at times it seems that children are particularly fond of them, perhaps perceiving at some level the flexibility that is inherent in having these constructions. Not only is (5) a children's rhyme, we find other similar examples for children, such as those in (15). Even at a very early age, children are taking part in one of the central mysteries of language: its PRODUCTIVITY (see Chapter 5). It is this productivity which allows us to say whatever we want to say or whatever occurs to us. This is one of the major differences between human language and animal communication systems, and it happens because we have language with a dual articulation and syntactic structure.

> (15a) And the leaf was on the twig, and the twig was on the branch, and the branch was on the bough, and the bough was on the tree, and the tree was in the hole, and the green grass grew all around.

> (15b) [Diminuendo until the last word]. In the dark dark wood there's a dark dark house and in the dark dark house there's a dark dark room and in the dark dark room there's a dark dark corner and in the dark dark corner there's a dark dark cupboard and in the dark dark cupboard there's a GHOST.

So however clever you may or may not be, you have mastered enough of language to allow you to deal with an infinite set of data by using a finite tool: your brain. This tells us something about language: it must be the kind of structure that can be created anew on every occasion and that can be interpreted anew on every occasion, and that means that language cannot be random, but must operate according to some learnable rules. It also says that your brain has coped with one of the major achievements that being human thrusts at it. Even if nearly all humans manage to do this, it is a significant thing to achieve in just a few years without overt teaching, and you can be proud of yourself.

Where next?

To study the kinds of rules that apply to allow you to create an infinite number of words (in those languages that allow this) you need to study morphology, and to study the kinds of rules that allow you to construct and understand an infinite number of sentences, you need to study syntax. Both of these fields require you to assimilate quite a large amount of jargon before you can start to understand the way in which complex structures can be created by means of simple rules, but you should not let that stand in your way. It can be immensely satisfying to see how a few basic principles can interact to give rise to a number of quite complex constraints, some of which you would never have realized you were applying unless you had studied linguistics. The more you look at the linguistic structures you use every day, the more you will be amazed by your own ability to manipulate language, both in terms of speaking it and in terms of understanding it. Not only are you able to sort out the ambiguity of things like *Visiting relatives can be boring*, you can ignore irrelevant readings. Sometimes this has disadvantages, so that you may fail to understand *The car raced along the street crashed*, until you see that it can mean *The car [which had been] raced along the street crashed* (see Chapter 21). But it is rare that you can catch your competence asleep in this way. At this point, you are starting to get involved in the psycholinguistics of how your brain goes about understanding these messages in real time, but also the pragmatics of how we arrange messages to make them most useful, and how we draw inferences from the messages we receive. But a study of morphology and syntax is a prerequisite for a thorough understanding of these other questions.

SOME POINTS TO PONDER

▶ Try to build meaningful long words using sequences of prefixes and suffixes. How long can you make them? How many prefixes or suffixes can be strung together? You will find that some suffixes allow for further suffixes to be added to them, while some seem to prevent any further additions.

▶ If you did not have available the kind of construction illustrated in (9), you might still be able to express the same thoughts, but it would be far more difficult. What kind of paraphrase would you need to use under such circumstances to express the relevant thoughts?

▶ The constructions in (5) and (9) tend to be used in different kinds of text from the construction illustrated in (10). Look for these constructions in texts, and see how common or how rare they are in news reportage as opposed to fictional texts as opposed to the text in comics, for instance. Why might differences arise?

▶ If we hear *I don't want to go and see my aunt because visiting relatives can be boring*, we automatically assign a meaning to 'visiting relatives' which is different from that we assign if we hear *I'm dreading having my aunt come to stay because visiting relatives can be boring*. How do you think we manage this? What would happen if *Visiting relatives* were at the beginning of the sentence?

READING AND REFERENCES

For introductions to the productivity of language, see Anderson (2004) and Pinker (1994) and chapter 3 of Baker (2001). For an introduction to the structure of words and sentences, see any good introduction to linguistics, such as Fromkin and Rodman (1988 [1974]), or more specific texts on morphology and syntax, such as Coates (1999) and chapter 1 of Poole (2002), or Tallerman (1998).

Anderson, Stephen R. (2004) *Doctor Dolittle's Delusion* (New Haven, CT and London: Yale University Press).

Baker, Mark C. (2001) *The Atoms of Language* (New York: Basic Books).

Bauer, Winifred (1997) *The Reed Reference Grammar of Māori* (Auckland: Reed).

Coates, Richard (1999) *Word Structure* (London: Routledge).

Derbyshire, Desmond C. (1979) *Hixkaryana* (Amsterdam: North Holland).

Fleischer, Wolfgang (1975) *Wortbildung der deutschen Gegenwartssprache*, 4th edn (Tübingen: Niemeyer).

Fromkin, Victoria and Robert Rodman (1988 [1974]) *Introduction to Language*, 4th edn (New York: Holt, Rinehart & Winston).

Pinker, Steven (1994) *The Language Instinct* (Harmondsworth: Penguin).

Poole, Geoffrey (2002) *Syntactic Theory* (Basingstoke: Palgrave).

Seuss, Dr. (1965) *Fox in Socks* (London: Collins).

Tallerman, Maggie (1998) *Understanding Syntax* (London: Edward Arnold).

Primitive Languages

What's the matter?

If you had been around in the 1950s, you could have looked in the *Guinness Book of Records* to find the language nominated as the most primitive language in the world. The 1955 edition of the *Guinness Book of Records* nominates Arunta, also called Aranda, an Aboriginal language from central Australia, for this honour. More modern editions of this work do not have a category of 'primitive language' at all. These days, if you try to find out what a primitive language is, you are likely to find one of three things (as you can check by doing a web search):

(a) comments on early versions of computer languages such as Java;
(b) discussions of languages such as Latin in relation to the modern Romance languages of French, Italian, Portuguese, etc., where 'primitive' means 'in an earlier state';
(c) denials that there is such a thing as a 'primitive language'.

Yet linguists are well aware that there are many people who believe that there are what non-linguists would call 'primitive' languages out there in the world, and that the notion of a primitive language still occasionally gets the kind of publicity that was more common in the 1950s. Both Blake (1981: 3) and Evans (1998: 159) report, on the basis of personal experience, on the kinds of comments that are frequently made by outsiders about these languages.

It is rather difficult to find out what a 'primitive' language might be. The obvious answer – that it is a language belonging to a primitive culture – becomes problematic when we realize that anthropologists deny that any culture is primitive. Instead, we need to ask what languages might be considered primitive by those who use the term. Some typical examples are given in Table 9.1. Note that most of those languages that are not called 'primitive' are European (or closely related to European languages), which may be revealing.

If this distinction is a meaningful one, then we ought to be able to find things which the languages in the first column share and which they do not

Table 9.1   What languages are called 'primitive'?

Languages often called 'primitive'	Languages rarely called 'primitive'
American Indian languages	English
Australian Aboriginal languages	Latin, Classical Greek
Khoe or Bushman languages of the Kalahari Desert	French, Italian, Portuguese, Spanish
Local languages in Papua New Guinea or Vanuatu	Dutch, German, Swedish; Russian
Maori in New Zealand	Sanskrit, Hindi; Persian (Farsi); Japanese; Arabic, Hebrew

share with the languages in the second column or vice versa. The search for such features will take up the first part of this chapter.

Is primitiveness defined in terms of linguistic patterns?

Linguists faced with this task are likely to think of linguistic features before any others. Are there linguistic patterns which are found in one of these sets of languages but not in the other? We might consider the numbers of sounds that the languages use or the grammatical patterns that they employ, for example.

We can start with the number of sounds various languages use. We might look at the number of vowel sounds there are in particular languages, for instance, and say that Dyirbal, an Aboriginal language of Queensland with only three vowels, looks as though it might not have enough vowels to be fully developed (English, to provide a point of comparison, has about 20, depending on the variety of English you speak). However, Classical Arabic also has only three vowels, so a low number of vowels does not define 'primitive' as opposed to a 'non-primitive' language. In any case, Maori, many languages of Vanuatu, Latin and Spanish can all be said to have five vowels (depending on how we count). Number of vowels does not seem to be a relevant criterion.

Neither is number of consonants. Maori, like many Polynesian languages, has a relatively small consonant inventory. Maori has ten consonants. (For comparison's sake, English has about 24, depending on the kind of English you speak.) But the Khoe language !Xū has 95 consonants (Maddieson 1984). So neither a small number of consonants nor a particularly large number of consonants defines the so-called 'primitive' set of languages. Neither is it defined by having an extreme number of consonants. Diyari, an aboriginal language of South Australia, has 22 consonants, pretty nearly the same as English.

What about the patterns these consonants and vowels can occur in? Diyari, for instance, never lets a word end in a consonant. But then neither does Italian, except on a few small words like *al* 'to the' and *in* 'in' and in some truncated words, and Japanese allows even fewer word-final consonants.

What about grammatical patterns? We have already seen (in Chapter 3, see also Chapter 11) that languages have two ways of marking who did what to whom and with what: either they use word order (like English) or they use marking on the noun (like Latin or German). We can make this a bit more complicated because sometimes the marking on the noun is an actual suffix or prefix, on other occasions it is a word which occurs alongside the noun, but the general principle is the same. However, the fact that the examples given here all refer to languages in one column of Table 9.1 shows that these patterns do not correlate absolutely with so-called 'primitiveness'. If we add that Warlpiri, an Aboriginal language of central Australia, behaves like Latin, while Tiwi, an Aboriginal language from Melville and Bathurst Islands in Northern Australia behaves like English, we can see that there is no general pattern here.

We have already seen that languages may have different numbers of word-forms for each verb lexeme. Again Latin with over 200 has far more than English with four (in most cases), but again we see that some of the languages of Vanuatu have far more, while Maori has only two.

As far as we are aware there are no linguistic features which will divide languages neatly into those which some people view as 'primitive' and those which they do not view in this way. That being the case, we could simply give up this distinction as meaningless. However, users of the term do seem to agree about some of the things that are true of a 'primitive language', so it is to those we turn next.

What people think 'primitive' languages are like

If you find descriptions of so-called 'primitive' languages from non-linguists, they tend to agree about certain features, though there are others where they disagree. These features are not of the same type as the ones that were considered in the last section, so it would be perfectly possible for the last section to be right, but for the idea of a 'primitive' language still to be a coherent one. We will argue, however, that the notion is not coherent by giving some examples which show the fundamental ideas about them to be misguided.

'Primitive' languages have tiny vocabularies

There is a myth that many languages have vocabularies of just a few hundred words, perhaps as few as two or three hundred. No language used as a first language by even a handful of people has ever been discovered of which this is true. Although we do not have reliable figures for most languages, we have some fairly good ones for Maori, which we can use as an illustration here. The major dictionary of Maori, even today, is one that was first published in the 1840s, not long after this first missionary contact with the Maori people. It has been irregularly updated since then, but no full dictionary of the language using modern methods of lexicography has been written. Such a dictionary is currently under development. The old dictionary contains about 16,000 words. One estimate we heard recently from someone in the know is that there are at least another 25,000 Maori words not listed in this dictionary: after all, the original writers must have missed some words, and the Maori language, just like the English language, has been adding new words since 1840. So that gives a total of about 41,000 words for Maori as a reasonable estimate. This might not seem much when compared with the hyperbole that we find on the covers of some English dictionaries, but note that the high numbers there are often said to be the number of definitions rather than the number of words – quite a different matter. We have already seen, though, (in Chapter 7) that Shakespeare used a vocabulary of about 20,000 words in his plays and poems. So a total of 41,000 words for Maori represents over twice the number of words that Shakespeare used. Would we want to say that Shakespeare had a tiny vocabulary? Almost certainly not. So it makes no sense to say that Maori has a tiny vocabulary, either.

Sometimes a problem is seen not so much with the number of words a particular language has, but with the fact that many of them are borrowed, often in a simplified form, from English, French, Portuguese, etc. However, English borrows many words from Greek, Latin, French and the languages of its colonies; Japanese borrows many words from Chinese and from English; even Icelandic, well-known for its resistance to borrowing, borrows from Danish and English. All languages borrow; the fact that some of the languages borrow from English is no more meaningful than that English borrows from Latin. Adding Latin words to English is often said to have benefitted English by increasing the size of its vocabulary; the same ought to be true of borrowing words from English in other languages.

'Primitive' languages have no grammar

It is not clear what is meant by 'no grammar'. As is pointed out by W. Bauer (1998), if you had a language with no grammar, then it would be impossible to make a mistake in that language. But it is always possible to make mistakes in speaking the language (even if you know which words to use), so every language must have grammar. If 'no grammar' refers to the number of word-forms for each lexeme, we have already seen that there is no correlation between this and expected 'primitiveness'. If 'no grammar' means there is not much to say about the grammar, then this is also demonstrably false. A quick look at library shelves will quickly unearth relatively short grammars of English, Latin, and Russian, but also relatively long grammars of languages such as Dyirbal, Maori, Yimas (Papua New Guinea). Even the long ones are by no means exhaustive. For anybody's native language, if we know enough about it (and that is often the problem), there is enough material to write a 500-page grammar with ease. The notion that some people's native languages have no grammar is always false.

Words in 'primitive' languages have no fixed meaning

A quick look in the *Oxford English Dictionary* will show that it lists 40 different meanings for the noun *shell*, for many of which it lists sub-meanings. If we were trying to learn English for the first time, we might find the word *shell* impossible to understand, and complain that it keeps changing its meaning, depending on whether it is a sea-shell, nut-shell, snail-shell, turtle-shell, sound-shell, the shell of the ear, the shell of a boat, an artillery shell, and so on. English speakers might justifiably say, though, that although we can see these are different aspects of the word 'shell', at some level this is all the same meaning. The same is almost certainly true of the words of languages we do not understand: things which seem different to us nevertheless display a unity to speakers of the language concerned. For example, in Navajo *dìnìʔ* can refer to deer, buffalo or antelope, but these are all large huntable animals, and the verb root *k'àà∫* can mean 'sharpen', 'cut a groove', 'bang together' (e.g. stones), 'sprain', or 'take part in a dancing ceremony', where the idea of things rubbing against each other is central (Hoijer 1974). Similarly, in Enga, a language of Papua New Guinea, *silyu* can mean any of 'hear, know, understand, sense, feel, experience' (Draper and Draper 2002), all united by a sense of acquiring knowledge through the senses. It must also be recalled that homophones (words which sound alike but are not related) are much more confusing to the foreign learner than to the native user: French speakers have no trouble with the fact that *sent* 'he/she/it feels/smells', *sans* 'without', *cent* 'hundred', *sang* 'blood' all sound identical, but an outsider might well be puzzled by this state of affairs.

There are no generalizations or no particulars in 'primitive' languages

We include the two sides of this complaint together to show that nobody can ever win! But in fact there are plenty of examples of so-called 'primitive' languages showing very clear divisions between similar things and showing robust generalizations (Evans 1998 provides some examples). It's rather as if a learner of English, having come across *cat, dog, hedgehog, horse, rabbit, weasel* and so on were to say 'but English has no word for living being'. English does have the word *creature*, it is just a relatively rare one. We have seen that there are areas where individual languages genuinely do not have words (recall the example of *græskar* from Chapter 7), but even then we were able to find a way of expressing the generalization. This is true of all languages. Details and generalizations are always available.

'Primitive' languages cannot express logical thought

One of the texts in the Nez Perce language of Oregon and Idaho reported in Aoki (1979: 17–19) tells of two coyotes having an argument. The first says that they are both coyotes; the second claims that he is not a coyote at all. So they go up to a ridge where people can see them.

When the first started walking . . . the people below said, 'There is a coyote going upstream.' Then the people came out and watched the coyote going. 'See?' said [the second coyote]. 'See what they said? You are a coyote.' 'Come, you too,' said [the first]. 'They will say the same of you. You are a coyote.' 'All right, I'll go,' and he too started walking along the trail. Then people said 'Ah, another one. There is another one.' Then he came to the first, saying, 'See? I am not a coyote. I am "another one".'

The text shows awareness of the way in which people use language, it sets up a situation and then finds the proof for the (at first sight ridiculous) postulate. Not only does this show delight in puzzles, in order to be a story worth telling, it has to show a coherent (though, as we and the Nez Perce people are fully aware, mistaken) thought pattern. The text indicates the ability to take another's point of view and argue from a different perspective, which shows advanced narrative skills and seems to be incompatible with the notion that logical thought cannot be expressed.

'Primitive' languages just cannot cope with the modern world

The final gauntlet thrown in the way of so-called 'primitive' languages is that they cannot cope with the modern world, that they are simply not suited to dealing with civilization. Aranda may not have words for the parts of the internal combustion engine; these languages have no words for computers, nuclear physics or genetic modification.

There are various ways in which we could respond to this challenge. The first is to ask how many of us could distinguish a tappet from a rocker arm or a camshaft from a crankshaft; how many of us could explain exactly the distinction between a meson and a gluon, or explain what an object-oriented programming language is? In other words, can we cope with the modern world? However, most of the objectors would find this irrelevant: English has words for these things, they would claim, while 'primitive' languages do not.

It is certainly true that if we look in the Maori dictionary referred to above we will not find words for all these things. But then we would not find words for them in English dictionaries written in the 1840s either. So no fair comparison is available. But when we push this, we discover that it is not true. University courses in computer science are taught in Maori in at least one New Zealand university. Kunwinjku has words to describe cars, and nuclear physics can be discussed in Warlpiri (Evans 1998: 166). In fact, any language can develop a vocabulary for talking about anything, as long as its speakers want to discuss that topic. The moment that speakers of Navajo or Chocktaw or Cree need to discuss genetically modified crops, they will find a vocabulary for doing so. Sometimes that vocabulary will be borrowed from English or another language, but usually it will be partly borrowed and partly made up from the resources of their own language.

Before we criticize other languages for not being able to cope, we must remember that Newton wrote his works in Latin rather than in English because he did not believe that English was capable of coping with the sophistication required for abstruse mathematical reasoning. Today such a notion seems absurd. English has become accepted as a language in which you can discuss almost anything (though not necessarily cultural phenomena associated with other people's cultures): the same potential exists in all other languages.

Conclusion

From all of this we must conclude that evidence for any of these languages being 'primitive' in the senses indicated is lacking. There may be cases where we cannot prove that a particular language has thousands of words in its vocabulary or that there are words for generalizations in a particular language, but it always turns out to be a problem of missing data rather than a real limitation on the part of the language concerned.

Some real primitive languages

Must we then conclude that there is no such thing as a primitive language at all? Not quite. There is something which seems like a primitive language, though ironically it arises only in non-primitive circumstances.

PIDGIN languages (the word *pidgin* is a pidgin pronunciation of the English word *business*) are languages which are spoken when people with different native languages come face to face and have to deal with each other, usually for trading purposes. Pidgins often take much of their vocabulary from one of the languages, and a great deal of their grammar from the other, but there are certain patterns of simplification which are shared by many pidgins from round the world, independent of the two languages which come together:

- Difficult consonant clusters are simplified, the vowel system is small.
- Endings such as the ones we saw in Latin are removed.
- Most words can be nouns or verbs or adjectives.
- Compounds are very common.
- Reduplication (the repetition of words or parts of words for grammatical purposes) is common.
- Tenses tend to get spelled out as separate words rather than being part of the verb (e.g. *baimbai* < *by and by* for future in some Pacific pidgins).
- Pronouns have a single form, not two or more as in English *I*, *me* and *my*, *he*, *him* and *his* or *she*, and *her*.

If these pidgins are used by large communities, they eventually get learned as a first language by children. At this point, these languages turn into CREOLES, and the children start adding in a lot of the grammatical complexity that is missing in the pidgin. So a pidgin really is a primitive language. It is simplified from two (or more) non-primitive languages, with the speakers of each using the kind of simplification you find in BABY-TALK and FOREIGNER-TALK (i.e. speech directed at babies and foreigners). Because pidgins arise in these very sophisticated settings, we have no evidence that pidgins resemble the kind of communication that was available before the development of the full language faculty in humans, though it may be tempting to think so.

Where next?

There are many languages of the world, especially languages that people are likely to think of as 'primitive' which are still undescribed. This is one of the major challenges for linguists in the twenty-first century: to describe as many of these languages as possible before they become extinct (see Chapter 13). Each of these languages is likely to contain some grammatical features which surprise us and show great sophistication in classifications, in the use of ways of making distinctions, in ways of marking relevant material grammatically. In order to undertake such work, you need a full grounding in formal linguistics, including phonetics, morphology and syntax, and an appreciation of the situations these languages exist in such as is delivered by the study of sociolinguistics.

Pidgins and creoles provide a fascinating area of study in themselves, partly because of the features these very disparate languages share, partly because of the insight into what counts as linguistic 'simplification', and partly as a reflection of the way in which humans cope when communication between people breaks down. Pidgins may be primitive in one sense, but they illustrate the drive towards communication which people share and the ways in which people can cooperate to come up with a new system.

Most importantly, though, you should be wary of any claims about 'primitive' languages. We hope we have shown you that any such claims are more likely to be the result of ignorance on the part of the person making the claim than any objective feature of the language for which 'primitiveness' is claimed. Do not make the mistake of equating the unknown with the simple or undeveloped. The opposite is likely to be the case.

SOME POINTS TO PONDER

▶ Why might English have been considered unsuitable for the expression of scientific thoughts in the seventeenth century? How did it become suitable? Is there any reason why Navajo or Warlpiri could not follow the same path towards becoming a suitable language for science?

▶ The hundred most frequent words of a language like English are mainly grammatical words: words like the, a, an, it, is, this, when, and and so on. Is it possible to create a language with no more than 200–300 words with which you can communicate relatively freely about everyday life? Can you imagine how such a language might work?

▶ If you were a Martian who had to write down English, you might say that English is a particularly stupid language because a single word can mean 'jetty', 'noble', 'person of equal status', 'look closely', while another can mean 'large furry mammal', 'naked', 'carry', 'put up with' and yet another can mean 'money paid for transport', 'just', 'place of entertainment', 'food', and so on. Would it be fair for you to conclude that English speakers cannot distinguish between people of equal status and jetties or food and places of entertainment? Would you be justified in concluding that English words do not have fixed meanings, but keep changing their meanings? What conclusions would be justified?

▶ How would you respond to someone who claimed that English was a primitive language in the fifteenth century because it could not be used for the discussion of advanced scientific concepts, because it had a small vocabulary and virtually no grammar?

READING AND REFERENCES

Several of the myths discussed in Bauer and Trudgill (1998) are relevant for this theme, as are the websites listed below. Most of the other references below are sources of information on the real complexity of languages. It may be of interest to take a grammar of a language which someone has described as 'primitive' and see how complex, nuanced and logical it is. Unfortunately, we could find no grammar of Aranda to make the point with reference to that language, although we do know that it has complex verbal paradigms (like the French example in Chapter 7). For a very interesting discussion of the ways in which English was deemed unsuitable for dealing with the modern world in the fourteenth to the seventeenth centuries, see chapter 5 of Knowles (1997). There is much of value on pidgins in Aitchison (1981, 1996). For more details, see Romaine (1988).

Aitchison, Jean (1981) *Language Change: Progress or Decay?* (London: Fontana).

Aitchison, Jean (1996) *The Seeds of Speech* (Cambridge: Cambridge University Press).

Aoki, Haruo (1979) *Nez Perce Texts* (Berkeley, CA: University of California Press).

Bauer, Laurie and Peter Trudgill (eds) (1998) *Language Myths* (Harmondsworth: Penguin).

Bauer, Winifred (1998) 'Myth 10: Some Languages Have No Grammar', in Laurie Bauer and Peter Trudgill (eds), *Language Myths* (Harmondsworth: Penguin), pp. 77–84.

Blake, Barry J. (1981) *Australian Aboriginal Languages* (London: Angus and Robertson).

Blake, Barry J. (1987) *Australian Aboriginal Grammar* (London: Croom Helm).

Dixon, R. M. W. (1980) *The Languages of Australia* (Cambridge: Cambridge University Press).

Draper, Norm and Sheila Draper (2002) *Dictionary of Kyaka Enga, Papua New Guinea* (Canberra: Australian National University).

Evans, Nicholas (1998) 'Myth 19: Aborigines Speak a Primitive Language', in Laurie Bauer and Peter Trudgill (eds), *Language Myths* (Harmondsworth: Penguin), pp. 159–68.

Guinness Book of Records (1955) (London: Guinness Superlatives).

Hoijer, Harry (1974) *A Navajo Lexicon* (Berkeley, CA: University of California Press).

Knowles, Gerry (1997) *A Cultural History of the English Language* (London: Edward Arnold).

Maddieson, Ian (1984) *Patterns of Sounds* (Cambridge: Cambridge University Press).
Romaine, Suzanne (1988) *Pidgin and Creole Languages* (London: Longman).

<http://dir.yahoo.com/Social_Science/Linguistics_and_Human_Languages/ Languages/Language_Groups/Contact_Languages/> <== This is a Yahoo page which links to several other pages dealing with pidgins and creoles.
<http://zompist.com/lang9.html> <== Answer 13 is right on topic!

Who Needs Grammar?

What's the matter?

I make every effort to never split infinitives. I certainly wouldn't use no double negatives. I agree that prepositions are things you shouldn't end sentences with. And I never start a sentence with *and*.

While the sentences in the above paragraph give examples of grammatical 'rules', they simultaneously break those rules. The notion of grammar implicit here is what we often find reflected in Letters to the Editor or in text corrections provided by proofreaders or teachers. As we see in Chapter 17 and the Conclusion, this is a *pre*scriptive notion of grammar, to be contrasted with the *de*scriptive approach taken by linguists (at least when they are in their offices or talking to the media, rather than in their homes or talking to their children). We will also see that whether or not any of these sentences seem 'wrong' may depend on factors such as the age, regional background, social context etc. of the language user. Judgements about correctness will change over time, so that some things that may have been heavily frowned upon when the authors were at school may be perfectly acceptable now. Indeed, some 'rules' are based on an old misconception that English is meant to behave like Latin, the medieval language of the learned. The split infinitive idea (outlawing anything between *to* and the verb) is one of these, but note that Latin couldn't in any case split infinitives because, for instance, *to love* is one unsplittable word, *amare*.

We might argue that rules such as the ones illustrated above are made to be broken, and that breaking them does not impair our ability to communicate. Indeed, 'breaking' them may actually communicate something about the type of person we are, that we want to identify with other people who use language in these ways, and so on. However, we additionally need to acknowledge that there are other rules or constraints that need to be more closely adhered to, because 'breaking' them could lead to dire consequences. Consider the possible combinations of the three words of the title of this chapter. The six sequences in (1) below are all possible, but competent users of the language will know that the first and last of these are the only ones allowed by the rules of how sentences are put together in English. They will also know that (1f) is more likely than (1a) because it makes more sense. A slippery distinction is often made in linguistics between 'grammatical' and 'acceptable' (e.g. Chomsky 1965: §1.2). The sentences in (1a) and (1f) are both grammatical, but (1f) is more acceptable.

(1a)   Grammar needs who?
(1b)   Grammar who needs?
(1c)   Needs grammar who?
(1d)   Needs who grammar?
(1e)   Who grammar needs?
(1f)   Who needs grammar?

Chomsky (see Box 10.1) illustrated the fact that judgements of grammaticality need not depend on meaning with his now famous example sentence

PERSONALITY

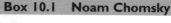

Box 10.1   Noam Chomsky

Noam Chomsky (1928–) has been a hugely influential figure in linguistics since the 1950s. In 1955 he completed a doctoral dissertation in linguistics called 'Transformational Analysis' at the University of Pennsylvania. Since then he has been on the staff of the prestigious Massachusetts Institute of Technology. He has received numerous honorary degrees and awards in recognition of his work not only in linguistics but also in politics – he has been hailed as one of America's most prominent political dissidents.

Chomsky's early contribution to linguistic theory was his distinction between the 'surface structure' of utterances and more abstract 'deep structures'. These structures are linked by transformational rules, which allow different surface structures (such as *The dog chased the cat* and *The cat was chased by the dog*) to be generated from the same deep structure (which would correspond to the meaning shared by the two examples). Chomsky showed how, with a limited set of rules of grammar and a finite set of words, we can produce an infinite number of sentences, including sentences we have never said or heard before. He argued that the basic faculties that allow us to use language in this way are innate, i.e., are part of our genetic structure, and part of what he calls 'Universal Grammar'. Universal Grammar refers to the fundamental aspects of language which we do not have to deduce from the language data we hear when we acquire our first language. Part of Universal Grammar is the Language Acquisition Device (LAD) that children use when they acquire the necessary words for their first language and work out the relevant settings of the parameters that determine the specific aspects of different languages. Chomsky argues that children can do this using a relatively small set of key examples.

Colourless green ideas sleep furiously. This sentence obeys the rules of English sentence structure in terms of how adjectives modify nouns, verbs are modified by adverbs, and so on, even though it does not make a lot of sense. Native speakers intuitively know that *Colourless green ideas sleep furiously* is qualitatively different from *Furiously sleep ideas green colourless* – this is reflected, for instance, in the fact that the former is much easier to say with a normal intonation pattern, whereas readings of the latter sound more like lists of disconnected words. Of course, examples of supposedly unacceptable sentences can often be made to seem more acceptable through provision of an appropriate context. (Imagine you are talking about a possible gatekeeper function for linguists in preserving correct grammar and the person you are talking to doesn't quite catch what you are saying. She asks, 'Grammar needs who?')

Assembly instructions

Kit-sets for furniture (and other construction toys for older children) generally come with a parts list and a set of instructions. If the parts list of a language is the set of words used by that language, then the grammar is the instruction set. If your build-it-yourself bookcase arrives with a parts list but no instructions, then the construction of a well-formed piece of furniture may be more difficult, if not impossible. If we have a set of words but no grammar then the construction of well-formed sentences is similarly compromised.

The language instruction set is useful not only in constructing sentences, but also in deconstructing them, in understanding what someone is saying to us. And understanding what someone says is not just understanding the words they use. Compare, for instance, *Tama would like to speak to you* and *You would like to speak to Tama.* These sentences share the same words, and the result of the situation expressed in them might be the same (i.e. the people referred to as *you* and *Tama* get together to talk), but our understanding of these sentences involves not just knowing what each word means but also recognizing how the words, as components of sentences, are combined. After all, *Max loves Alice* does not mean *Alice loves Max.* Success in communicating the message depends on speakers and listeners working with the same instruction set. It is this type of shared knowledge which constitutes part at least of what we call *grammar.*

It is not just the individual words that have to fit a certain construction pattern, but groups of words are joined together to form subparts of a sentence, just as groups of items in a parts list need to be assembled to form, say, the back of a bookcase and the sides of the bookcase before back and sides are put together. English has a basic sentence order of *subject-verb-object* (see Box 10.2), which can be found in *Felix is starting his writing, The dutiful boy has finished a long and informative thank-you letter,* and *He posted it.* Although these sentences have the same overall subject-verb-object structure, their parts look quite different. For instance, the subject in the examples can

TERMINOLOGY

BOX 10.2 Grammatical terms

There are a number of common grammatical terms that are found in descriptions of many of the world's languages, though they may refer to slightly different things depending on the language being described. The most basic of these terms refer to the grammatical roles of the various elements in a sentence. So the *subject* of a sentence determines some of the aspects of the form of the verb in English and is frequently the doer of the action or activity expressed by the verb, the (direct) *object* is the person or thing that is acted upon, while *indirect objects* include recipients. For instance, in the sentence *Lee and Pat are sending a postcard to their neighbour*, *Lee and Pat* form the subject, and it is the fact that they are a plural entity (i.e. more than one) that determines the verb form *are sending* rather than *is sending*. The phrase *a postcard* is the object, and *to their neighbour* shows the indirect object. However, the grammatical subject is not always the doer of the action, as shown by the passive form of this sentence, *A postcard is being sent by Lee and Pat to their neighbour*, where *a postcard* is the subject.

Different verbs combine with differing arrays of other parts. Compare, for instance, the verbs *sleep, snore, watch, open, give, send*. Ask someone to give you the simplest sentence they can think of using each of these. You will probably find that the first two only have a subject (*Max is sleeping; Jo is snoring*), the second two have a subject and an object (*Jack is watching television, Mary opened the door*), and the last two have a subject, an object and an indirect object (*Peter gave the present to his dad, Felicity sent the letter to granny*). Of course, these verbs are not restricted to these constructions (for instance a recipient could be 'understood' in *Sam sent the letter*), but there do appear to be preferences for the kinds of constructions entered into by different verbs. This can be demonstrated by asking people to assign the six verbs above to nonsense frames like *The purk is ___ ing; The purk is ___ ing the splod; The purk is ___ ing the splod to the shub.*

be a proper name *Felix*, a noun phrase *the dutiful boy*, or just a pronoun *he*. Our instruction set has to allow multiple legitimate ways of building a particular kind of phrase (a noun phrase in this instance), and we know that these different phrases are in an important sense equivalent, even though we also know that they are different.

Because in English the different roles associated with a verb (loosely, roles such as subject and object, or doer and done-to) tend to appear in particular positions relative to that verb, a function of English grammar is that it tells us where to look for the elements filling these roles. However, this is something that has to be learnt (rather than being in-born), as different languages do this differently. Table 10.1 illustrates how a small selection of languages might order the elements we have been discussing.

But this is not the only way in which the grammars of different languages can vary. In some languages, the order of these elements can be very flexible. For instance, if we wanted to make a sentence in German that said that 'A gave X to B' we could have at least the following orders: *A gave X B; X gave*

Table 10.1 Basic word order in a selection of languages

Order of elements	Example languages	English equivalent
subject-verb-object	English, Italian, Swahili	The purk is watching the splod
subject-object-verb	Farsi, Japanese, Turkish	The purk the splod is watching
verb-subject-object	Hebrew, Maori, Welsh	Is watching the purk the splod

A B, B gave A X. The only constraint appears – at first sight – to be that the verb has to be in second position (though not even this is reliable, since if the sentence was 'When A gave X to B . . .', then the verb would be in final position). You might think that this flexibility in word order would lead to chaos – after all, if either A or B or X can come before the verb, then doesn't that mean that any of them can be the subject? So how would we know what the speaker means? Fortunately German makes use of a different grammatical device for indicating the roles played by different elements in the sentence. Where English (like many other languages) uses ordering of elements, German uses word endings and different forms of some words, as Table 10.2 shows (and see also Chapter 3 for discussion of how such differences between languages arise through language change).

What the English translation fails to show is that German indicates the roles of the noun phrases (*the man, the passport, the officer*) through differences in some of the words. In this case the marking is on the articles, *der, den, dem*, all translated here as 'the'. Other word types such as adjectives and nouns can also take different endings to show these roles, though this is not evident in the examples. So no matter where in the example sentences the phrase 'the man' appears, it is marked as being the subject by the form of the article: <u>*der*</u> *Mann*. The choice between the German orderings in the table is largely a question of which element the speaker wants to focus on. The first example uses the normal or 'unmarked' order, and the others allow the speaker to bring different elements into the foreground.

Other differences between languages include the fact that while English has *pre*positions (e.g. *with* comes before [pre-] *stripes* in *the tiger with stripes*),

Table 10.2 Word order and word endings in German

German	literal English translation
Der Mann gab den Paß dem Beamten	the man gave the passport the officer
Dem Beamten gab der Mann den Paß	the officer gave the man the passport
Den Paß gab der Mann dem Beamten	the passport gave the man the officer

other languages have *post*positions (so the equivalent of *with* comes after [post-] *stripes: the tiger stripes with*). Interestingly languages that put the verb after the object tend also to have postpositions rather than prepositions.

So the instructional set of grammar includes (at least) instructions about how to use word order and word endings. Some languages use mostly one or mostly the other, many languages use both. For instance English, which we have seen uses word order to show the roles of sentence elements, also uses some endings, e.g. to show number agreement, as in the difference between *snore* and *snores* in *John and Mary snore* vs. *John snores*. It might seem that this marking of the third person singular present tense by adding *–s* is redundant (see Chapter 11), since word order and expectations about roles played by different elements before and after the verb mean that *John snore* is just as comprehensible as *John snores*. But sometimes there are situations in which the *–s* seems to matter – compare *I heard John snores* and *I heard John snore*.

Language programs

Is grammar really like the instructions that come with kit-set furniture, or is it more powerful than that analogy might suggest? A single set of instructions might let us build a bookcase, but will it let us build a coffee table, a chair, a piano stool? Grammar might perhaps be more like a sophisticated computer program, a set of procedures for producing and understanding language that not only builds one sentence or set of sentences, but which contains rules that make it capable of building an infinite number of sentences (see Chapter 8).

Comparisons are sometimes made between human language as a reflex of human intelligence, and computer programs as a component of artificial intelligence. One challenge for computer programmers is to develop software that will allow computers to interact (usually with their human operators) using 'natural' (rather than programming) language. This challenge has occasionally been issued quite explicitly, with contests bearing prize money for programs that are so good that the judges interacting with the computer through a computer terminal are not able to determine whether their conversation partner is human or machine. However, the so-called 'First Law of Artificial Intelligence' is that the hard problems are easy, and the easy problems are hard. That is, things that humans might find hard are easy for computers, such as doing complicated sums, while things that we tend to achieve without much effort, such as recognizing faces, playing tennis, doing up buttons or using human language, prove to be difficult for computers. So language is generally acknowledged to be one of the hard-for-computers/easy-for-people problems, and we still need to rely on computer languages (rather than human languages) in order to interact with computers. Some programs that initially seem convincingly like human conversation partners tend to *mimic* language understanding by picking out key words from the human contribution to a 'conversation' and soon betray their true identity through unimaginative repetition.

There are two factors involved in grammar programs, both for computers and for humans, and it is the different balance of these factors that is perhaps critical. These are memory and decision making. Computers are good at memory but poor decision-makers; humans are good at decision-making but relatively poor at the memory part. As a result, computer-based grammars often give too many possible analyses, and cannot be easily constrained to choose the most likely one. For instance, the phrase *Time flies like an arrow* allows for a good degree of ambiguity, since *time, flies* and *like* can all be different parts of speech (cf. *the flies, it flies*). It has been claimed that there may be over 100 possible analyses of this phrase (Altmann 1997: 85). These include the usual interpretation, i.e. 'time proceeds as quickly as an arrow proceeds' (cf. *Jonah runs like a stallion*), but also 'measure the speed of flies in the same way that you measure the speed of an arrow' (*slice through logs like butter*), 'measure the speed of flies in the same way that an arrow measures the speed of flies' (*leap tall buildings like Superman*), 'flies of a particular kind, time-flies, are fond of an arrow' (*fruit-flies like a banana*), along with many others.

The point about these examples is that they are all, with smaller or larger stretches of the imagination, possible interpretations of the phrase *Time flies like an arrow*. They are possible because they all adhere to the rules of grammar. What the human mind brings to the problem is the ability to assess the plausibility of the possible interpretations and to make decisions about what is more likely.

Mind grammar

While computers can entertain a wide range of possible interpretations of a sequence of words, humans tend to encounter difficulty when memory is an issue. Consider for example the sentences in (2):

(2a) He gave the girl a present
(2b) He gave the girl he met a present
(2c) He gave the girl that he met in Wanganui a present
(2d) He gave the girl that he met in Wanganui around Christmas and New Year a present
(2e) He gave the girl that he met in Wanganui while visiting his parents for ten days around Christmas and New Year a present

While understanding the sentences in (2a–c) is easy, the sentences in (2d) and (2e) start to get tricky. Although the grammar allows each of these sentences, and many more beside (and the examples in (2) give a sense of how the grammar can lead to an infinite variety of sentences – see also Chapter 8), the issue for comprehension is that longer and longer stretches intervene between some of the basic elements in the sentence, namely between 'He gave the girl' and 'a present'. Our grammar as a language processing system needs to see the relationship between these elements, and our human memories find it difficult to manage this. Of course, in normal language use we would allow for these constraints by using a different ordering: *He gave a present to the girl that he met . . .*

So memory is an issue for the human language processing system, and this is reflected in the actual use made of different grammatical possibilities, so that human language perhaps makes less use of the range of possibilities than an artificial system might do. When it comes to decision-making, the process we follow seems to depend on the decision. It appears that we consider, at least briefly, many meanings of an ambiguous word such as *bugs*, even when some of those might not make much sense in the context in which the word is used (Swinney 1979):

(3) Rumour had it that, for years, the government building had been plagued with problems. The man was not surprised when he found several spiders, roaches and other bugs in the corner of his room.

With larger pieces of language, such as phrases and sentences, we are often more likely to commit to one analysis, to minimize the memory load. This means that many ambiguities may go unnoticed, at least by editors, as (4) and (5) show.

(4) No one was injured in the blast, which was attributed to the buildup of gas by one town official.
(5) The summary of information contains totals of the number of students broken down by sex, marital status and age.

But it also means that some of our decisions can turn out to be the wrong ones, as shown by temporary misunderstandings that you may experience as you read (6–8).

(6) The horse raced past the barn fell.
(7) The cotton clothing is usually made of grows in Mississippi.
(8) The prime number few.

Examples of ambiguities like these are discussed further in Chapter 21, where it is claimed that we have grammatical preferences (e.g. for *raced* in example (6) as a main verb – cf. *The horse was racing . . .* , rather than as a participle *The horse was raced*), and that these result in the misreadings.

Where next?

This chapter has considered some of the features of grammar, and has pointed out how individual languages make different use of these features, such as word order and word endings. We have considered grammar as a set of instructions for the construction of sentences and as a program for generating language, and we have highlighted the differences between computer-based and human processing of language. The title of the chapter poses the question of who needs grammar. It should be obvious from our discussion that we all need grammar – not grammar as a set of rules that we are aware of, nor as a set of rules that we can use to determine whether someone is using language 'properly', but grammar as the implicit rules by which we produce and understand language and which allow us to communicate successfully with other speakers of our language. In this sense, then, we already have 'grammar'. In another sense, of course, we can learn much more about grammar and about how the grammars of different languages are not the same but are nevertheless based on similar principles. We can learn about the grammatical description of language through introductory linguistics texts or courses, and we can learn about the grammatical description of languages by studying those languages.

SOME POINTS TO PONDER

▶ What might someone mean when they say that a particular language has 'no grammar'? (See Bauer 1998.)
▶ What does it mean to say that someone uses 'poor grammar'?
▶ Ask some of your friends or relatives to give a real verb instead of the ___ing part of: (a) *The purk is ___ing*; (b) *The purk is ___ing the splod*; (c) *The purk is ___ing the splod to the shub*. Can you group the verbs given for (a), (b) and (c) into sets with similar meanings? E.g. for (a) you might get 'bodily action' verbs like *snore* or *cough* or 'grooming' verbs like *wash* or *shower*. Do you get different types of meaning for the three groups? Does this mean there is a relationship between sentence structure and meaning?
▶ Play a game of 'consequences': player 1 writes down the first two words of a sentence, then folds the paper so only the second word is visible. Player 2 adds a word and then folds the paper again so that only their word is visible, and so on for ten or 15 words. Unfold the paper and see what the entire 'sentence' looks like. Play again, but this time player 1 writes three words and leaves the last two showing, then player 2 adds one and leaves the last two showing, and so on. Play several times, with different numbers of words visible each time. What do the results tell you about how words are strung together to make sentences, i.e. about 'grammar'?

READING AND REFERENCES

Good introductory overviews of what makes human language what it is can be found in Aitchison (1998), Altmann (1997) and Pinker (1994). The latter includes more detail than has been provided here of some of the challenges issued to computer programmers to develop software that uses natural language in a convincingly human-like way. The examples of the analysis of *time flies like an arrow* come from Altmann, who gives considerably more possible analyses than the few listed above. The *bugs* example comes from Swinney's study of how we process ambiguous words.

Aitchison, Jean (1998) *The Articulate Mammal* (London and New York: Routledge), especially chapter 9.

Altmann, Gerry T. M. (1997) *The Ascent of Babel* (Oxford: Oxford University Press), especially chapters 7 and 8.

Bauer, Winifred (1998) 'Some Languages Have No Grammar', in Laurie Bauer and Peter Trudgill (eds) *Language Myths* (London: Penguin), pp. 77–84.

Chomsky, Noam (1965) *Aspects of the Theory of Syntax* (Cambridge, MA: MIT Press).

Pinker, Steven (1994) *The Language Instinct* (London: Penguin Books), especially chapter 7.

Swinney, David A. (1979) 'Lexical Access during Sentence Comprehension: (Re)consideration of Context Effects', *Journal of Verbal Learning and Verbal Behavior*, 18: 645–59.

Mobile Messages

What's the matter?

When we talk to our students about the form of child language that is known as telegraphic speech, they nowadays look at us in blank bewilderment. Talk to them about a form of communication called a txt mssg and they have no problem. Telegraphic speech is a form of language which keeps the important bits and leaves out some of the less important ones, as in *Mummy read book*. This is how people used to write telegrams or telegraphic dispatches, now largely superseded by e-mail and text messaging. Interestingly, the tradition of the telegram (still associated with 100th birthday messages from the Queen or the best-man's speech at weddings) has not yet died, since at least one cellphone provider offers a service by which text messages are used to send a telegram, the attraction being that the recipient gets a hand-delivered message on paper.

The first telegram was transmitted in 1844 by the inventor of Morse code, Samuel Morse. It has been widely claimed that an early linguistically clever telegram was sent by Sir Charles Napier when he gained control of the Indian province of Sindh (now part of Pakistan). To disguise the message, it was written in Latin: *peccavi*, meaning *I have sinned*, homophonous with *Sindh*.

What telegrams and text messages have in common is the need to send a communication by the most efficient (usually cheapest) means possible, which they do by exploiting predictability and redundancy in language.

Language has predictability

Text messaging and telegrams work (usually) because we know what words can be like, and how they can be put together to make larger units. That is, thr's a cnsdrbl amnt of prdctblty in lngge.

Of course, some words are more predictable than others, and the contexts in which we use words have a major impact on their predictability. To see this, ask some friends to complete each of the following sentences by adding a word:

(1) Never look a gift horse in the _____
(2) A stitch in time saves _____
(3) John took the bread out of the _____
(4) Mary turned over the page in her _____
(5) Max had never seen such a filthy _____
(6) Josie wanted to get a new _____
(7) Just look at that _____

Your group of friends will probably offer a smaller range of completion words for sentences nearer the top of this list (assuming they are being cooperative – there are always some who give other parts of the anatomy for the sentence in (1)). This is because these sentences are more predictive of the continuation. Some, notably proverbs such as (1) and (2), have entirely predictable continuations. Other sentences constrain the choice in terms of meaning and/or grammar, while others leave the options considerably more open.

More broadly speaking, some words are more predictable simply because they are used more. Again you could convince yourself of this by asking your friends to put the following words into two sets of five – those that they think are used a lot, and those that are used rarely: *again, anvil, dirge, great, house, juror, pluck, right, small, wince.* You should find that *again, great, house, right,* and *small* are put into the set of frequently used words, while the others are listed as more rarely used. Some areas of language-related research are particularly sensitive to such frequency differences. In psycholinguistics, for instance, word frequency has been shown to have a strong effect on how rapidly readers or listeners can recognize a word. For reasons such as this, there are a number of published tables of 'frequency norms', based on surveys of the words that occur in language corpora. In one (Kučera and Francis 1967) *again, great, house, right,* and *small* all have a frequency count of greater than 500 instances per million words, while *anvil, dirge, juror, pluck* and *wince* occur fewer than five times per million. Of course, frequency counts are based on analyses of a selection of actually occurring texts, and what is true for one set of frequency norms may not be true for all language users or at all times. However, the general pattern tends to be right, as the first set of examples demonstrates.

You may have noticed that the words above all have the same number of letters. When researchers are testing people's sensitivity to word frequency, they generally try to keep other factors such as word length as constant as possible, so that these factors do not affect how easy it is to recognize the words (for instance, longer words take longer to read, which may make them slower to recognize). But over the English language as a whole, a 'law' attributed to Zipf (1935) maintains that frequently used words are shorter than words that are used less often. (A 'law' here means a tendency rather than an absolute rule.) For instance, Figure 11.1 plots the frequencies (per million words of text, from the Kučera and Francis norms) of a random selection of words (in fact the words in the first sentence of this chapter) against the letter length of the words.

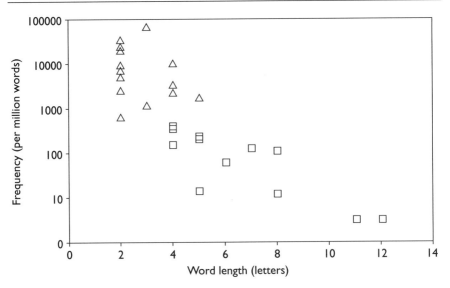

Figure 11.1   Word length (in letters) plotted against frequency of occurrence (per million words) for a set of 26 English words

The shortest words include most of the grammatical words, such as articles (*the, a, an*), conjunctions (*and, but*) and prepositions (*in, on, by*), as well as general referring words like pronouns (*I, you*). The ten most frequent words in the one-million word Wellington Corpus of Spoken New Zealand English (Holmes et al., 1998) are – in descending order – *the, and, I, to, a, you, that, it, of, yeah*. Short grammatical words are used more frequently than individual examples of other word types, i.e. content words such as nouns (*alligator*), verbs (*entertain*) and adjectives (*nonchalant*), though not all instances of these types are particularly long (*cat, eat, shy*). In Figure 11.1, the grammatical and general referring words are shown by triangles, the content words by squares. Note that although there is some overlap in the lengths of these two groups, the general finding is supported – short words tend to be grammatical words, long words tend to be content words.

Under-exploitation

There are other ways in which predictability surfaces in language statistics. For instance, in Chapter 7 we showed that you can understand between 71 per cent and 84 per cent of most English texts knowing only the most common 1000 words of English. Also, although English words use a total of around 1300 different syllables, about a quarter of what we say can be managed with just 12 syllables (including *the* and *-ing*). In other words, there is under-exploitation of the language's possibilities.

A more recent notion of predictability, which our students are likely to be familiar with from text messages, and one which involves under-exploitation, is found in predictive texting. Clever software, dictionary information and statistics about likely word-shapes are installed in mobile phones, helping text users to compose messages more quickly than they might otherwise, given that the 26 letters of the alphabet are encoded onto just eight digits (2–9) on a telephone keypad (Table 11.1). The digit–letter correspondences have long been in use in telephone systems, for example to make freephone numbers more easily memorized, even when the letter string is longer than the number (for instance, remembering 0800 LINGUIST for an expert linguistics consulting service is easier than remembering 0800 546484).

Table 11.1   Digit–letter correspondences on telephone keypads

2	ABC	6	MNO
3	DEF	7	PQRS
4	GHI	8	TUV
5	JKL	9	WXYZ

Although each digit has at least three corresponding letters, mobile phone technology allows users to enter words without having to multi-tap, e.g. without having to choose between the letters ABC after pressing the digit 2. This, again, is because of redundancy in the language – there are relatively few words that correspond to particular number sequences, even though each number could stand for one of three or four letters. After all, not all possible letter combinations correspond to words in the language, some letter sequences occur more frequently than others, and some words are more frequent than others. Consider, for instance, what your mobile phone is likely to display as you enter the number sequence 43556. The first digit, 4, could be G, H or I, and your mobile phone is most likely to suggest 'I', which is a word. The first two digits could give GD, GE, GF, HD, HE, HF, ID, IE, IF, but only four of these match possible word beginnings (GE, HE, ID, IF), plus the possible (unpunctuated) abbreviation IE. Because 'HE' is a word, and other words beginning HE- are quite likely, your phone will probably suggest this for 43. The next digit gives J, K or L, but some combinations of these with GE, HE, ID, IF just won't work in English (how many words begin with IDJ or IFK?). The mobile we tried offers 'GEL' at this point – again this is a possible word and this factor seems to outweigh the presence of more frequent words beginning HEL- or IDL- (e.g. 'HELD', 'HELP', 'IDLE'). Entering another 5 (J, K or L) gives 'HELL' (the mobile offers no alternatives now, showing not surprisingly that the Spenserian *gelliflowre* is not in its dictionary), and the final digit 6 (potentially M, N or O) gives 'HELLO'. The net result is that if you want to text the five-letter word 'HELLO', you only need to enter the five digits 43556. What makes this interesting (for us as linguists and for mobile phone manufacturers from a technological point of view) is that there are 243 (3^5) potential letter sequences corresponding to the sequence 43556, yet only one of these gives an actual word of English.

Getting the right word using predictive text is not always straightforward, since some number sequences are ambiguous. Interestingly perhaps, 5477 could give you 'LIPS' or 'KISS', as well as 'LISP' and 'LIPP' (as in 'LIPPED'). 'ALONE' and 'ALOOF' also share a number sequence, as do 'PINTS' and 'SHOTS'. The disambiguator key on the phone allows you to rotate between these alternatives, though for some phones it has been claimed that this is necessary for fewer than 3 per cent of words being entered. These odds are helped by the use of information about the frequency of use of different candidate words – for example 'WATER' is more likely for 92837 than (in order) 'WAVES' and 'WAVER' and these words are offered in this order by the disambiguator key.

Language has redundancy

Of course, predictability implies a certain amount of redundancy. That is, certain parts of a text may be redundant or unnecessary because they are predictable. Text messaging makes use of this, but which parts of a text are left out? At one level the omissions seem to be very similar to telegrams: a message like 'see you at 12' instead of 'I will see you at 12 noon' expects the receiver to common-sensibly understand that the sender is confirming a meeting (and so 'I will' is redundant) and exploits the fact that the participants to the communication have some common understanding that this will be 12 noon rather than 12 midnight, that it will be 12 as a time rather than 12 as a house number, and so on.

In addition, though, text messaging saves on space by cutting out redundant letters, or by using a short-hand code for words, often exploiting letter pronunciations, so that 'see you at 12' becomes 'CU @ 12'. A study carried out by one of our Psychology colleagues (Weatherall 2004) looked at over 1300 text messages forwarded by volunteer participants. The ten most frequently used 'text' forms were *u, 2, im, r, ur, da, lol, 4, th,* and *tb,* which illustrate a number of ways in which texts are frequently shortened, such as leaving out letters, as in *th* and *da* (both for *the; da* also reflects a common non-standard pronunciation), using letter-for-word homophones such as *u* and *r,* number-for-word homophones like *2* and *4,* omission of apostrophes as in *im,* and abbreviations such as *tb (text back), ttfb (text the f*** back),* and *lol (laugh out loud).* These last three examples also show how aspects of the interaction are managed by text users. A further frequent form of shortening involved phonetic spellings of words, such as *ova, cum, dunno.* Interestingly, though the text messages in the study contained many such 'text' forms, they still only averaged 70 characters, when the maximum character length of a message allowed by the phone company was 160. Clearly, the language of text messaging has developed its own forms that are not (or no longer) determined by the constraints of the communication channel, while they still illustrate the redundancy of language.

Text messaging also exists in other languages, of course. The example below is from French. (This was constructed for teaching purposes. Our thanks to Elizabeth Warren for permission to reproduce it here.)

(8) Txt: GHT 1 nouvo CD 2day. C Gnial!
    French: J'ai acheté un nouveau CD aujourd'hui. C'est génial!
    English: I bought a new CD today. It's great!
    Txt: Keske tu fé 2m1 ?
    French: Qu'est ce que tu fais demain?
    English: What are you doing tomorrow?
    Txt: JM b1 ton fR. Il é 5pa
    French: J'aime bien ton frère. Il est sympa.
    English: I really like your brother. He's nice.

Note that the conventions included here are that capital letters and (usually) numbers should be sounded out, and that <é> stands for a number of spellings. French language purists probably have something to say about the inclusion of English text forms like *2day*.

Not all parts of a message are equally redundant. For another example, consider which of the following seems easiest to understand.

(9) D_ t_e_ r_a_l_ b_l_e_e _h_ s_o_y _e _o_d
(10) C_n y_ _ pl_ _s_ sh_w m_ h_w t_ d_ th_t
(11) _ _e_ _oe_ _ _e _e_ _ _u_o_ia_ _ _a_ _

In (9), every second letter is omitted, so consonants and vowels are more or less randomly affected. In (10), the vowel letters are left out, and in (11) it is the consonants that are omitted. Most people will find (10) easier to reconstruct than (9), with (11) the most difficult. This would suggest that in English the vowel letters are the most redundant. This is not unique to English – the writing systems of Semitic languages (e.g. Arabic) often omit vowels quite regularly.

Of course, redundancy – marking the same thing in more than one way in a single message – means that we can understand a lot of language even in imperfect conditions, which is more often than not how we experience language (e.g. in noisy rooms, through dirty spectacles, etc.). Predictability plays a role here too. For instance, note from the text in this sentence how context means that we don't need to see all of a word in order to recognise it.

Language has structure

The predictability and redundancy found in language is made possible by the fact that language is structured on a number of levels at the same time (see also Chapters 8 and 10). For instance, word order gives us information about the relationship between a verb and its subject in English, with the subject normally preceding the verb, as in *My brother took the cheese*. But when we use a pronoun to refer to something or somebody that has already been introduced into the conversation, we use a form that is appropriate to whether the something or somebody is the subject, object, etc. of the sentence, as in *He took the cheese.* So the fact that the person being referred to in this sentence is the grammatical subject of the sentence (the 'doer' of the verb) is marked both by the position of the pronoun and by the form of the pronoun. So when a child is learning English as their first language and is still sorting out the forms of different related words like pronouns, and says *Him take the cheese,* we still know who is doing what because the word order information is consistent with the interpretation we had before, while *The cheese takes him* is more likely to lead to a different, nonsensical interpretation.

But structure at other levels also has important roles to play, as we saw with texting and in particular with predictive text, where the success of the technology depends on some letter combinations being much more likely (in the sense of being words) than others. Interestingly, an earlier technological advance, the manual typewriter, was driven by somewhat different needs. On these typewriters, each letter was printed by a separate metal bar striking an ink ribbon when a key was pressed. If the typist went too quickly, then two or more bars could collide, causing the typewriter to jam. The standard QWERTY layout of the typewriter was developed (by Christopher Sholes in the nineteenth century) to slow typists down and avoid such jamming. The technology therefore paid little heed to the structural organization of language. A later alternative (probably too late, because the QWERTY layout had become so well established) was developed by Dr Dvorak in the 1920s (see Figure 11.2).

Figure 11.2   Dvorak keyboard layout

Based on a combination of ergonomic and linguistic considerations, the Dvorak keyboard places the most frequently used letters on the 'home' line (the second line up), and has all the vowels under the left hand, so that typists are more likely to alternate hands when typing. These considerations are aimed at increasing speed and accuracy while reducing the risk of repetitive-strain injury.

Users of a language develop intuitions for the structural possibilities of their language, which prove helpful in completing crosswords and other language-based puzzles and games. For instance, puzzle fanatics will frequently make use of knowledge about what consonant sequences are possible at the beginning of an English word, or what vowel letters can occur in sequences of two identical vowels. Some acquaintance with simple letter frequencies can be useful in playing Hangman, so a strategy when setting a word is to choose less frequent letters, but one for guessing a word is to start with the more frequent letters. In Table 11.2 the letters of English are ordered according to their frequency in the British National Corpus (BNC) (a 90 million word corpus of British English), as indicated in the second column. The frequency ordering of letters depends on which texts are being analysed, and so alternative published rankings will have slight deviation from the order in the table. However, in a game like Scrabble the frequencies of letters in a corpus, where many words occur more than once, might not be as useful as their frequencies over a vocabulary list (since this provides the alternatives in the game). The third column accordingly shows the relative ranking of the letters in headwords from the *Concise Oxford Dictionary* (9th edition, 1995). Note that the letters that have the most different rankings are <t> and <h>, demoted from 2nd to 6th and 9th to 15th respectively – these two letters tend to be overrepresented in a corpus, since the word 'the' makes up about 6 per cent of all the words in a text. The makers of Scrabble seem to have been sensitive to this sort of difference, as there is a slightly stronger relationship of Scrabble letter scores with headword rankings than with BNC rankings.

Table 11.2   Letter frequency rankings and Scrabble scores

Letter	BNC rank	Headword rank	Scrabble score	Letter	BNC rank	Headword rank	Scrabble score
E	1	1	1	M	14	14	3
T	2	6	1	F	15	18	4
A	3	2	1	P	16	13	3
O	4	5	1	G	17	16	2
I	5	4	1	W	18	20	4
N	6	7	1	Y	19	19	4
S	7	8	1	B	20	17	3
R	8	3	1	V	21	22	4
H	9	15	4	K	22	21	5
L	10	9	1	X	23	23	8
D	11	12	2	J	24	25	8
C	12	10	3	Q	25	26	10
U	13	11	1	Z	26	24	10

Where next?

In this chapter we have outlined a few aspects of predictability and redundancy in language. It is partly because of these features and because they are in turn founded on the structural organization of language that we are able to use language with such success, even in the normal noisy conditions of communication. These properties of language can be exploited, for commercial gain (text messaging) or for fun (text messaging, language games). It is interesting to note that as technology has become more reliable (i.e. less data is lost through interference and general 'noise' in the transmission pathway), so exploitation of the redundancy and predictability of language has increased. It is interesting also to conjecture how much further this can go before messages become uninterpretable.

The structural organization of language goes beyond the patterns of letters (or sounds) in a word, and we have also seen a few examples of this. A fuller appreciation of linguistic structure and redundancy results from the study of the grammar of language, for which the reader is directed to any good introductory text on linguistics, as well as to grammar books for specific languages.

The examples in (9)–(11) above were constructed from the following originals (though you may have come up with alternatives):

(9)   Do they really believe the story he told
(10) Can you please show me how to do that
(11) When does the next tutorial start

SOME POINTS TO PONDER

▶ If you didn't try out the completion task for sentences (1)–(7) at the beginning of this chapter, do so now. Do you get the kinds of results that the information in this chapter suggests you should?

▶ Go to the website listed under Wilson in the references below, and select five five-letter words with Kučera and Francis frequencies of greater than 300 per million, and five with frequencies lower than 50 per million. Get friends and family to repeat the grouping exercise you did for *again, anvil*, etc. earlier in the chapter. Are the two sets grouped as you'd expect? Repeat with words in other frequency groups (e.g. greater than 200 per million and lower than 100 per million). Do your groupings accurately reflect the frequency counts? If not, why not?

▶ Choose a paragraph at random from a newspaper and do a frequency check on the words, using the website under Wilson or the Kučera and Francis book. Work out the lengths of the words and do a plot like Figure 11.1. Do your data support Zipf's law?

▶ Why is there redundancy in languages (such as marking third person singular on the present tense of a verb in English as well as in the pronoun in *he walks*)?

READING AND REFERENCES

For further information on frequency counts, see Baayen (2001) and Baayen et al. (1993). Most of the frequency data quoted in this chapter come from an early study by Kučera and Francis (1967; see also Wilson 1988). The New Zealand English data are derived from the Wellington Corpus of Spoken New Zealand English (Holmes et al. 1998). Zipf's law is discussed in many texts on linguistics and the psychology of language, and the original discussion of this and related phenomena can be found in Zipf (1935). Discussion of the merits and demerits of different typewriter keyboard layouts can be found in Brooks (2000).

Baayen, R. Harald (2001) *Word Frequency Distributions* (Dordrecht: Kluwer Academic).

Baayen, R. Harald, R. Piepenbrock, R. and H. van Rijn (1993) *The CELEX Lexical Database* (CD-ROM) (Philadelphia, PA: Linguistic Data Consortium, University of Pennsylvania).

Brooks, Marcus (2000) *Introducing the Dvorak Keyboard,* http://www.mwbrooks.com/dvorak (accessed 18 October 2004).

Holmes, Janet, Bernadette Vine and Gary Johnson (1998) *The Wellington Corpus of Spoken New Zealand English: A Users' Guide* (Wellington: School of Linguistics and Applied Language Studies, Victoria University of Wellington). See also http://www.vuw.ac.nz/lals/research/corpora/wcs.aspx (accessed 18 October 2004).

Kučera, H., and W. N. Francis (1967) *Computational Analysis of Present-day American English* (Providence, RI: Brown University Press).

Weatherall, Ann (2004) '"Whr r u? tb!" A preliminary study of language use in young people's text messages', *Wellington Working Papers in Linguistics*, 16: 78–92.

Wilson, Michael D. (1988) 'The MRC Psycholinguistic Database: Machine Readable Dictionary, Version 2', *Behavioural Research Methods, Instruments and Computers*, 20: 6–11. Available on-line at http://www.psy.uwa.edu.au/mrcdatabase/uwa_mrc.htm

Zipf, G. K. (1935) *The Psycho-biology of Language: An Introduction to Dynamic Philology* (Boston, MA: Houghton Mifflin).

Part III

Language and Society

How Do We Lose Languages and Does It Matter?

What's the matter?

Ned Maddrell, the last speaker of Manx, died on 27 December 1974. Manx is a Celtic language which used to be spoken by people from the Isle of Man, a tiny island situated between England and Ireland. Now Manx is a dead language with no native speakers. Cornish met the same fate two centuries earlier, and though there are efforts to revive it, they are almost certainly doomed to failure for reasons we explore in this chapter. In Australia, it is estimated that 90 per cent of the approximately 250 indigenous Aboriginal languages spoken before 1800 are already dead or moribund (heading for death). In the USA and Canada, 80 per cent of the estimated 187 Native North American languages once spoken are extinct or destined for extinction. This is a sad catalogue for linguists.

How did things get to this state? Is English the 'killer' language that this list of its linguistic victims suggests? Why should anyone other than a linguist care about the loss of a language? And, if they do, what steps could they take to reverse what often looks like look an inevitable progression towards linguistic annihilation? (See box 12.1.) These are some of the questions we address in this chapter.

Language shift

The sad story of language loss takes a number of forms. Chapter 16 describes the very familiar pattern of language shift over three or four generations which seems almost inevitable when a family moves to a new country where their mother tongue is not spoken. Almost everyone knows a family who have had this experience. Our Chilean friends, Maria and Juan, arrived in New Zealand in the 1970s with their seven-year-old daughter, Katarina. Maria spoke good English, Juan only a little, and Katarina none at all. Within six months, despite the family's use of Spanish at home, Katarina's English was fluent, with only the faintest trace of a Spanish accent. By the time she reached her teens, Katarina sounded like a native speaker of New

BOX 12.1   Terms for language loss and revival

LANGUAGE SHIFT refers to the gradual or sudden move from the use of one language to another (Crystal 2000: 17). Some linguists use this term only for language shift by a whole community; others use it for individuals too.

LANGUAGE DEATH has occurred when a language is no longer spoken naturally anywhere in the world. Language shift for the Australian Greek community may result in Greek being no longer spoken in Australia, but Greek will not suffer language death while there are native speakers in Greece. If Welsh was no longer spoken in Wales, however, it would be a dead language.

LANGUAGE LOSS refers to a decrease in language proficiency. The term is generally used for loss of proficiency at the individual level. Languages such as Manx have totally disappeared because all those who once spoke Manx gradually lost proficiency in the language until there were no speakers remaining. Of course, particular individuals may also suffer loss of proficiency in a language that continues to be spoken by others.

LANGUAGE REVIVAL is the result of successful efforts to reverse the stages leading to language shift or language death. When a language is reclaimed from being dead or very close to death the process is sometimes referred to as LANGUAGE REVITALIZA-TION. Hebrew, now spoken by millions in Israel, is the best-known case of successful language revitalization.

Zealand English and she categorically refused to use Spanish. She replied to her parent's Spanish with English, and they gradually gave up the battle to maintain Spanish in the home. Thirty years later, Katarina is married to an English-speaking New Zealander and no one would suspect she was once a fluent Spanish speaker. Her children speak only New Zealand English. In barely three generations, Spanish has disappeared from the verbal repertoire of this family.

A former student, Despina, called in to see us recently. Despina is a third-generation Greek New Zealander, and her two children speak Greek. How did she manage to challenge the inevitable erosion of the ethnic language which is the typical pattern for immigrant groups? The answer is complicated, but her story illustrates some of the factors which contribute to language shift and what can be done to inhibit the process.

Numbers matter

Despina belongs to the Wellington Greek community. As a child she lived in a street where most of the neighbours were Greek immigrants and many of the shops were run by Greek families. People spoke Greek to each other in the streets and at church. The community held regular festivals and got together for dancing, singing and other community activities. The contrast to Katarina's situation is obvious. If you belong to a community where there are people around who use your ethnic language, the chances of its surviving are much greater.

Greek was used by people from the community not just at home, in shops, and in the street, but also at church, in community newsletters, and at Greek school. On Saturday mornings Despina went to Greek school to learn to read and write Greek. When she left school and started university, she went back as a teacher in the Greek school (and incidentally transformed their teaching methods to focus on interactive ways of maintaining spoken Greek). So, because of the size of the community and people's commitment to maintaining the language, Greek was supported by a number of institutions which helped it survive, and which gave the Greek language some status in the community. All this is relevant in explaining why some languages resist language shift longer than others.

Attitudes matter too

Despina has been more successful than most in maintaining Greek, even in the Wellington Greek community. True she had more opportunities to hear and use Greek than Katarina had for Spanish, and she had a vibrant community to support her efforts. What's more, she married another Greek speaker which meant her children's chances of learning Greek were greatly improved. But Despina was also remarkable in her personal commitment to maintaining Greek. She loved the language and she was passionate about not losing it. A positive attitude and high motivation are factors which cannot be underestimated in language maintenance. They led her to return to Crete where her paternal grandmother still lived. In Athens, where she went to work for a while, she met her husband, and so when they eventually returned to New Zealand with two small children, Despina brought with her considerable extra linguistic resources for the local community. Despina and Katarina are at the two extremes of the language maintenance and shift continuum. They illustrate some of the complexities of explaining why the grandchildren of some immigrants to a country can still speak their grandparents' mother tongue, the ethnic language, while others are monolingual in the majority language of the country where they now live.

Language death

If Despina's children eventually shift to English and abandon Greek, she will be sad, but the Greek language will survive. Even if it eventually disappears from vibrant communities like Melbourne (the largest Greek community outside Greece), it will survive in Greece where millions of native speakers are not threatened by the predominance of another language in schools, universities, the law courts, the newspapers, the radio and television, and so on. But Ned Maddrell was the last speaker of Manx and the language died with him. Similarly Menomini, a native North American language, has fewer than 50 fluent speakers. When they die, that's it. The language has disappeared for ever as a living language. Every two weeks, somewhere in the world, a language disappears completely. Some linguists estimate that by the twenty-second century the world's languages will literally be decimated, dropping from around 6000 to around 600 (Krauss 1992). How could this happen? And should we care?

Money makes the world go round

If we ask why languages get wiped out, the single most comprehensive answer is an economic one. Colonization, for instance, is generally motivated by the need for new land or a bigger labour force, and it accounts for the disappearance of thousands of languages around the world. Because English speakers have been such determined colonizers, English has been dubbed 'the killer language'. In many places, it has left a trail of linguistic destruction. Indigenous languages have been obliterated, along with their speakers in many cases, in the United States of America, Canada and Australia. Where languages have survived the onslaught of English, it has been because the native populations are too large to eradicate (e.g. India, Africa), and where multilingualism is normal, so that English has been absorbed as simply one code among others, each of which has its own uses and appropriate contexts. Not everyone assumes, in other words, that learning a new language means abandoning the old one.

The decline of Maori – a case in point

In New Zealand, the Maori language was almost annihilated in the early twentieth century. The story of its initial decline and of its survival into the twenty-first century illustrates some of the factors that affect all indigenous languages faced with an invading force of English speakers. The Maori tribes of the nineteenth century were a bellicose lot (as documented in Belich 1998 and reflected in the title of the book and film *Once Were Warriors*), so, despite many losses during colonial wars with the British, they were certainly not physically annihilated by British troops. Much more devastating were the diseases that the colonizers brought with them which reduced the number of native speakers of Maori dramatically in the period between 1840 and 1900. In 1800, before the colonizers arrived, there were approximately 250,000 Maori people. By 1900, this had dropped to around 50,000. And just as important, these Maori speakers now constituted about 5 per cent of the total population of New Zealand, as opposed to 100 per cent before colonization.

Colonization also meant Western-style, school-based, education, and the Maori people embraced literacy and education with great enthusiasm. Indeed, at one point, it is reported that more Maori people than Europeans could read and write in New Zealand (McKenzie 1985). In the long run this proved, inevitably, to be another factor which contributed to the erosion of the Maori language. Many Maori leaders and well-meaning parents supported the use of only English in the education system – even in rural schools where the majority of the children were Maori. As the numbers of

Maori people declined and the use of English spread to more and more domains, Maori became increasingly confined to Maori homes, and to the rituals of the Maori meeting house and marae (the area around and including the meeting house where formal welcomes are performed). And even Maori homes were infiltrated by English, first on the radio and then on the television – indeed one linguist labelled TV 'cultural nerve gas' (Krauss 1992). By the 1970s, although the Maori population had grown again to almost 400,000, only about 18 per cent of Maori people could speak fluent conversational Maori, and most of those were over 45 years of age, with many living in remote rural areas (Benton 1981). So, while economics (in the form of colonization) was perhaps the primary reason for the decline of Maori, demographics (the decimation of Maori caused by war and disease, together with a steady increase in the number of English speakers), compulsory education (in English), gradual domain encroachment (of English as the usual language in church, work, the media and government, and so on), and the loss of status which inevitably accompanied this erosion of its value, all contributed to the steady disappearance of Maori from everyday interaction. This story, with slight variations, could be repeated all over the world to account for the loss of indigenous languages.

Why should we care?

Does it matter if we lose a language? As long as we can communicate does it matter which language we use? As linguists, we believe it does matter. When we lose a language we lose more than just a code for communicating with others.

Perhaps the most obvious reason for a linguist to mourn the disappearance of a language is that the loss of a language means the loss of potential information about what is linguistically possible in human languages. How many or how few distinct sounds can a language make use of? (see Chapter 9). What are the constraints on human articulatory capabilities? Ubykh is a Northwest Caucasian language which has 81 distinct consonants – a remarkably large number (English has only 24). However, in the 1990s, Ubykh had only one remaining speaker, so this testimony to linguistic diversity was destined to be lost.

Until 1959, when people discovered the Amazonian tribe who speak Hixkaryana, a Carib language, linguists had speculated that no human language used a word order which involved the object (O) at the beginning of the sentence and the subject at the end (S) with the verb (V) in between: i.e. OVS (see Chapter 10). Hixkaryana scuttled that theory and forced descriptive and theoretical linguists to think again about linguistic possibilities. And perhaps even more importantly, this discovery forced cognitive linguists to reconsider the range of formal constraints on human cognition, and the kinds of rules the human brain can cope with. Information on possible cognitive limitations on human thinking is relevant in a number of areas, including research on the brain, where it suggests ways of treating brain damage, and information technology, where the limits of what human beings can conceptualize clearly affects what is possible in computer programming.

Perhaps more obviously interesting to non-linguists are examples from languages which record semantic distinctions that are not commonplace. So Polynesian languages, such as Maori, provide speakers with ways of signalling whether they are addressing one person, two people, or three or more people, and with inclusive ('you and me') and exclusive ('me and others') pronouns, which make it easy to indicate who is expected to help when you say something like 'we need to organize dinner'! Some American Indian languages provide affixes on the verb which indicate how much trust the listener should put in the information being offered: for example, Nettle and Romaine (2000) describe how Tuyuca makes such distinctions, and sentences (1)–(3) illustrate just three of those available (there are more!).

(1) díiga apé-wi [visual affix]   'I saw him play soccer with my own eyes'

(2) díiga apé–yi [apparent affix]   'I have seen evidence that he played soccer: e.g. the shoe print on the playing field, but didn't see him play'

(3) díiga apé-hiyi [inferential affix]   'It is reasonable to assume he played soccer'

It has also been argued that it is not just linguists and anthropologists who should be distressed by the loss of a language. Languages encode information. When we lose a language which makes subtle distinctions between plants on the basis of their medicinal properties, or which encodes important biological and environmental knowledge which may not be obvious to outsiders, we lose information which may be very difficult to retrieve. Nettle and Romaine (2000) point out that 25 per cent of the prescriptive medicines used in the USA are derived from plants that grow in the world's rain forests, and that are most easily identified in languages which are at great risk. Australian Aboriginal people know how to survive in the desert; encoded in their languages is information about which plants to eat and which to cook, which provide water, and so on. As the languages disappear, the information is harder to retain, and it gradually disappears too.

Finally, another important reason for deploring language loss is the fact that when people lose their language, their distinctive socio-cultural identity is also put at risk. Language and culture are clearly closely related, as the discussion above has indicated. These are crucial symbols of identity and the loss of a language and the related erosion of cultural identity is often devastating. People whose language has been swamped by another often lose confidence in their abilities and develop poor self-esteem. While many other factors are also relevant, language loss in such cases is at least a contributing factor in educational and socioeconomic underperformance. So, assuming these arguments are convincing, what can be done about language loss?

Language revival

Over the last century many linguists have become concerned about the wholesale loss of languages on a world-wide scale, and they have begun to take steps to stem the flood. At the most basic level, some linguists are trying to describe languages which are at risk. For example, Vanuatu, one of the most multilingual countries in the world, is the focus of interest of a number of linguists who are documenting languages such as Naman, Tape and Ura, which will otherwise disappear without trace (see, for example, Crowley 2001). Another valuable step is to produce writing systems for languages which are still spoken, but are at risk, in order to make it possible to produce educational materials which can be used to teach children using these languages. Preserving traditional stories, for example, is valuable, since many will disappear when the old people die, and they also make good teaching materials for schools that want to use the children's mother tongue.

Crowley argues that in these situations, the role of the linguist is a sensitive one. The wishes of the speakers of the languages being describing must always guide the linguist's activities. Offers to record and write down culturally treasured stories are generally welcome. If people see value in having a writing system, developing an orthography for an unwritten language is also a good way of preserving it. This will often have greater obvious appeal to speakers of a language than an offer to document the grammar or write a dictionary – however important a linguist might think these activities! Pointing out the dangers of not using the threatened language with children is also important. People generally do not realize how quickly language loss occurs. And straight facts are valuable, too, as a stimulus to action, as demonstrated by the effect of dramatic figures produced by a linguist on the extent of Maori language loss in the early 1970s (see below). But, finally, maintaining or reviving a language depends to an extraordinary extent on the behaviour and attitudes of its speakers. Linguists can only help.

Maori in New Zealand

People often point to success stories, such as the revival of Hebrew in Israel, and wonder why other peoples cannot replicate them and rescue their dying languages. But Israel was a special case in many, many ways (Spolsky 1996). There was enormously strong and determined political will involved in establishing the creation of a new state. For primarily ideological reasons, then, as the symbol of the new nation of Israel, Hebrew was adopted and adapted to fit the role of national language. It was steadily introduced as the language of schooling, and large groups of committed adults determined to bring up their children speaking Hebrew as a first language. Such circumstances are not easy to duplicate.

The relative success of the survival of Maori in New Zealand is a much more typical story. In the 1960s, Maori looked doomed to destruction. Most Maori people spoke English as their first and usually their only language. A survey undertaken by a linguist, Richard Benton, for the New Zealand Council for Educational Research, estimated that there were only 70,000 fluent Maori speakers remaining in a population of 400,000 Maori people. His research made it clear that the language was in danger (Benton 1981, 2001). At this time, too, a committed group of young Maori people, supported by some older Maori and some Pakeha (New Zealanders of European origin) activists, began a vociferous campaign to assert the value and importance of Maori language and culture, leading to a 'Maori renaissance' in the early 1970s. One of the first steps that was taken in response to the demands of Maori people for attention to the plight of their language was the establishment of bilingual schools where, for the first time since the turn of the century, children could use Maori in the classroom. Bilingual schools were first established in a few rare areas where Maori was still used in the community. Two of our recent students attended one of these schools in the northeast of New Zealand, and as a result they are among the very tiny group of remaining native speakers of Maori in New Zealand. It was a great pleasure to hear them talking to each other in class with impressive levels of confidence and fluency.

Using the language in school, then, is one obvious way to revive a language. Maori is now used in a number of primary and secondary schools as a medium of instruction, and is taught in many more as a second language. More radically, it is used at a small number of tertiary institutions known as 'wānanga' or Maori universities where not only the language but the ways of teaching and learning are distinctively Maori. Most effective of all, however, has been the introduction of Maori as the language of pre-school education. New Zealand's 'kohanga reo' or 'language nests' have been widely regarded as a great success story. Begun on a voluntary basis in the 1980s by a small group of committed Maori parents and grandparents, they now receive government funding and they can be found throughout New Zealand (Benton and Benton 2001). The children who attend them certainly gain fluency in Maori (although the precise level of fluency reflects the Maori proficiency levels of the adults who teach them). The problem of course is that when they reach school age, there is often no way for this fluency to be maintained.

There is now also a Maori television channel, which broadcasts a range of programmes judged to be of interest to a Maori audience, with some using the Maori language. There are also a number of Maori radio programmes, though they do not consistently use the Maori language. People have the right to use Maori in Parliament and in court – it is an official language of New Zealand. Very few do, however, and there is typically a good deal of grumbling when people exercise this right. Maori is still used on most marae for ritual welcomes and formal speeches, but the amount varies greatly in different places, and in some consists of little more than a few token formulaic phrases.

Despite these limitations, and the lack of opportunities to use and hear the language, and the need for more resources to teach the language well, it seems that the erosion of Maori has been at least slowed down. Recent surveys suggest that though native speakers are rare, Maori is much more widely spoken as a second language than it was 30 years ago. A survey of 5000 Maori people by the Ministry of Maori Development in 2001, for example, indicated that 42 per cent of the Maori population over 15 years old reported they could speak some Maori, though only 9 per cent reported being fluent, and 59 per cent of Maori people over 15 years old reported that they could understand some Maori. Things could be worse.

Where next?

This chapter has painted a depressing picture of language erosion. We have identified some of the reasons why languages wax and especially why they wane, as well as some of the potential effects of language loss, both in global and individual terms. As linguists, not surprisingly, we deplore the loss of linguistic diversity, and we have suggested that there are other reasons for attempting to stem the tide of language eradication which appears to be sweeping steadily across many vulnerable populations.

Linguists clearly have a role and indeed a responsibility in assisting people to resist the extermination of their languages. But what could you as an educated layperson do if you wished to help? Having read this chapter, you could provide facts to startle people. Many people are totally unaware that we face the decimation of the world's linguistic resources over the next century. And many more do not see such losses as a problem. This chapter has provided you with some ammunition to challenge false assumptions. Perhaps most importantly, we all need to develop and encourage positive attitudes to linguistic diversity. Rather than seeing multilingualism as a 'problem', we should value it and seek ways of preserving rather than eliminating linguistic variation. We should be pleased when we hear people using a language we don't understand on the bus or in a shop; the speakers may be keeping alive a precious linguistic resource. Let's hope they succeed, since there is no doubt that, as the number of languages contracts, the world will become a very much less interesting place.

SOME POINTS TO PONDER

▶ Do you know any families where a language other than English is used in the home? Are these families deliberately and consciously attempting to maintain their family languages? If so, what strategies are they using?

▶ Do you think that television programmes in a minority language can be useful in spreading the language? Why (not)?

▶ Are you convinced that there is a case for attempting to preserve languages which are threatened? If so, which arguments did you find most convincing? If not, how would you frame a counter-argument?

▶ If you are convinced that there is a case for attempting to preserve threatened languages, what specific steps could you take to help?

READING AND REFERENCES

There are many books on the issues covered in this chapter. Three of the most readable are Crystal (2000), Dalby (2002) and Nettle and Romaine (2000), which explores the links between language and biodiversity very thoroughly.

Belich, James (1998) *The New Zealand Wars and the Victorian Interpretation of Racial Conflict* (Auckland: Penguin).

Benton, Richard A. (1981) *The Flight of the Amokura* (Wellington: New Zealand Council for Educational Research).

Benton, Richard (2001) 'Whose Language? Ownership and Control of Te Reo Māori in the Third Millennium', *New Zealand Sociology*, 16(1): 35–54.

Benton, Richard and Nene Benton (2001) 'Reversing Language Shift in Aotearoa/New Zealand, 1989–1999', in Joshua A. Fishman (ed.), *Can Threatened Languages Be Saved? Reversing Language Shift Revisited: A 21st Century Perspective* (Clevedon, OA: Multilingual Matters), pp. 423–50.

Crowley, Terry (2001) 'Language, Culture, History and the Fieldworker: "What I did on my Christmas holidays on Malakula?"' *Anthropological Forum*, 11(2): 195–215.

Crystal, David (2000) *Language Death* (Cambridge: Cambridge University Press).

Dalby, Andrew (2002) *Language in Danger* (London: Allen Lane).

Duff, Alan (1994) *Once Were Warriors* (Auckland: Tandem Press).

Krauss, Michael (1992) 'The World's Languages in Crisis', *Language*, 68: 4–10.

McKenzie, D. F. (1985) *Oral Culture, Literacy and Print in Early New Zealand: The Treaty of Waitangi* (Wellington: Victoria University Press).

Nettle, Daniel and Suzanne Romaine (2000) *Vanishing Voices* (Oxford: Oxford University Press).

Spolsky, Bernard (1996) 'Conditions for Language Revitalization: a Comparison of the Cases of Hebrew and Maori', in Sue Wright (ed.), *Language and the State: Revitalization and Revival in Israel and Eire* (Clevedon, OH: Multilingual Matters) pp. 5–29.

<http://www.terralingua.org/> & <http://www.ogmios.org/5content.htm> <== information on endangered languages

What Shall I Call You?

What's the matter?

Young children are usually given very clear directions about what to call people – as well as what *not* to call people. But young adults often face problems in this area. When you meet her again as an adult, what do you call the friend of your parents who was *Mrs Landy* when you were five? Using her first name *Pat* seems too familiar, but *Mrs Landy* seems too formal and unfriendly. What do you call your mother-in-law? Many people find that calling her *Mum* does not feel comfortable, but, again, using her first name seems over-familiar. How do you react when the butcher calls you *dear* or the bus driver addresses you as *love*? Do you consider it patronizing, over-familiar, or just friendly? And when you are talking to your friends in school, how do you refer to your father if he is the school principal? *Dad* seems inappropriate in class while calling him *Mr Wallace* sounds very odd.

Difficulties in deciding what to call someone nicely highlight the sociolinguistic norms which guide our behaviour, but which we are generally unaware of. It is only when we hit a problem that we reflect on the complex patterns that allow us to thread our way confidently through the maze of alternatives most of the time. Difficulties arise when how well we know someone conflicts with their social role in a particular context, for instance, or when there does not seem to be an appropriate address term in the language for a particular relationship. In English, depending on the variety you speak, it is often possible to duck the problem by avoiding using any name at all. But in some languages such choices have to be made every time you open your mouth to address someone. This chapter explores some of the sociolinguistic patterns revealed by the use of appropriate and inappropriate terms of address, and in doing so identifies the wide range of social factors that are relevant in selecting a term which will not offend – unless it is intended to do so!

Before reading further you might like to make a list of all the terms of address you can think of that different people might use to a middle-aged married woman doctor with two children whose name is Elizabeth Anderson, and whose husband is Mike Scott. (See end of chapter for some possibilities.)

Being friendly vs. keeping your distance

At the end of each day Elizabeth Anderson switches off her computer and leaves her Birmingham doctor's surgery at about 5 o'clock. As she leaves, her partner in their practice says *Goodbye, Elizabeth* (she replies *Goodbye, Neil*), their secretary says *Goodbye, Dr Anderson* (she replies *Goodbye, Jane*) and the caretaker says *Bye, Mrs Anderson* (to which she responds *Goodbye, Ken*). As she arrives home she is greeted by *Hi, mum* from her teenage daughter, Helen, *Hello, love. Have a good day?*, from her father, and *Did you miss the bus again, Beth?* from her husband. Later in the evening someone from the local tennis club calls to ask if she would like to join. *Good evening, is that Mrs Scott?* he asks. *No, it's Ms Anderson, but my husband's name is Mike Scott*, she answers, *What can I do for you?* Finally a friend calls, *Hi, Liz, how's things?*

In the course of a day, we all play many parts, and these different social identities are typically reflected in the names we are called. Terms of address and reference are important resources in these constructions. The choices in the example above reflect some of the different social identities that one person may perform, as well as the influence of a range of different social contexts in which she performs them. Elizabeth Anderson is called a range of names in the example, depending mainly on how well she knows the person addressing her, but also on the social role she is playing. As a middle-aged successful doctor, she is addressed respectfully by her secretary and the building caretaker. Her roles as mother, daughter and wife all elicit different address terms, and the fact that she has not adopted her husband's last name leads to an error by someone who assumes this norm (see Chapter 15 for further discussion of the social significance of the choice between *Mrs* and *Ms*). Friends generally call her *Liz*, while at work she is addressed as *doctor* or *Dr Anderson*.

Selecting a term of address or reference involves making sociolinguistic judgements about the kind of relationship we have with others. In most Western societies, the most important judgement we make these days is how well we know someone – a dimension known in sociolinguistics as the solidarity or social distance dimension. We can represent it by a scale and locate people along it according to how well we know them (see Figure 13.1).

Intimate ————————————————————— **Distant**

High solidarity   Low solidarity

Low social distance   **High social distance**

e.g. best friend, sister   e.g. stranger, bus driver

Figure 13.1   The solidarity dimension

In modern English, the range of choices facing us on the basis of where people are located on the scale is relatively simple. We generally choose between first name (FN), e.g. *Neil*, which we use when we know the person well, or title plus last name (TLN) e.g. *Mr King*, if we don't know them well. At the far end of the scale, of course, with complete strangers, we don't have to make this choice since their name is not known. In other languages, however, when the degree of solidarity is a factor in selecting between pronouns, ignorance of a person's name is irrelevant, and avoidance is generally not an option (Lambert and Tucker 1976). So, speaking French, the choice between *tu* and *vous* (alternative forms of the pronoun 'you' for addressing an individual) reflects an assessment of the closeness of your relationship with the person addressed. Simplifying somewhat, if you know them well you use the *tu* pronoun, but in addressing a stranger, a shop assistant or a bus driver, *vous* is generally the appropriate pronoun. The same is true for the choice between *du* and *Sie* in German, between *tu* and *Lei* in Italian, between *ty* and *vy* in Russian, and between *sen* and *thkhven* in Georgian. In fact there are many languages which require the speaker to make a choice of this sort in addressing someone, and in Shakespeare's time English speakers also made a similar choice between *thou* and *you*. At the start of the play, for instance, Hamlet addresses Horatio with *you*, but later pledging his friendship, he switches to *thou* (Brown and Gilman 1989: 178).

> Give me that man
> That is not passion's slave, and I will wear him
> In my hearts' core, ay in my heart of heart,
> As I do thee.   (*Hamlet*, III.ii.73–6)

The pronoun forms indicating greater solidarity (*tu, du, ty, thou* etc.) have been labelled the T forms, while the more distant forms are the V forms (Brown and Gilman 1960).

So far so good, but, in fact, the choices are not at all straightforward. How well do you need to know someone before they merit first name or the T form? The answer differs in different cultures, in different societies, and in different eras or time periods. So, for instance, in Japanese, a culture where respect for others and for their privacy is given great weight, use of TLN is normal for a much wider range of acquaintances and colleagues than in New Zealand and the USA, where people tend to use FN to each other from when they are first introduced. The British English pattern falls somewhere between these two. No more than a generation ago, for instance, on housing estates in Lancashire, it was normal for neighbours to address each other by TLN, even after 15 years of living side by side. This pattern is changing over time in the direction of the New Zealand and American norms; in other words, young people tend to move to FN more quickly these days, even with people they don't know well. And this pattern is also evident in another area – the solidarity dimension is gradually encroaching on the status or respect dimension.

How important is status?

Example from the television programme *The West Wing*:

Context: The US president walks into the office of his Chief of Staff.

Chief of Staff: Mr President

President: I've decided you're right, Leo. I'm just going to ignore that troublesome man. . . .

The Chief of Staff, Leo, has known the President Jed Bartlett for over 20 years, yet even when they are talking one-to-one, he addresses him as *Mr President*. As long as they are relating to each other in their roles as President and Chief of Staff, formality and the respect due to the highest office in the land prevails. It is interesting to reflect on where else we hear people addressed by their title plus last name in the twenty-first century.

School pupils still tend to use TLN for their teachers in primary schools. The combination of a large age difference together with the status of the teacher's role means that the children are expected to demonstrate respect. This is expressed through non-reciprocal address terms: the child uses TLN (e.g. *Good morning, Miss Smith*), but the teacher addresses the child with FN (e.g. *Good morning, Jill*). Similarly, university students talking to the Vice Chancellor or the Dean will generally use their TLN (e.g. *Good afternoon, Professor Johnston*) or even just their title (e.g. *Thank you, Vice Chancellor*). And despite the fact that they may have known them for decades, older people typically use TLN to their doctor and lawyer. Even in New Zealand, a society where the solidarity dimension has made great inroads on the status/respect dimension, and where people are very reluctant to recognize status differences, the bank manager still gets TLN from most! The status or respect dimension can be represented as a vertical scale (see Figure 13.2).

The fact that some secondary school pupils and most university students now use FN to their teachers, especially their young teachers, attests to the erosion of the importance of the status dimension. An American university lecturer – we'll call him Jim Keller – arrived in New Zealand in the late 1990s and attracted considerable comment when he insisted his students address

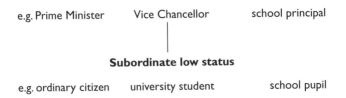

Superior high status

e.g. Prime Minister   Vice Chancellor   school principal

Subordinate low status

e.g. ordinary citizen   university student   school pupil

Figure 13.2   The status dimension

him as *Dr Keller* rather than *Jim*. He argued that this requirement was not simply a demand that students show him respect, but, because he did a good deal of one-to-one teaching, he felt the more formal address term assisted in maintaining a distance between himself and his mainly young and female students. This example nicely illustrates the sociolinguistic complexity of such choices. The same term can signal both respect and social distance.

The conflict between social distance and respect has been resolved in different way in different periods of history. In earlier centuries, even members of the same family used TLN to the head of the household. For example, in *Pride and Prejudice*, Mrs Bennet expresses the view that her daughters are all very clever. Her husband responds:

'I must so far differ from you as to think our two youngest daughters uncommonly foolish'.

Mrs Bennet replies

'My dear Mr Bennet, you must not expect such girls to have the sense of their father and mother.'   (Austen 1813: 21)

It seems inconceivable today that a wife would address her husband with TLN, but a little reflection identifies situations where, even in the twenty-first century, this may occur – most obviously perhaps in a very formal setting where people are performing a role rather than relating to each other on a personal dimension.

Context is crucial

In July 2000, the American sisters Venus and Serena Williams ended up facing each other in the semi-finals of the Wimbledon women's singles. The British *Daily Telegraph* (5 July) reported that the match raised problems for the referees' office who devoted time to deciding how to call out the advantage in deuce games. The normal call in this formal British setting would have been *Advantage Miss Williams*. The officials debated the options of *Advantage Miss Serena Williams* against *Advantage Serena Williams*. The paper reported that *Advantage Serena* or *Advantage Venus* was definitely not an option. In other words, the formality of the situation dictated the use of the more formal term. The decision was made in favour of the fuller form *Advantage Miss Serena Williams*.

A law court is another very formal setting where those who are performing an assigned role are required to follow carefully prescribed behavioural rules. Who may talk, about what, when, and for how long is largely pre-determined; in other words, many aspects of the talk are tightly constrained by the formal purposes of the speech event. Moreover, the judge, the lawyers, the accused, and the witnesses are required to use certain ratified terms of address. In court, people are frequently addressed or referred to by their roles (e.g. *Your Honour, my learned colleague, Mr Hobbs*) as well as or even instead of their names (e.g. *the witness may now stand down*), and the formulae used in referring to people are very full and explicit. Such contexts have been labelled 'status-marked settings' (Ervin-Tripp 1972), since people's roles and statuses are the basis for determining the way they will be addressed and referred to in such settings.

This pattern holds in other formal situations too. In ceremonies where ritual dominates, for instance, the roles of the participants are typically formally signalled by the way people are addressed and referred to. On formal occasions, etiquette books tell us that a bishop is appropriately addressed as *Your Lordship,* a duke as *Your Grace,* and a countess as *Your Ladyship.* During a graduation ceremony the Chancellor will refer to the Vice Chancellor by her title rather than as *Sylvia,* the name he uses when chatting in the robing room before the ceremony. The fact that there is an audience also emphasizes the formality and the requirement for people to perform in their ritualized roles rather than as individuals. This sociolinguistic requirement is exploited in the famous *Monty Python* sketch where John Cleese performs the role of inter- viewer in a staged formal TV interview with an art critic, Sir Edward Ross (played by Graham Chapman). John Cleese introduces his guest very formally as *Sir Edward Ross* but then, appealing to the benefits of reducing formality, he drops the *Sir* and steadily moves to increasingly less formal address forms, progressing from *Edward,* to *Ted,* and then to *Eddie-baby,* at which point the interviewee protests. As usual the *Monty Python* sketch pushes the boundaries and indicates that, while most people are willing to tolerate and even welcome some relaxing of formalities in such contexts, the use of *Eddie-baby,* an intimate nickname, goes well beyond the bounds of accept- ability in a public televised interview. This example also demonstrates that the analysis of address terms into just two categories, FN and TLN, is an over- simplification. There are many other terms available for different purposes.

Strategic selections: endearments and insults

Eddie-baby is clearly a nickname, the kind of name used only between inti- mates or within the family. Many people have names of this kind which they sometimes regard as appropriately used only by family and close friends. Many English nicknames are shortened versions of FN (e.g. *Rob, Liz, Meg, Tom*) or LN (e.g. *Brad* from *Bradford, Rich* from *Richards*), or end in *–y/ie* (e.g. *Jenny, Robbie, Laurie*) or in Australia in *–o* (e.g. *Jacko, Johnno*). More intimate nicknames often focus on a physical or psychological trait. When outsiders use such intimate nicknames, it feels as if they have 'taken a liberty'; the social distance dimension is clearly in evidence here. So while in many Western societies, the use of FN has extended over time to more and more contexts and relationships, alternative terms of address have often developed to mark the boundary between intimates and others. On the other hand, there are also terms which can be used to signal social distance and respect for those whose names we do not know.

A: What do you call a man with a shotgun?

B: Sir.

This well-worn joke demonstrates that the names we call people are often determined by the effect we want to have. Terms such as *sir, madam* and *ma'am* show respect and they are often used by sales people or those involved in service occupations such as porters, receptionists and taxi drivers as useful ways of addressing customers whose names they don't know. The same applies to men whose rank one is unsure of. One etiquette book writer remarked wryly, 'However exalted an officer's rank, he can always be addressed as "sir"' (Pine n.d.). For women whose name (or rank!) is unknown, *ma'am* is more widely used in the United States of America, and especially in the south, while *Madam* is generally more common in Britain, and interestingly *ma'am* seems to be spreading in New Zealand usage, where once such terms of respect were relatively rare.

At the other end of the social distance spectrum are terms like (*my*) *love, duckie, darlin'* and (*my*) *dear,* all of which can be heard in different parts of England in superficially similar contexts to *sir* and *madam,* i.e. between people providing a service and their customers. The difference is that the customers are typically less well off than those who attract *sir* and *madam,* and the services provided are often those on public transport, and in less exclusive shops. These terms of endearment, associated with intimate, family relationships, have become general terms of address in many contexts, among working-class people in particular. The endearment terms are used to indicate good will and friendliness, even to strangers. Again this demonstrates the extension of the solidarity dimension among some groups of people to embrace a much wider set of addressees than is encompassed by other groups.

There are subtle gender differences in such usages, too. Men from other areas travelling to the north of England are often taken aback to be addressed as *love* by a male bus conductor or the train steward. And it is interesting to reflect on who calls you *dear.* An American study of 650 service encounters found that women were much more frequently addressed as *dear* (or *hon*) than were men, a pattern the researchers associated with women's less statusful position in society (Wolfson and Manes 1980). In general, *dear* is used reciprocally with someone who is very close, but non-reciprocally to someone of subordinate status, e.g. to someone younger. This imbalance is highlighted by considering how the butcher would react if you responded by calling him *dear. Dear* carries connotations of either intimacy or power depending on the context. When used to an equal who is not an intimate, it may therefore be experienced as patronizing.

Another sub-category of terms of address is terms of abuse or insult. As the discussion has suggested, it is possible to insult someone by using an overly intimate term. Non-reciprocal usage is still the norm where there is a recognized power or status difference. Thus addressing the Prime Minister as *mate,* or addressing an adult as *boy* or *girl* is usually offensive. The term *girl's blouse,* for instance, is an example of an insult used between men in a rugby changing room (Kuiper 1991). However, this also highlights the fact that ritual insults and jocular abuse may be a marker of solidarity or rapport – especially between males (Poynton 1988).

Young people also regularly exchange such insults. The list on the left in Table 13.1 is just a small selection from the terms recorded in actual interactions of groups of London teenagers from a range of social backgrounds (Stenström et al. 2002). Most readers will no doubt be able to add many more such terms. The list on the right is a small selection from terms collected from New Zealand university students (Roberts 1997) who were asked to write down metaphorical terms of address (and reference) that they used for the opposite sex.

Interestingly, the table illustrates that terms of abuse often make use of animal and body-part imagery. And while it still seems to be the case that the range of such terms directed towards women is more extensive than that for men, the gap appears to be narrowing (see also Chapter 15).

Table 13.1   Terms of insult

Terms recorded in the usage of UK teenagers	Terms cited by NZ university students
you silly bastard	dog
you fat wanker	cow
you fucking arsewipe	bitch
dickhead	tart
you fuckin' slag	pig
peanut head	rat
you flat-chested cow	asshole
bitch	prick
you burk	cunt

Names in non-Western cultures

We mentioned above that the pronoun system in some languages forces the speaker to signal explicitly how they perceive their relationship with their addressee. Addressing another person in French or German or Russian, for instance, involves a choice between a T pronoun which signals intimacy or condescension and a V pronoun which indicates social distance and/or respect. It is not always easy to know which pronoun to use since the patterns differ in different communities. Within Canada, for example, the range of people for whom *tu* as opposed to *vous* is appropriate varies from city to city, and in urban compared to rural regions, and there are interesting stories about the conditions for shifting from *vous* to *tu* (Coveney 2003). It has been said, for instance, that above a certain critical height on a mountain, climbers shift to *tu*. The reliance on others' skills engenders a degree of intimacy which is appropriately expressed with the T form.

Many Asian cultures place greater emphasis on the respect dimension than on solidarity. In Bengali society, for instance, young people should not address a superior by first name. And, because she is regarded as subordinate to her husband, a Bengali wife is not permitted to use her husband's name. She addresses him with a term such as *suncho* 'do you hear?', and when she refers to her husband in conversation, she uses a circumlocution. One nice example of this practice is provided by the Bengali wife whose husband's name was *Tara*, a word which also means 'star'. Since she could not call him *Tara*, his wife used the term *nokkhotro* or 'heavenly body' to refer to him.

Where next?

We have provided many examples in this chapter to illustrate the diversity of address terms in different social and cultural contexts. But underlying all the examples are the apparently universal dimensions of solidarity and respect. We select the appropriate term of address on the basis of our relationship to the addressee in a specific social context, i.e. how well we know the person, what social role we are playing in relation to them, whether the setting is formal or not, and what we want to achieve. It is also important to note that patterns vary in different cultures and they change over time. The respect dimension is more heavily emphasized in many Asian communities, for instance, than in Western society, but it was accorded much greater weight in earlier centuries in many English-speaking communities. It is interesting to speculate on whether the encroachment of the solidarity dimension will eventually constitute another Western influence on Asian culture in places like Hong Kong, Tokyo and Kuala Lumpur, and whether change is inevitably in the same direction. What kind of circumstances might lead to a reversal of the pattern in the West, for instance, and a reinstatement of the emphasis on the respect dimension? Studying the sociolinguistic norms for terms of address in different cultures provides some useful starting points in answering such questions.

Possible address terms for Elizabeth Anderson

> *Madam, ma'am*
> *Dr Anderson, Doctor, doc*
> *Ms Anderson, Mrs Anderson*
> *Mrs Scott, Ms Scott*
> *Eliza, Liz, Lizzie, Beth*
> *Mum, mummy, ma*
> *Auntie Liz, Aunt Elizabeth*
> *love, dear, sweetie, honey....*
> *idiot, fool, silly woman......*

SOME POINTS TO PONDER

▶ Write a list of all the names people call you, i.e. address you by. Can you account for the different choices using the dimensions of social distance/friendship and status/respect? If not, what other factors are relevant? If you have friends from different cultural backgrounds from your own, you could compare their answers to yours.

▶ Are there people who present a problem when you have to decide what to call them (e.g. your parents' friends)? How do you resolve the problem and what factors are most important – age difference, social distance, status, context?

▶ Choose a television programme which involves a relatively formal setting: e.g. law court, police station, classroom, doctor's surgery, and examine the way people address and refer to each other. Are the patterns you observe accounted for in the discussion in this chapter?

▶ If you know a language which uses the T vs. V distinction, can you formulate the rules for choosing T vs. V? Are they similar to the patterns in English for choosing first name or title plus last name? If they differ, can you say why?

▶ It has been suggested that we have more terms of address (names, nicknames, terms of endearment) for those whom we like most. Is this true in your experience? What about names for people you do not like? It is interesting to check out this hypothesis using a literary text (e.g. a Shakespearean play or a modern novel). Does the range and number of names correspond to the closeness of the relationship?

READING AND REFERENCES

Most introductory sociolinguistic textbooks include some discussion of terms of address and the social dimensions of solidarity and status or respect. See, for example, Holmes (2001) and Wardhaugh (1998). Spencer-Oatey (2000) provides a more elaborate and sophisticated discussion of the concepts of solidarity (which she calls 'rapport') and power, with particular attention to cross-cultural factors. Mühlhäusler and Harré (1990) provide a very scholarly approach with a philosophical orientation.

Austen, Jane (n.d. [1813]) *Pride and Prejudice* (London: Blackie).

Brown, Roger and Albert Gilman (1960) 'The Pronouns of Power and Solidarity', in T. A. Sebeok (ed.), *Style in Language* (Cambridge, MA: MIT Press) pp. 253–76.

Brown, Roger and Albert Gilman (1989) 'Politeness Theory and Shakespeare's Four Major Tragedies', *Language in Society*, 18 (2): 159–212.

Coveney, Aidan (2003) '"Anything *you* can do, *tu* can do better": *Tu* and *Vous* as Substitutes for Indefinite *On* in French', *Journal of Sociolinguistics*, 7 (2): 164–91.

Das, Sisir Kumar (1968) 'Forms of Address and Terms of Reference in Bengali', *Anthropological Linguistics*, 10(4): 19–31.

Ervin-Tripp, Susan (1972) 'Sociolinguistics Rules of Address', in John B. Pride and Janet Holmes (eds), *Sociolinguistics* (Harmondsworth: Penguin) pp. 225–40.

Holmes, Janet (2001) *An Introduction to Sociolinguistics*, 2nd edn (London: Longman).

Kuiper, Koenraad (1991) 'Sporting Formulae and What They Tell Us: Two Models of Male Solidarity', in Jenny Cheshire (ed.), *English Around the World: Sociolinguistic Perspectives* (Cambridge: Cambridge University Press) pp. 200–9.

Lambert, Wallace and Richard Tucker (1976) 'Tu, Vous, Usted: a Social-Psychological Study of Address Patterns (Rowley, MA: Newbury House).

Mühlhausler, Peter and Rom Harré (1990) Pronouns and People: The Linguistic Construction of Social and Personal Identity (Oxford: Blackwell).

Pine, L. G. (n.d.) Written and Spoken Guide to Titles and Forms of Address (Kingswood, Surrey: Elliot's Right Way Books).

Poynton, Cate (1988) 'Terms of Address in Australian English', in Peter Collins and David Blair (eds), Australian English (Brisbane: University of Queensland Press), pp. 55–69.

Roberts, Mary (1997) 'Metaphor: or Brick Shithouses, Studmuffins and Horny Old Goats'. Paper presented at the Twelfth New Zealand Linguistics Society Conference, 26–29 November 1997, University of Otago, Dunedin.

Spencer-Oatey, Helen (2000) 'Rapport Management: a Framework for Analysis', in Helen Spencer-Oatey (ed.), Culturally Speaking: Managing Rapport through Talk Across Cultures (London: Continuum), pp. 11–46.

Stenström, Anna-Britta, Gisle Andersen and Ingrid Kristine Hasund (2002) Trends in Teenage Talk: Corpus Compilation, Analysis and Findings (Amsterdam and Philadelphia: Benjamins).

Wardhaugh, Ronald (1998) An Introduction to Sociolinguistics, 3rd edn (Oxford: Blackwell).

Wolfson, Nessa and Joan Manes (1980) 'Don't "Dear" me!', in Sally McConnell-Ginet, Ruth Borker and Nelly Furman (eds), Women and Language in Literature and Society (New York: Praeger) pp. 79–92.

Do Women and Men Speak Differently?

 (the large "14" chapter number appears in the top right)

What's the matter?

> Men are from Mars, Women are from Venus.   (Gray 1992)

Do women speak differently from men? This seems a simple question, but, as often with apparently simple questions, the answer is in fact complicated. Many people would answer, 'Yes, they certainly do' – including John Gray, who wrote the book *Men are from Mars, Women are from Venus.* He argued that women and men communicate so differently that they might as well come from different planets. However, a more accurate answer to the question, 'Do women speak differently from men?' is the sociolinguist's response, 'It all depends' (see Box 14.1).

Most obviously, it all depends on what you mean by 'differently' – what kinds of differences matter, and how big a difference counts? Can something

---

PERSONALITY

Box 14.1   Deborah Tannen

Deborah Tannen is an American socio-linguist who published a popular book on language and gender, *You Just Don't Understand*, which was on The *New York Times* best-seller list for nearly four years. It has been widely interpreted as supporting claims that women and men speak differently, but the discussion in her book is more circumspect and takes careful account of context. She is a Professor of Linguistics at Georgetown University, where she teaches courses on discourse analysis as well as language and gender.

as apparently insignificant as using 'ng' [ŋ] rather than 'n' [n] at the end of a word like *playing*, or the use of words like *cute* or *quite* signal your gender? Or do the differences need to involve more noticeable behaviours, such as interrupting other speakers or hogging the talking time? Some people believe women speak more 'properly' and 'correctly' than men, for example. Others have claimed that women are more polite than men. But how do we decide what counts as 'more polite'? It certainly isn't just a matter of who says 'please' and 'thank you' most often!

Answering the question of whether women and men speak differently also depends on where the talk is going on and who is involved. Women may speak differently from men when they are in a public setting, such as a school meeting, or in a formal context, such as a job interview, but more similarly at home in private. Do women and men talk differently from their children? Do women in the netball changing room talk differently from men in the rugby changing room? The answers are almost certainly 'yes'. We know that social context make a difference to the way people talk, and there is some evidence that context affects women's and men's speech differently.

Finally, the answer even depends on whether you think that being a woman or a man is a straightforward matter of biological classification, as opposed, for example, to believing that people signal their gender identity by the ways they dress and behave, including the way they speak. Categories like 'woman' and 'man' may be less relevant than categories such as 'masculine' and 'feminine' when we are concerned about ways of talking.

Do women speak more 'correctly' than men?

If you actually try counting how often a group of English-speaking women and men use the sound 'ng' [ŋ] as opposed to 'n' [n] at the end of words like *running, clapping* and *swimming*, it is likely that you will find that women use more of the [ŋ] and men use more of the [n] pronunciation. Figure 14.1 shows the average results for a sample of women and men in the city of Porirua, near Wellington, the capital of New Zealand.

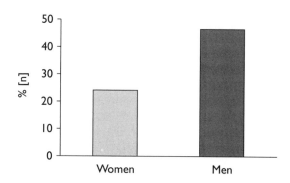

Figure 14.1 **Percentage vernacular (n) pronunciation by women and men in a New Zealand speech community**

Notice that everyone uses some of each pronunciation – no one uses [n] all of the time – but the women typically use more of the more careful, 'proper' or standard 'ng' [ŋ] pronunciation, while men use more of the colloquial, 'careless' or vernacular 'n' [n] pronunciation. The same pattern turns up in surveys of English all over the world. In Newcastle upon Tyne, for instance, men more often than women end words like *stop* and *clap* with a 'p' which is 'glottalized' (i.e. they cut the air off abruptly in the wind-pipe as they say the 'p'). This is a non-standard or vernacular pronunciation. And this pattern – men's greater use of vernacular forms and women's preference for standard forms – carries over into other features of the language too (see Box 14.2). So women also tend to use standard *grammatical* features more often: e.g. *I didn't do anything wrong* rather than the less standard *I didn't do nothing wrong*.

The pattern is not restricted to English either. Although your French teacher no doubt taught you to carefully pronounce the [l] at the end of the words *il* and *elle*, French Canadians in Montreal often omit it. But French Canadian men typically leave off the [l] more often than French Canadian women. And in Mombasa, women use more standard Swahili pronunciations than men.

Yes but . . . what about the context? We tailor our speech to fit the situation; we talk differently to our grandparents compared to our friends, and we talk differently in class and in a coffee bar. Obviously, then, generalizations about women's and men's speech need to take notice of contextual influences. Gender differences of all kinds certainly reduce dramatically when people are recorded talking to their friends in a relaxed context, as opposed to in a formal interview with a complete stranger. Similarly there is evidence that women and men respond differently in different contexts. This might explain women's greater use of standard forms in a formal interview – perhaps they treat the interviewer with greater respect or less familiarity than the men, for instance.

Another intriguing explanation that has been suggested for women's greater use of standard forms is that their usage *defines* the standard. In other

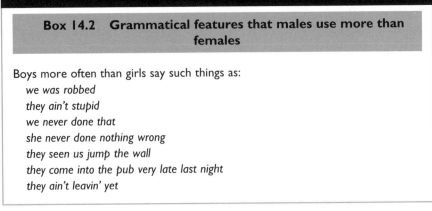

ILLUSTRATION

Box 14.2   Grammatical features that males use more than females

Boys more often than girls say such things as:

we was robbed
they ain't stupid
we never done that
she never done nothing wrong
they seen us jump the wall
they come into the pub very late last night
they ain't leavin' yet

words, it is not so much that women use more standard forms but rather that the forms that women use become the standard forms because the community expects women to model the 'correct' forms. Women are usually the care-givers, after all, and, in many communities, women are expected to model all kinds of 'good' behaviour. This could explain the way in which new vowel sounds gradually become accepted as part of the standard language – women introduce new pronunciations and children imitate them – but it is harder to see how it could explain patterns like [ŋ] vs. [n] where what is standard has been cemented in place by the written language for centuries.

And what about women who don't follow these patterns? When we actually examine the way any individual speaks, we often find that they use language in sophisticated ways, and that their gender identity is only one aspect of a complex picture. Look at excerpt (1), for instance. Can you guess the gender of the speaker?

(1) and she goes + she kept tryin' to push away from me I says you better put those arms down because that's fightin' material for me . . . and she goes oh what have I have I done she goes um she says you can't fuckin' do nothin' to me and I says d'you wanna bet

This is a short excerpt from a story told by a working-class New Zealand woman, Geraldine, who clearly challenges the norms described above. Geraldine uses vernacular forms just as frequently as men in her social group, and the effect is to construct a tough 'masculine' identity or image. She consistently uses the vernacular pronunciation [n] rather than [ŋ], for instance, and she also uses a number of vernacular grammatical forms and swearwords. So here we have a woman who does not follow the standard patterns, but rather exploits them to help construct a masculine gender identity for herself as a participant in the events she is recounting. We return to this point in the last section.

Do women speak more politely than men?

When one of the authors started learning Japanese, she was told that because she was a woman she had to learn a special vocabulary. The 'women's word' for 'father' was *otoosan*, while men used *oyaji*; men said *kuu* but women said *taberu* for the verb 'eat', and so it went on. Actually, it didn't go on very far, since the number of such paired alternatives turned out to be rather small. And what is more, she discovered that many modern young Japanese women used the 'men's' words without being burnt at the stake. Much more important for sounding like an authentic Japanese woman was acquiring control of the language of politeness. What was generally regarded as an appropriate way for a Japanese woman to speak involved becoming familiar with a complex set of styles and word forms, and making sophisticated choices between them on the basis of factors such as the relative status of the speaker and addressee, the social situation, and even the topic of conversation. While all Japanese speakers were aware of these sociolinguistic subtleties, it seemed that women were expected to use them to express greater degrees of politeness and deference than men.

People have often claimed that women are generally more polite than men, more considerate of the feelings of others, and more responsive to the needs of others. But like the claims about the greater 'correctness' of women's speech, it is easy to challenge such generalizations when you look at the complexities of any specific situation.

Swearing is generally considered to be rude and offensive behaviour. And there is certainly evidence that women tend to swear less than men – at least in the contexts where researchers have studied this behaviour. But, once again there are lots of 'buts'. Swearwords can serve a range of functions – most people use them when they are really annoyed or frustrated, but some people use them to strengthen a much wider range of expressions, as in (2):

(2) Shit that was good
What a shit-hot game
Bugger I've dropped the pin
Don't fuckin' look at me like that
That's fuckin' fantastic
You're a bloody marvel
Abso-bloody-lutely mate!

People generally swear more in relaxed situations, and gender differences tend to reduce dramatically as the context becomes less formal. In the pub, on the sports field and in the sports changing room, even in some 'chat rooms' on the internet, where people generally interact as equals, swearing is quite frequent. And although the evidence that is available suggests that, in general, males swear more than females in these contexts, it has also been found that young women swear more when they mix with men than when they are in all-women groups, and young men tend to reduce the amount of swearing in the company of women. Each 'accommodates' to the other's patterns – or perhaps to what they believe are the other's norms.

Another 'but' relates to workplaces. Swearing is considered more acceptable in some workplaces than others. And though it seems that blue-collar workplaces tend to tolerate a greater level of swearing than white-collar workplaces, factors such as team membership seem to be more important than gender. In one New Zealand factory, for instance, both men and women used swearwords in their exchanges with other team members, but they didn't swear when talking to people from outside their own team. And even between team members, the amount of swearing varied. The same point was nicely illustrated in the Ken Loach film *The Navigators*, which deals with the trials faced by a gang of railway line repairmen when British Rail restructured. In the gang which was the film's focus, swearing was well tolerated, but there was one character, the cleaner, who used the word *fuck* and its variants (*fucked, fucking* etc.) far more often than anyone else. And this was clearly a source of amusement to the others. So again, things are often not as neat as they first appear.

When you want your mother to lend you her car, you are likely to adopt another politeness strategy, namely, softening your request with 'hedges' such as *perhaps, might, could, just, possibly, I wonder, maybe*, and so on:

(3) I *just wondered* if you were likely to be using the car tonight, Mum.
Do you think *perhaps* I *could possibly* borrow the car tonight, Mum?
I *thought maybe* if you weren't going out that *maybe* you *might* let me borrow the car *for a little while* later Mum?

The use of hedges to soften utterances is another feature which has often been identified with the way women talk. But you can undoubtedly think of situations in which a man might also use a well-hedged utterance, especially if the favour was a big one! While the evidence suggests that women tend to use hedges more often than men, this may well be a reflection of the fact that they are more often than men in a position where they need to be polite. In other words, relative power and status are typically at least as important as gender in accounting for why people use hedges.

Do women talk more than men?

The conventional wisdom in many societies, as reflected in their proverbs, suggests that women talk more than men (see Box 14.3). The reality is, as

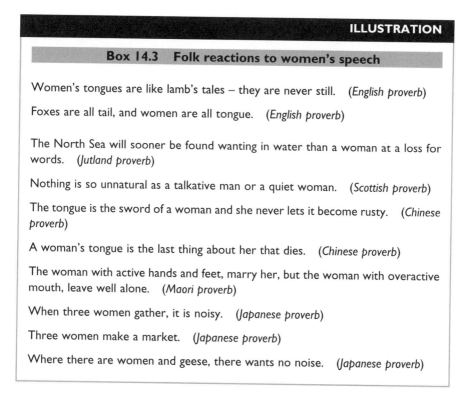

ILLUSTRATION

Box 14.3   Folk reactions to women's speech

Women's tongues are like lamb's tales – they are never still.   (*English proverb*)

Foxes are all tail, and women are all tongue.   (*English proverb*)

The North Sea will sooner be found wanting in water than a woman at a loss for words.   (*Jutland proverb*)

Nothing is so unnatural as a talkative man or a quiet woman.   (*Scottish proverb*)

The tongue is the sword of a woman and she never lets it become rusty.   (*Chinese proverb*)

A woman's tongue is the last thing about her that dies.   (*Chinese proverb*)

The woman with active hands and feet, marry her, but the woman with overactive mouth, leave well alone.   (*Maori proverb*)

When three women gather, it is noisy.   (*Japanese proverb*)

Three women make a market.   (*Japanese proverb*)

Where there are women and geese, there wants no noise.   (*Japanese proverb*)

you might expect, nowhere near so clear-cut. Again we encounter a raft of 'buts' or ways in which 'it all depends!' When do you talk most? The answer is probably something like 'when I am most relaxed' or 'when I am interested in the topic' or 'when I am talking to my friends'. In other words, the obvious contextual factors that were discussed in the previous sections are all likely to be relevant: is it a formal situation or a casual conversation? are you in a public or in a private setting? are you talking to a friend or to your boss or to a complete stranger?

What we know from research about women and men's talk suggests that men tend to dominate public and formal contexts – they talk more in public meetings and formal seminars, they ask more questions at conferences, and they tend to dominate formal business meetings. Women, by contrast, tend to talk more in private. Studies of couples at home (and there are not many such studies, it should be said!) indicate that the women work hard to try to get their partners to engage in conversation, while the men tend to be relatively taciturn in more private contexts.

There has been a good deal of speculation about the reasons for this – no doubt you can think of a wide range of explanations. One which has been widely cited is that men talk more in contexts where it will contribute to their mana or status, while women use talk to establish connections or rapport. A related reason is based on the idea that women and men tend to use talk for different purposes. Men, it is claimed, tend to see talk as a means of getting things done – conveying and obtaining information, and getting things organized. Women use talk to build, develop and maintain relationships. The weaknesses of such generalizations are obvious. The contexts in which we get things organized and establish rapport clearly overlap. Indeed, language is so complex and subtle that we are often doing all these things at once. In any situation people achieve a wide range of things though talk. In a formal meeting, for instance, people not only gather and convey information, they also signal their status – as meeting chair, for instance, or as 'expert' on a topic, or as a bored secretary. In a chat over coffee, which might look like a 'gossip' session focused on maintaining a friendship, there is often a good deal of useful information being transmitted and discussed. So labelling situations as formal or informal or treating the functions of talk as one-dimensional is self-evidently misleading.

Much the same arguments apply to the issue of who interrupts most. Popular myth says women 'never let a man get a word in edge-wise' and there are many TV comedy shows and stand-up comedians who make use of this widespread belief in representations of the nagging wife who peremptorily cuts off her husband's attempt to speak. Again the research which has been undertaken presents a much more complicated picture. There is certainly some evidence that men interrupt women more in situations where the men hold a more powerful position, and even where both are apparently equal participants in an interaction. But the most interesting issue that has arisen from this research is 'what counts as an interruption?' If someone enthusiastically breaks into your sentence with a supportive comment, does that count as an interruption? If it does, then obviously we need to revise the idea that interruptions are a 'bad' thing. One study showed, for instance, that the talk between a group of women friends typically involved a lot of overlapping speech, and yet the women did not report that they felt 'interrupted'. So, more usefully perhaps, we need to distinguish between supportive interruptions and unsupportive interruptions which break the flow of someone's talk, or perhaps change the topic. But even that is not easy, as you will find if you try to classify interruptions. Does it count as an interruption, for instance, if the speaker keeps talking despite someone else's attempt to take over the floor? The answer is not straightforward. Like generalizations about who talks most, generalizations about men's and women's patterns of 'interruption' should be treated with caution.

Gender identity

In this final section, we ask a more fundamental question, 'How do you know if someone is male or female?' The answer – it depends on what kind of gender identity they are 'constructing' or conveying – provides a somewhat different set of lenses for considering the issue of whether women and men speak differently. Most obviously we classify people as women or men by how they appear, though we all know how misleading that can sometimes be. People usually wear clothes that signal their gender identity – though this differs in different eras, and in different cultures. Despite the acceptance of the Scottish kilt on formal occasions, Westerners are often taken aback to see the military personnel of Fiji and the male chiefs in Tonga wearing 'skirts'. Even mini-skirts are not an unambiguous gender signal since (often labelled as 'tunics') they have frequently been male rather than female garb in the past. Context is crucial in accurately interpreting signals of gender identity.

Behaviour is another way of signalling gender identity, and speech is obviously an important resource for this purpose. High pitch tends to be associated with women, for instance, though not just for biological reasons, since the pitch continuum has a wide area in the middle where women's and men's pitch ranges overlap. People have good control over where in the pitch range they locate their speech. To sound more 'feminine' people typically use higher pitch, while lowering the pitch contributes to a more 'masculine' impression. On the radio, the current New Zealand Prime Minister, Helen Clark, is frequently mistaken for a man on the basis of her low-pitched voice, an attribute which she doubtless exploits in a context where leadership has been strongly associated with men until relatively recently. Indeed, Margaret Thatcher, the first female British Prime Minister, was given lessons to lower the pitch of her voice so that she sounded more authoritative. This is a clear indication that we can use speech to 'construct' a particular kind of social identity, and this includes our gender identity.

High pitch is associated, then, not so much with 'women' as a group as with 'femininity' as an aspect of gender identity. Similarly, pragmatic particles, such as *you know* and *I think*, pragmatic devices such as tag questions (*isn't it, didn't you, eh*), and supportive feedback (e.g. *yeah, mm*) can be used to express social meanings such as tentativeness, rapport and friendliness. Speakers draw on these social meanings in their construction of relatively feminine or relatively masculine gender identities. This is a fruitful way of considering how people make use of the resources of language to manage their way through social situations.

Taking this approach, we find that people tend to emphasize different aspects of their social identity in different contexts, and even at different points in the same interaction. So, for instance, a middle-aged, middle-class woman who is the manager of a company may draw on features associated with masculine, authoritative speech when she opens a company board meeting. But at a later point in the meeting when she wants to emphasize the collegiality of the senior team, or to present a more feminine identity, she may make use of more linguistic features associated with 'feminine' speech. Many of these linguistic choices will almost certainly be relatively unconscious; particular pronunciations and most grammatical features are rarely under conscious control. The decision to use certain intensifiers (such as *vastly* or *utterly*) or hedges (such as *possibly* or the tag *eh*) may be more conscious, and certainly the selection of swearwords is a more conscious matter. But overall the construction of gender identity in a social setting is generally achieved with relatively little awareness of the process, though we may have a clear idea of what we are trying to achieve. The tough, masculine identity constructed by Geraldine in example (1) above was achieved through her use of exactly such features – her vernacular pronunciations and vernacular grammatical features, and her use of swearwords all contributed.

Consider the example in (4), an excerpt from an interaction which took place in a New Zealand workplace. How would you respond in this case if you were asked to identify the gender of the speaker?

(4) actually I- I wanted to- get your advice about that I want to do a bit of a wee sort of ra ra speech at the beginning of like of planning day tomorrow we ARE stretched people ARE starting to feel the pressure but it's it's just the kind of thing you know it's- if if we want to be in the business you're gonna have to live with it you know that kind of thing . . .

In this short excerpt, the speaker uses a relatively large number of 'hedges' (*a wee sort of, you know, just, that kind of thing*) to indicate the tentative nature of the suggestions being proffered. But forms like *you know*, and *that kind of thing* not only serve as hedges, they also claim common ground with the person addressed. These devices are generally regarded as typical of feminine rather than masculine styles of speaking. Yet in this case the speaker is a man. He is talking to his manager, a woman, and he uses a range of hedging devices to construct a relatively feminine identity which emphasizes his relatively subordinate status in this particular interaction, while also appealing to their relationship as colleagues. In other words, he uses stereotypically 'gendered' linguistic resources to achieve his desired effect.

This approach encourages, then, an appreciation of the skilful ways in which people exploit linguistic resources to construct an appropriate social identity in a dynamic and on-going way in interaction. Just as there are women who at certain points choose to convey a 'tough', powerful or author-itative identity, so there are occasions when men choose to construct a more 'feminine' identity. While adjectives such as *divine* and *heavenly*, and address terms such as *sweetie* and *darling* conjure up stereotypes of gay men, it is also true that many middle-class, heterosexual men use words associated with 'women's language' in contexts such as an interaction with a more powerful person, or in a context where they want to be particularly persuasive. Looking at the way we talk from this perspective provides a much more dynamic and subtle view of interaction.

Where next?

The material in this chapter has suggested a host of reasons for treating the bland claim that women and men speak differently with some caution. The obvious response is to ask a raft of further questions. Which women and men are being compared? In what kinds of social contexts? And exactly which linguistic features are involved? Similarly, claims that men 'just can't under-stand' women can be treated with scepticism. We can all make use of rela-tively masculine and feminine ways of talking when it suits us. Finally, it is important to give careful thought to how we interpret any differences we find: one woman's 'indecisive hedge' is often perceived as another man's 'judicious qualification'. And the same behaviour may be classified as 'helpful and articulate' from a man but 'loquacious and verbose' from a woman. Perception is all. We need to be careful that we don't don culturally gender-biased spectacles when we consider the research in this area.

SOME POINTS TO PONDER

▶ Listen to radio interviewers. Some tend to listen politely and allow the interviewee to finish what they want to say while others interrupt their interviewees more often. Are there gender differences that you notice or do other factors explain the different styles? Could any of the interruptions be described as 'supportive' rather than 'disruptive'?

▶ Do the vernacular grammatical forms shown in Box 14.2 occur in your dialect of English? Have you heard 'tough' girls use such forms and if so what effect do they have in your community?

▶ Do you think swearwords are always offensive? Why do you think most societies generally accept swearing from men more readily than from women?

▶ Can you think of contexts in which you adopt more masculine or more feminine speech? What are the changes that you make in your speech when you want to sound more 'masculine' or more 'feminine'?

▶ Do you think social class is more or less important than gender in accounting for the way we speak? How would you test out whether you are right?

READING AND REFERENCES

Talbot (1998) is an easy-to-read introduction to language and gender. Tannen (1990) is a very popular book on the topic. Slightly more demanding are Coates (1998), Holmes (1995) and Romaine (1999).

Coates, Jennifer (ed.) (1998) *Language and Gender: A Reader* (Oxford: Blackwell).

Gray, John (1992) *Men are from Mars, Women are from Venus* (New York: HarperCollins).

Holmes, Janet (1995) *Women, Men and Politeness* (London: Longman).

Holmes, Janet and Maria Stubbe (2003) *Power and Politeness in the Workplace* (London: Pearson).

Romaine, Suzanne (1999) *Communicating Gender* (Mahwah, NJ: Lawrence Erlbaum).

Talbot, Mary M. (1998) *Language and Gender: An Introduction* (Oxford: Polity Press).

Tannen, Deborah (1990) *You Just Don't Understand: Women and Men in Conversation* (New York: William Morrow).

Sexist Language and Linguistic Sexism

What's the matter?

Can a language be sexist? To what extent are we constrained by the language or languages we speak? Does language affect the way we think about certain things or the way we perceive certain groups of people? These are questions which linguists have pondered for many centuries. Current thinking suggests that language *does* have an important influence on the way we perceive and even create social reality, even if it does not act as a strait-jacket for our thinking (see Chapter 22).

Every language provides well-established categories that mean we don't have to invent them for ourselves, and well-worn grooves for our thinking so we don't have to think every issue through from scratch. Often this is useful and saves time. Sometimes, however, especially if the categories encode misleading, socially unacceptable, or unjustifiable assumptions, it is potentially dangerous. When linguistic categories exclude, marginalize or discriminate against people on the basis of their gender, or when language creates or promotes an irrelevant or unfair distinction between women and men, we are dealing with 'sexist language'. When, for instance, women, rather than men, are referred to using terms such as *peach, crumpet, plum,* and *tart,* while men are referred to by terms such as *wolf, goat,* and *shark,* the underlying assumptions (about women as satisfying appetites, and men as rapacious predators) are clearly contestable.

Similarly, established usages which exclude sections of the population, or which treat one group as the central core exemplar of a category, must be considered unsatisfactory in any society which prides itself on being democratic and valuing equity. Consider the following sentences.

(1) Man alone among the animals uses language to communicate.
(2) Each student will have the opportunity to discuss his project with his supervisor.

When presented with sentences such as these, most people 'think male'. In other words, people construct male images, even though conservatives argue that the words *man* and *he* in these sentences are 'generic' words which include both women and men. As this example suggests, in most societies it is women more often than men who are the butt of sexism, including sexism encoded in language.

But, one might argue, languages change in response to social conditions, and, as we illustrate below, alternative forms emerge or new forms are invented to resolve such equity problems. So is there really a serious problem with sexist language? While it is true that language does evolve in response to changes in social attitudes and behaviours, there *is* nevertheless a serious issue here. Language is a complex and sophisticated instrument, and people use it in very subtle ways, not only to express attitudes and reflect social conditions, but also to construct, maintain and reinforce certain social 'realities'. Well-established linguistic categories encourage certain ways of thinking and viewing the social world, and thus contribute to the creation of that world. Learning to identify the unacceptable assumptions underlying the use of terms like *chairman, career woman* and *lady doctor* is an important critical linguistic skill.

Invisible women

Many people object to so-called generic usages such as *man* and *he* (illustrated in (1) and (2) above) because they treat men as the paradigmatic case or the norm, and thus render women invisible. These people argue that such terms do *not* include both women and men, they are better described as 'false generics'. The following example makes this point even more clearly:

(3) 'Man loves to hunt. He sees it as a tradition and a right. He believes that deer herds should be managed so he and his son after him, can hunt them'. (*Mountain Management,* New Zealand Department of the Environment, 1986)

It is hard to imagine any woman identifying with the 'man' described in this rather extreme example. And in the twenty-first century, we would expect such a paragraph to be written more sensitively, using terms such as *people* and *they* rather than *man* and *he*. In fact, many people would now use *their* instead of *his* in sentence (2); *they, them* and *their* are the new generic pronouns in English, as illustrated by sentences such as (4).

(4) Everybody's got their own style.

The substitution of *their* neatly avoids the use of the false generic *his,* as well as the cumbersome, non-sexist *his or her*. One recent study showed, for instance, that use of generic *he* in the official documents of a New Zealand government department dropped from 98 per cent in the 1960s to 7 per cent in the 1990s, while use of generic *they* correspondingly rose from 0 per cent to 81 per cent (Brown 2000). Another study of spoken New Zealand English confirmed that generic *they* was also widespread in speech in the 1990s;

79 per cent of the pronouns following non-gendered words such as *anyone, anybody, nobody, no one, person, somebody, someone,* and *whoever* were forms of *they* rather than the prescriptively 'correct' conservative form *he* (Holmes 2001a).

These overtly sexist usages thus seem to be steadily disappearing, especially in speech. More problematic and difficult to challenge are terms that we might call 'pseudo-generics' – terms which masquerade as generics but which tend to be associated with male images, and which therefore subtly exclude women. Phrases such as *the man in the street, the tax man* and *as good as the next man* illustrate this phenomenon, where there is no rational justification for using *man* rather than *woman,* but conventional usage has established the male term as the norm. Inevitably this simply reinforces the widespread assumption that the basic, default or normal human being is male (as reflected in the Genesis myth where Adam was created first and Eve was created from one of his ribs). And, at least from the perspective of those who support equality between the sexes, this is far from satisfactory.

Are suffixes sufficient?

False generics delete women from the linguistic map by claiming to include them in the male term. One might expect, then, that those who oppose discriminatory language would welcome the fact that many languages provide a range of affixes which offer a means of explicitly marking gender on a noun. But this apparent solution often proves to be a chimera when one looks more closely at what is going on.

In most respects the same objections that have been discussed in relation to the false generic *man,* apply to the suffix -*man.* So the words *fireman* and *policeman* reliably evoke male images; hence, the widespread adoption of alternatives such as *officer* for -*man* in such contexts. Similarly, the Australasian term *postie* provides a satisfactory gender-neutral term for the person who delivers the mail or post. Terms such as *chairman, spokesman* and *foreman,* however, have proved more problematic. Example (5), which was noted by an observer at a council meeting, strikes some people as odd for similar reasons that claims that 'man is the only animal who breastfeeds his young' seems odd.

(5) Male local authority councillor thanking female chair of the authority:
'You have been a capable and decorative chairman'.(Austin 1990: 285)

In addition to the covert and insulting sexism embedded in the use of the term *decorative,* a quality irrelevant to the role of chair, there is also the incongruity of an adjective which implies 'female' (since people don't usually describe men as *decorative*) with the term *chairman* which for many listeners signals 'male'. Attempts to substitute the neutral suffix -*person* in such contexts have not always succeeded. Rather, *chairman* and *spokesman* are widely regarded as the 'unmarked' or normal terms, while *chairperson* and *spokesperson* tend to be perceived as 'marked' or unusual. So since the marked terms tend to be used when women take these roles, the purpose of the new terms is subtly undermined or subverted. *Chairperson* is not a neutral term like *director*, which does not signal gender; *chairperson* signals 'female' with, of course, the additional implication of 'unusual'. *Foreperson* is another such term which, in addition to signalling 'female' and 'unusual', is also widely regarded as stylistically clumsy. Nevertheless, despite this rather depressing picture of the ways in which non-sexist initiatives are often less than totally successful, there is also some evidence that more acceptable alternatives such as *chair* for *chairman*, and *spokeswoman* as well as *spokesperson* as alternatives to *spokesman*, are steadily establishing themselves (Holmes 2001a; Romaine 1999).

However, this is clearly not a straightforward matter. Is it better to be rendered invisible by a term which covers both female and male, or is it preferable to be marked as an unusual or odd case by suffixes such as *-ess* (e.g. *poetess*) or *-ette* (e.g. *usherette*) or *-ix* (e.g. *aviatrix*)? Even when an apparently neutral form is the norm, underlying sexist assumptions can often be uncovered, as illustrated by the example in Box 15.1.

ILLUSTRATION

Box 15.1   The sexist litmus test story

A man was driving his son to school and they had a terrible accident. The son was rushed to hospital and straight into the operating theatre. The surgeon looked at the boy and said, 'My god, it's my son.' How can this be explained?

While *surgeon*, *pilot* and *doctor* are apparently unmarked for gender, the covert social presumption is often that the incumbents are male – as indicated by such phrases as *lady doctor*, *woman pilot* and *female surgeon*, which are uncompromisingly condemned by those concerned about issues of gender equity. On the other hand, the term *actress* – which clearly signals 'female' – is strongly endorsed by those who want to make the presence of women in the performing arts more visible.

More subtle linguistic inequality

Suffixes signal gender differences quite explicitly, so that it is easy to identify ways in which women are treated differently from men. But there are other ways in which language use discriminates much more subtly between the sexes by developing connotations, categories and contrasts which we often accept without question or a second thought. In this section we consider a number of ways in which language discriminates more subtly against women, and where it is clearly the underlying sexist attitudes and assumptions that are the target of critical linguistic analysis, rather than overtly sexist usages.

Imagery and reference terms

One area which very clearly illustrates how sexism is linguistically encoded is the metaphors people use to refer to women and men, and the choices they make in constructing gendered images. Most obviously, perhaps, different gender identities are constructed and moulded by imagery which describes women and men as different kinds of objects (e.g. *old bag, prick, dick, blouse*) or animals (e.g. *bitch, kitten, cow, bunny, chick, shark, wolf, stud, stag*) or food (*peach, plum, tart, crumpet, studmuffin*). In general, the connotations of the terms used for women tend to be more pejorative or patronizing than those used for men (though context is an important factor in assessing attitudinal messages). Even superficially negative terms for men, such as *shark, wolf* and *stud*, often have a compensatory covert complimentary feature (such as 'skilled' or 'wily', 'powerful' or 'potent'). Interestingly, too, the term *dog*, originally defined as referring to 'an unattractive person of either sex', is now used almost exclusively to refer to an unattractive woman (Talbot 1998: 123–4). Overall, then, the evidence indicates that terms used to refer metaphorically to women as food, objects or animals are more prolific, as well as more negative than equivalent metaphorical terms used for men (Romaine 1999).

A similar pattern is evident in the semantic development over time of terms available to describe and refer to women compared to men more generally. A remarkably consistent trend emerges: namely, terms used for women tend to acquire negative and often sexual connotations, while pejorative terms used for both women and men tend over time to become specialized for women. Terms like *girl*, which originally referred to either sex, have become specialized for reference to women and then acquired pejorative, demeaning and sexual connotations. Terms like *harlot*, originally used to refer pejoratively to men, have changed to refer only to women, and have also acquired sexual connotations. Terms such as *hussy*, originally used to refer positively to women, have acquired both negative and sexual connotations. And, finally, in more recent usage, terms such as *tart*, first used to refer to women in a complimentary way, have developed into terms used for female and later male prostitutes (cf. *whore*). The general pattern that terms associated with women steadily acquire negative and sexual connotations is apparent, with a further extension in some cases to gay men, who are thus placed even further beyond the social pale.

Negative social attitudes to both women and gay men are evident from such patterns. Linguistic research in this area in English, for example, has overwhelmingly demonstrated that there are far more derogatory terms available to describe women than men, and that the majority of those have negative, sexual connotations (Schulz 1975; Stanley 1977). So insulting words like *slut, whore* and *bitch* have until very recently been used mainly to refer to women, and even today their extension to refer to men tends to be confined mainly to the gay community. If language constructs our social reality and contributes to the creation of our social identity then the prolificness of such terms is another sad indication of sexism at work in English-speaking societies.

Non-parallel pairs

Another area where linguistic analysis has identified covert sexism is in the different associations of apparently equivalent terms. The way that language encodes differences in societal attitudes to women and men is apparent in the contrasting meanings of the pairs in Table 15.1. Although historically these words were the masculine and feminine counterparts to each other, the meanings of each member of the pairs have become quite different over the centuries. The pattern of 'semantic derogation' of women referred to above is equally clear here (Shulz 1975; Stanley 1977). The female term in these lists of apparently 'equal' pairs has acquired negative and often sexual connotations over time. Where the male terms have positive connotations such as 'power' and 'independence', the female terms are systematically lesser in status, and regularly connote dependence, which is sometimes sexual. These patterns obviously reflect the fact women are generally regarded as of inferior status to men and as primarily sexual beings or possessions.

Table 15.1   Non-parallel terms

master	mistress
courtier	courtesan
Sir	madam
bachelor	spinster
governor	governess

Ladies, women and girls

A third type of subtle linguistic discrimination is illustrated by the development of patronizing connotations for superficially polite terms. The word *lady* is a good case in point – it is a very slippery linguistic term. On the surface it seems polite; we talk of *ladies* and *gentlemen,* and we refer to *the cleaning lady* and *the tea lady* rather than *the cleaning woman* and *the tea woman.* But it is interesting to ask why we need such a polite form for women but not for men. The apparently equivalent term *gentleman* is vanishingly rare, while *lady* is still very much in evidence in many varieties of English. The short answer is that it serves firstly as a useful euphemism for the term *woman,* which many people feel is too direct and rude; and secondly it is used to raise the status of demeaning occupations.

Referring to someone as a *woman* still sounds rude to many people. Children are often corrected when they use it and told to substitute *lady.* Moreover, like some of the false pairs discussed above, the term *woman* often has sexual overtones. Note the different connotations, for instance, of the phrases *man of the world* and *woman of the world.* The former suggests much wider experience and knowledge (possibly including sexual experience), the latter mainly suggests sexual promiscuity. It is only in very recent years, and still not in all contexts, that the term *woman* is coming to be considered acceptable as the equivalent of *man*.

The euphemistic status of the substitution of the term *lady* for *woman* is apparent as soon as one considers phrases such as *lady doctor, lady editor* and *lady judge*. In phrases such as *cleaning lady* the term *lady* is used to attribute status to the referent; there is no need for it in the context of more prestigious professions. Moreover, as noted above, the fact that many people feel the need to signal the gender of the doctor, editor or judge when she is female but not when he is male is yet another indicator of covert sexism and of the 'male as norm' principle.

Not just a problem with English

We have used English to illustrate the issues which arise in analysing linguistic sexism because it is the language that we can assume most readers will be familiar with. But the same kinds of issues arise in all languages. Where one gender group is less powerful than another, then the attitudes and assumptions inevitably associated with subordinate status will be mirrored in the ways that the community refers to, describes and addresses members of that group. The community's language becomes a way of encoding and reinforcing attitudes and values, and in everyday use in specific situations the language is thus constantly constructing the subordinate group's inferior or secondary status.

Languages with grammatical gender face additional problems, though the basic issues are the same. French, for example, faces genuine issues of linguistic sexism. Like other languages which signal noun classes using categories labelled 'feminine' and 'masculine', problems arise when there is a conflict between natural and grammatical gender which the designated group find unacceptable. Many women are unhappy, for example, with occupational titles such as *le pharmacien*, 'the pharmacist', which are grammatically masculine. If they feminize them to *la pharmacienne* they are frequently classified, not as a pharmacist, but as a pharmacist's wife. Interestingly, grammatically feminine forms exist for *hairdresser, charwoman, maid* and *factory worker*, while terms for *President, engineer, doctor, lawyer* do not have universally accepted feminized forms. French speakers in Quebec have been fighting this battle for some time, and they have simply created their own feminine forms such as *la professeure*, ('teacher', 'professor') a word which formerly existed only in the masculine form *le professeur*. Recently, even the more conservative European French have begun to challenge the forces of the Academie Française, with women in the cabinet of Socialist Prime Minister Lionel Jospin calling themselves 'Madame la Ministre' (see Hellinger and Bussman 2001).

So the patterns that we have illustrated for English are also identifiable in other languages. The 'male-as-norm' presumption is frequently evident, together with the development of derogatory and demeaning associations for terms used to refer to women, and the covert sexism which derives from socioculturally based assumptions concerning appropriate social roles for women and men. English does not have a monopoly on linguistic sexism.

Can the fight against sexist language succeed?

The Ms-story

'In the mouths of sexists, language can always be sexist.'

(Cameron 1985: 90)

Cameron's point – that it is sexist attitudes that are the issue rather than sexist language – explains why the fight against sexist usages is on-going, a battle which is constantly being subverted. People's attitudes are the basic problem – but when these are encoded in language they are often more difficult to challenge. One obvious illustration of this point is the story of the alternative non-sexist title *Ms*. The terms *Miss* and *Mrs* overtly signal a woman's marital status, but there is no such distinction in titles for men. Note too that men do not have 'maiden' names nor any equivalent of them. This kind of linguistic discrimination has been a target for feminist reformers for many decades.

The term *Ms* was introduced as a genuine parallel to *Mr*, a term which does not signal the marital status of the person referred to. It has had variable success in different countries and eras, but it is true to say that it has not achieved its intended aim. Rather than replacing *Mrs* and *Miss*, *Ms* has typically become a third term in the system of titles for women and it has developed a wide range of different meanings. Recent sociolinguistic research indicates that *Ms* is frequently interpreted as a title for a divorced, separated or widowed woman, or a woman in a de facto relationship, and that for some people it signals 'feminist' or 'lesbian'. The following example illustrates the widespread negative response to *Ms*-usage from some men when it was first introduced:

(6) A is a male member of the business community, B is a female client.
  A: Now that will be Miss, won't it?
  B: No, Ms.
  A: Oh, one of *those*.   (Example from Austin 1990: 282, italics in original)

One recent survey suggested that many younger women now try to avoid such labels altogether. When forced to use a title, the majority reported they preferred *Miss*, though there was also an indication that some women adopt *Ms* when they marry. The history of the term *Ms* is thus a salutary example of how societal prejudices can subvert attempts to fight linguistic sexism.

Guy: a re-emerging generic problem?

When we bring up the topic of sexist language in our linguistics courses, many of our students reassure us that it is really no longer a problem. They would not dream of using generic *he* – it sounds really old-fashioned, they claim. And they can accurately identify usages of pseudo-generic *man*, and replace them with more inclusive terms such as *human beings* or *people*. But language is a lot more slippery than we often realize. Consider examples (7) and (8).

(7) Hey you guys it's time we hit the road.
(8) Pay attention guys – we need some help here.

Does the term *guys* refer here only to men? If you can use *guy* to include women then how does this differ from so-called generics such as *he* and *man*? And how come it is the male term which has been extended to refer to both sexes rather than the female equivalent *gals*? Clearly we need to be vigilant if we are genuinely concerned to identify subtly sexist usages as they creep into the language.

Slippage

A final illustration of the subtlety with which linguistic usage can exclude women is what has been called 'slippage', as illustrated in example (9).

(9) 'People won't give up power. They'll give up anything else first – money, home, wife, children – but not power' (Miller and Swift 1990: 55).

With an example like this, it rapidly becomes apparent that, despite the use of the generic term *people*, the author has men rather than women in mind in discussing who has power. It is interesting to watch for such revealing slips in newspaper and magazine articles. Similar, but more obvious, sexist bias is apparent in discussions which refer to *surgeons, lawyers* and *scientists* as *he*, but *nurses, secretaries* and *teachers* as *she*. Revealingly, it is typically the lower-status occupational titles that are associated with women. From the point of view of gender equity, the assumptions encoded in such usages reinforce gender stereotypes; they contribute to societal perceptions that certain jobs are more suitable for women than other (usually higher-status and better-paid) jobs.

Sexism is always a choice

Deborah Cameron, a British feminist linguist, has argued that when speakers are faced with a range of variants, there is no neutral or unmarked choice. Rather, she asserts, 'every alternative is politically loaded, because the meaning of each is now defined by contrast with all other possibilities' (Cameron 1994: 26). So, for instance, referring to a woman as *Mrs Smith* is just as significant and just as much a choice as using *Ms Smith*. Most obviously, *Mrs* signals 'married' while *Ms* provides no such information. But, more subtly, the choice of *Mrs* reinforces conservative linguistic patterns and undermines attempts to remove a sexist label from the language.

It is equally significant that in some areas there is an absence of choice for ways of indicating gender. Why, for instance, does the noun *blonde* reliably signal female, and why is there no male equivalent? What is the male equivalent of the word *nymphomaniac* or of the American English term *broad*? What is the male equivalent of *misogyny*? Why does English provide no familiar word for 'hatred of men'? The analysis of lexical gaps can be just as revealing as the analysis of false choices or pseudo-pairs such as *governor* and *governess*.

Adopting this kind of critical approach to identify linguistic gender bias, some linguists argue that language not only reflects and maintains sexist attitudes, it also actively contributes to the construction of a sexist social reality. If women as a group are considered less powerful and influential than men in a society, then inevitably that social fact will be reflected in the way women are referred to and addressed linguistically. We use language to distinguish and create important social categories; so every linguistic choice is a political choice. Our linguistic selections may positively reinforce and maintain linguistic discrimination, or alternatively they can contest, challenge or subvert societally based sexist assumptions.

Where next?

Language is not just a passive mirror of social 'reality'. It is an expressive resource which is shaped and honed by centuries of sociocultural conditioning. As reflective language users, we all need to be aware of the ways in which our thinking may be channelled along well-worn grooves reflecting attitudes which are no longer acceptable in a society which claims to value and promote gender equality.

It is clearly possible to explore such claims by consciously raising your own awareness of the ways in which language is used around you. Do the people you mix with use titles such as *Mrs* or *Ms* and if so which do they prefer? What is the standard usage in your local newspaper? It will be interesting to observe whether the trend towards dropping such titles, already evident in some young New Zealanders' practice, becomes more widespread. Similarly it is fascinating to try to spot lexical gaps – another area where semantic analysis clearly makes a useful contribution. The next step for some readers may be active challenge and contestation: i.e. bringing to people's attention the underlying assumptions which unequal usages betray, with the goal of exploiting the opportunities language offers to influence social attitudes and even social behaviour. A little activism to challenge sexism is certainly one interesting response to the question 'where next?'

SOME POINTS TO PONDER

▶ Ask a number of your friends and family whether they think the following sentences are acceptable or not. Ask them to say why.

1. Ms Sophie Walker was elected chairman for a term of three years. She graciously agreed to serve.
2. [*On airline*] Now guys, just a few words from our captain, Catherine Harrison. She's a real peach.
3. [*At the bowling club*] Everyone should tidy up his own dishes. Then the men can wash up and the girls can dry.

Think about what their responses tell you about attitudes to forms such as *Ms, chairman*, generic *his,* as well as the attitudes encoded in such sentences. What might a feminist linguist say in commenting on the responses you collected?

▶ Video your favourite TV programme. Then note down all the adjectives or adjectival expressions used to describe women vs. men in the programme. Is there a pattern?
▶ Check through the newspaper for descriptions of women vs. men and see if there are any differences in the number of titles and last name (e.g. *Mr Halsall, Dr Jones*) and the number of first names used for women vs. men. Is there a pattern? If so, what does it tell you?
▶ After reading this chapter do you think sexist language is an issue? If not, how would you argue against the position taken in the chapter?

READING AND REFERENCES

There are several accessible sources for further reading in this area. Chapter 12 of Holmes (2001b) is a good place to start. Talbot (1998), Gibbon (1999), Romaine (1999) and Pauwels (1998) provide further interesting information.

Austin, Paddy (1990) 'Politeness Revisited: the Dark Side', in Allan Bell and Janet Holmes (eds), *New Zealand Ways of Speaking English* (Bristol: Multilingual Matters), pp. 276–95.
Brown, Tim (2000) 'Changes in the Use of Sexist Pronouns in Government Documents'. Unpublished Honours terms paper (Wellington: Victoria University of Wellington).
Cameron, Deborah (1985) *Feminism and Linguistic Theory* (London: Macmillan).
Cameron, Deborah (1994) 'Problems of Sexist and Non-sexist Language', in Jane Sunderland (ed.), *Exploring Gender: Questions for English Language Education* (London: Prentice Hall) pp. 26–33.
Gibbon, Margaret (1999) *Feminist Perspectives on Language* (London: Longman).
Hellinger, Marlis and Hadumod Bussman (eds) (2001) *Gender across Languages: The Linguistic Representation of Women and Men*, vol. 1 (Amsterdam: John Benjamins).
Holmes, Janet (2001a) 'A Corpus-based View of Gender in New Zealand', in Marlis Hellinger and Hadumod Bussman (eds), *Gender across Languages: The Linguistic Representation of Women and Men*, vol. 1 (Amsterdam: John Benjamins), pp. 115–36.
Holmes, Janet (2001b) *Introduction to Sociolinguistics*, 2nd edn (London: Longman).
Miller, C. and K. Swift (1990) *Words and Women*, 2nd edn (Harmondsworth: Penguin).
Pauwels, Anne (1998) *Women Changing Language* (London: Longman).
Romaine, Suzanne (1999) *Communicating Gender* (London: Lawrence Erlbaum).

Schulz, Muriel R. (1975) 'The Semantic Derogation of Woman', in Barrie Thorne and Nancy Henley (eds), *Language and Sex* (Rowley, MA: Newbury House), pp. 64–75.

Stanley, Julia P. (1977) 'Paradigmatic Women: the Prostitute', in D. L. Shores, and C. P. Hines (eds), *Papers in Language Variation* (University of Alabama: University of Alabama Press), pp. 303–21.

Talbot, Mary M. (1998) *Language and Gender: An Introduction* (Oxford: Polity Press).

What Language Do You Use to Your Grandmother?

What's the matter?

(1) Grandmother to grandchild, Polly:

> Mi know dat woman is kenge and wicked . . . leavin' husband wid tree pickney, hungry and maga, lickin' de pickney for nuttin', kenge man, dey not even got proper niem
>
> (*Gloss*: I know that woman is weak and wicked . . . leaving her husband with three child hungry and thirsty, hitting the child for no reason, puny man, they don't even have proper names.)

Unless you are a speaker of Patois (especially if you did not have the gloss), you might well wonder what this utterance is all about. Polly has no trouble understanding her grandmother's Patois, even though she uses Cockney English to her friends and the rest of her family most of the time, and a variety of English which is much closer to standard English at school. Patois, or Jamaican Creole as linguists call it, is her grandmother's usual and preferred way of talking (though she understands standard English too), and so most of the time Polly uses Patois when she talks to her. Most people know someone like Polly – people for whom the choice of what kind of language to use with their grandmothers is just the tip of the iceberg in terms of when and how they choose from the wide array of linguistic possibilities in their verbal repertoires.

People who live in countries where English is the majority language typically know a number of people who use a language other than English, such as Croatian or Somali or Bengali or Samoan, to their grandmothers. Obviously these people are at least bilingual, and when they talk to their grandmothers, they usually choose from their linguistic repertoire the language she will find easiest, or that she prefers, or perhaps even the only language that she understands well. There are exceptions to this pattern, of course. Some children feel embarrassed or self-conscious using a language other than English in public and semi-public places such as on the bus, or when they are with their friends. Some people report that when they are upset and angry they choose the language in which they can most easily express themselves, regardless of their addressee's preferred language. And, on occasion, choice of language may reveal a person's aspirations to be similar to, or different from, the person they are talking to.

There are many factors which influence our choice of which language to use, or which variety or style of language to use in different circumstances; the linguistic range of the person we are talking to is just one of them. This chapter describes some of these influential factors, and tries to convey something of the sociolinguistic richness and complexity of our everyday language choices. We also identify some of the factors which lead to a reduction in linguistic diversity, when language shift occurs and a community's multilingual repertoire contracts, at least for a period.

Matching language to context

(2) Torilwo belongs to the Erromangan community in Vanuatu, an archipelago of about 80 islands in the South Pacific. Vanuatu is one of the most multilingual countries in the world with almost 100 different languages spoken by just 200,000 people. Torilwo uses the Sye language of Erromanga to talk to his grandmother, as well as to his mother and father and brothers and sisters. It is the language of his village, and the language he uses with his friends, and many of his other relatives. When he goes to school Torilwo uses English because his parents decided he should get his education in English rather than French (the only other choice in most of Vanuatu). They predict that English will be more use to Torilwo in the long run since they know more outsiders who use English, and they have seen more books and advertisements in English than French, and they know English is essential for a job working with computers, which is what Torilwo wants to do when he leaves school. Torilwo's family are Catholic, however, and they go to a church where the priest uses French to say mass, although he gives his sermons in Bislama, the lingua franca of Vanuatu. Next year, Torilwo will move to Tanna, another island, for his upper primary education, and there, interacting with friends outside school, he will learn Lenakel, the local village language, and he will also extend his knowledge of Bislama. Everyone learns Bislama in Vanuatu at some stage, because it is essential to communicate with anyone outside your own small community. Torilwo is multilingual, and so is everyone else in Vanuatu.

When sociolinguists study patterns of language use in bilingual and multilingual communities, they often begin by examining the languages used in some basic, and possibly universal, social settings or 'domains'. You can probably easily guess at least three of these – the home, the school or education domain, and the workplace. We can obviously add a domain that we might call the friendship or leisure domain, which may include sport, the pub or regular bar, the beach, and so on; and for many communities, we can also add the religious domain or church. Other possible domains are shopping, politics and the law – you can probably add more. In communities where two or more languages are used regularly, there are usually well-established patterns of use for each of these domains. Everyone knows which language is appropriate or usual in each domain; it is part of what you learn as you grow up in the community. You not only learn how to speak and understand several languages (labelled by Chomsky 1965 your 'linguistic competence'), you also learn how to use them appropriately in different situations (your sociolinguistic or 'communicative competence', as Hymes 1972 called it). So if Torilwa dozed off in school, and suddenly woke up to find the teacher standing over him looking furious, he would immediately make an excuse in English, not in Sye or Bislama, which would have earned him another telling off.

Although there are patterns of this kind, sociolinguists have found that when people interact in multilingual communities they often use more than one language in a particular domain. So, for example, when they go shopping, people in Singapore use not only colloquial Singapore English (referred to locally as 'Singlish'), but also local Chinese dialects, especially in the markets, often switching between languages not only within one domain, but even within one conversation. Switching between language like this can be described as 'code-switching' or sometimes 'code-mixing'. It is a skilled and effective way of conveying a range of meanings, often through a series of rapid choices of language (see Chapter 19).

(3) *Context:* store in Western Kenya. Brother is store owner, sister is customer. CAPITALS are used for speech in Lwidakho and lower case for speech in Swahili.

    1. Brother: GOOD MORNING, SISTER.
    2. Sister: GOOD MORNING.
    3. Brother: ARE YOU ALRIGHT?
    4. Sister: YES. JUST A LITTLE.
    5. Brother: Sister, now today what do you need?
    6. Sister: I WANT YOU TO GIVE ME SOME SALT.
    7. Brother: How much do you need?
    8. Sister: GIVE ME SIXTY CENTS WORTH.
    9. Brother: And what else?
  10. Sister: I WOULD LIKE SOMETHING ELSE, BUT I'VE NO MONEY.
  11. Brother: Thank you, sister. Goodbye.
  12. Sister: THANK YOU. GOODBYE.   (Romaine 1994: 62)

The brother and sister begin their conversation with greetings and small talk using their common tribal language Lwidakho (lines 1–4). Then the brother, who owns the store, switches to business and uses Swahili, the language of business transactions and lingua franca of the area, to ask his sister 'what do you need?' In this way, he skilfully signals that he is now operating as a businessman not a relative, with all that implies about what kind of treatment his sister can expect. His sister, however, persists in using their tribal language, saying *I want you to give me some salt* in Lwidakho. In this way she keeps their family relationship relevant, despite her brother's effort to switch to a transactional relationship. The choice of verb (*give*) and use of personal pronouns (*I, you, me*) also emphasizes the direction she wants the exchange to take (she could have answered instead, for instance, *some salt, please*). The remaining utterances repeat the same pattern with each speaker staunchly maintaining their effort to define the relationship as personal vs. transactional. The brother persists in his transactional role even in the face of his sister's explicit statement that she would like to buy more but has no money (line 10), and most significantly in his use of Swahili for his farewell (*Thank you, sister. Goodbye.*) which would most appropriately be given in Lwidakho.

Two points are worth spelling out here. Firstly, the switching from Lwidakho to Swahili within this conversation is perfectly appropriate in such multilingual communities. We can duplicate the pattern observed at the beginning of this example in speech communities all over the world. In places such as Norway and Switzerland, where the codes involved are different dialects rather than different languages, the greetings will be in the local dialect and the business will be transacted in the standard variety. But the basic pattern of using the local variety for small talk and personal information, and the standard variety, lingua franca or official language for the business transaction, is very widespread. In other words code-switching within a conversation is perfectly normal in multilingual communities.

The second point relates to the manipulation of these norms. Both the brother and the sister in this example 'break the rules' for their own individual purposes. The sister persists in Lwidakho at the point where a switch to Swahili would have been expected and normal (line 6). We can deduce (from line 10 especially) that her motivation is to appeal to her personal relationship with her brother to get special treatment and a cheaper price for the goods she needs. Her brother refuses to respond to this appeal, and persists in Swahili, even when the talk returns to the interpersonal thanks and farewells. His underlying message is clear, though it is never made explicit: 'don't expect favours from me where business is concerned, even though we are related'. All this is conveyed implicitly simply by choice of language. The example illustrates the significance of knowing what are the norms in a community, since departure from those norms generates inferences which convey important additional layers of meaning.

The patterns of language choice described so far, and the range of social factors which influence those choices, as well as the opportunity to manipulate those patterns for a variety of interesting reasons, are typical of many – perhaps most – multilingual communities around the world. We could construct similar case studies for people living in most African and Asian countries, as well as the West Indies and many of the communities of the south Pacific. You might like to read about your favourite African country and try to construct a case study of your own modelled on (2) from Vanuatu above. There is, however, another story to be told about bilingual communities, and that is a story of language shift (see Chapter 12).

Losing your language

(4) One of the authors was recently driven home from the airport by a taxi-driver, Ivanic, who had emigrated to New Zealand eight years earlier from the former Yugoslavia with his wife, his mother, and his 11-year-old daughter to escape 'ethnic cleansing'. Serbo-Croatian was his mother tongue and he spoke good English. His daughter, he said, had acquired English in about six months with no trace of an accent, and she still spoke good Serbo-Croatian. His son, Tomas, was born in New Zealand and is now six years old. As a result of Ivanic's determination to maintain his mother tongue, the normal language of the home domain is Serbo-Croatian, and Tomas is now fluently bilingual with no trace of a 'foreign' accent in either language. His vocabulary is extensive in both languages, partly because he has developed the habit of asking for the Serbo-Croatian word for new English words he learns in school rather than using the English word at home, which he knows his father does not like. Ivanic reads to Tomas in Serbo-Croatian every evening, and has taught him to read in both Cyrillic and Roman script. Tomas is outstanding at maths although he has had no help with this at home. His father has taught him to play chess and he has started to play against the computer. Ivanic said that after losing to the computer every time for several weeks, Tomas can now win about one time in three.

This is an encouraging account of the successful defence which a determined family can put up against the in-roads of the majority language when they move to a new country where their language is not used. Tomas uses Serbo-Croat to his grandmother since she does not speak much English. More importantly, he uses Serbo-Croat almost all the time in the home, providing a sound basis for the development of fluent bilingual competence, with all the associated cognitive and social benefits (see Chapter 19). Sadly, however, on the basis of what we know about patterns of language shift in immigrant communities, it is almost inevitable that over the next ten years Tomas's bilingual fluency will gradually erode.

The sad story of language loss takes a number of forms. Ivanic's story is likely to follow the typical pattern for an immigrant community. When people move to another country where their language is not spoken, the majority language of the new country gradually infiltrates the home, with children as the subversive second column. Another story is the disappearance of indigenous languages, such as Aboriginal languages in Australia, and Native American and Canadian Indian languages in north America, following invasion or colonization by a more powerful or economically dominant linguistic group (see Chapter 12). (The two scenarios are not always entirely unrelated, since those who move to another country may also be fleeing persecution or economic hardship caused by more powerful forces.) In both cases, the language of the political minority is put under threat, and the overwhelming result is that, if steps are not taken to preserve it, the minority language disappears within three, or at most four, generations.

Choosing your language

In the novel *White Teeth* Zadie Smith provides a sympathetic account of the challenges facing young British Black people whose grandparents migrated to Britain from Jamaica in the 1960s. The language they brought with them was Jamaican Creole, or Patois, their preferred name for it, and though it shares a number of structural and lexical features with standard English, it also has many distinctive features. Example (1) on p. 169 illustrated some of the linguistic features of patois (see also: Box 16.1).

ILLUSTRATION

Box 16.1 Some linguistic features of Patois or Jamaican Creole

- Vocabulary items: e.g. *lick* meaning 'hit' and *kenge* meaning 'weak, puny'.
- Stress and intonation patterns are different in Patois from those of standard English.
- The sound at the beginning of words like *the*, *they* and *then* is pronounced [d].
- The sound at the beginning of words like *thanks*, *thin* and *three* is pronounced [t].
- Vowels and especially diphthongs are distinctive: e.g. the vowel in *boy* is much more rounded in Patois than in British standard English; the vowel in *pain* is pronounced more like standard English *peon*.
- Plural forms don't have s on the end.
- Tenses aren't marked by suffixes on verbs, e.g. *walk* and *jump* in Patois compared to *walked*, *walks*, *jumped* and *jumps* in British standard English.
- Pronouns are distinctive: e.g. *mi* is used for standard English *I*, *me* and *my*; *dem* is used for standard English *they*, *them* and *their*.

One of the main characters in *White Teeth* is Irie Jones. Irie's grandmother speaks Patois consistently throughout the book. Interestingly, Irie, unlike many grandchildren, tends to respond to her grandmother's Patois with standard English, the variety she has acquired in school.

(5) Hortense leant against the oven with hands on hips. 'You look like Mr Death, your new lover. How you get here?'. . .
     'Er . . . Bus. Number 17. It was cold on the top deck. Maybe I caught a chill.'
     'I don' tink dere's any maybes about it, young lady. An' I'm sure I don' know why you come 'pon de bus, when it take tree hours to arrive an' leave you waitin' in de col' an' den when you get 'pon it de windows are open anyway an' you freeze half to death.'
     Hortense poured a colourless liquid from a small plastic container into her hand. 'Come 'ere.'
     'Why?' demanded Irie, immediately suspicious. 'What's that?'
     'Nuttin', come 'ere. Take off your spectacles.'

Hortense approached with a cupped hand.
'Not in my eye! There's nothing wrong with my eye!'
'Stop fussin'. I'm not puttin' nuttin' in your eye.'   (Smith 2000: 383)

Note that there are a few features in this example which do not fit the description of patois in Box 16.1. Can you spot any of them? (Answer at end of chapter.)

In this excerpt Hortense does not consistently use all the features described in Box 16.1, perhaps because, after two decades in England, her Patois has moved a little along the continuum towards standard English. Or, alternatively, this may simply reflect a misperception on the author's part. After all, *White Teeth* is fiction, and Zadie Smith is not a trained linguist, though she has an excellent ear for the rhythms of Patois which are conveyed skilfully in the novel.

It is equally interesting to reflect on why Irie is depicted as consistently using standard English rather than Patois (e.g. *nothing* vs. *nuttin*). This is clearly a deliberate decision on the author's part since it is apparent throughout the book, and may be a literary device to emphasize Irie's ambitions, which are to get a good education and to become a qualified scientist. Her language may also reflect the fact that she does not want to identify with her grandmother, since she associates Hortense with poverty, lack of education, and most of all religious extremism. Her grandmother is a fanatical Jehovah's Witness, and throughout the novel her predictions about the imminent catastrophe which is about to end the world determine her every action. Perhaps it is not surprising that Irie generally responds to her grandmother in standard English.

Language choice is a subtle but powerful means of conveying not only identity, but also attitudes and values. Irie's choice of variety to talk to her grandmother can be interpreted as conveying a desire to identify with the educated majority (an interpretation supported by the fact that she goes to some lengths to get her ethnically distinctive hair straightened). Young British Black women and men can select from a broad linguistic repertoire which ranges from standard English learned in school to broad Patois learned at home, and provides many shades of black and white linguistic associations in between. The linguistic continuum from creole to standard English provides a rich resource for expressing a precise position on any topic. The parallel with the choices available to those who control a multilingual verbal repertoire are obvious. Perhaps not so obvious, but just as much a parallel, are the choices available to those who are apparently monolingual.

Style-shifting and language choice

Those who live in English-speaking communities and whose mother tongue is English often do not recognize that they too possess a wide linguistic repertoire, and that they select from it according to who they are talking to and when, and what they want to achieve, just as the Kenyan brother and sister did in (3). This is perhaps understandable since the stylistic shifts involved are not so clearly marked or as easy to recognize as shifts which involve distinct languages.

Sociolinguists have provided many dramatic illustrations of the way we change our speech style in different social contexts. For example, Allan Bell (1984) demonstrated that the same person read the news in quite different ways on different radio stations. When the news reader was on the commercial pop station, he used a more casual pronunciation than when he was speaking on the more conservative national radio network. So words like *last* became *las'*, phrases such as *will not* became *won't*, and so on. In a Welsh travel agency, another sociolinguist, Nik Coupland (1980), found that the travel agent skilfully, though unconsciously, matched her pronunciation to that of her clients, whether they were of higher or lower social background than the travel agent herself. This kind of responsiveness to the addressee is especially noticeable (and understandable) when it is in a person's interests to appeal to their audience. Good ratings are important for the news readers, and audience appeal means more business for people in the retail sector.

It is not surprising then to find that teenagers in monolingual communities are also skilled at choosing appropriate ways of talking to their grandparents. Teenagers who want good communication with their grandmothers tend to avoid current in-group slang, computer jargon and fashionable music terminology, since these will quickly render their talk incomprehensible to older people. Swearing often marks in-group membership, and is typically more frequent in the speech of young people than older people. Hence, most teenagers tend to avoid swearing in front of their grandparents – though there are always exceptions and exceptional circumstances. Some grammatical expressions tend to be more common in exchanges between younger rather than older people, and informal phrases such as *you know* and *innit* are less frequent in conversations between the young and the very old. They are markers of solidarity, however, so those who have a close relationship with their grandparents could well use even these colloquial markers on occasion. The underlying presumption here is that we tend, even in modern urbanized societies, to express respect for older people, and the ways in which we do so extend to avoidance of very colloquial and casual language. In other communities, this respect is expressed more proactively. So, in Samoa, for example, expressing yourself appropriately in interaction with your grandparents involves not only avoiding a disrespectful casual style, but making a deliberate choice to use a respectful style. And there are many other languages, such as Japanese and Javanese, with similar patterns.

Styling your language

Recent research has shown that people change the way they talk even within the same context talking to the same people, according to the kind of image or identity they are projecting or constructing, and which aspects of their identity they want to emphasize. So, talking to a friend, a young Maori woman moved along a continuum from more standard New Zealand English at the beginning of their chat to a variety which signalled her Maori ethnicity and her working-class origins as she discussed topics such as sport and visiting the pub, and other leisure activities which she associated with her Maori mates. When she described a fight she had been involved in she unconsciously adopted a masculine tough way of talking, e.g., *'she says you can't fuckin' do nothin' to me, and I says d'you wanna bet'* (see Chapter 15).

In multilingual communities, as suggested above, different languages are also available as resources for the same complex identity construction, along with conveying other messages such as 'we belong to the same group' or 'this is a business transaction' as indicated in (3). In the film *Monsoon Wedding,* for example, there are many scenes where characters shift smoothly between Hindi and English, subtly conveying a range of affiliations and social (caste) identities as they do so, with a myriad of complex religious, educational and cultural metaphorical allusions for those familiar with the Indian context. The film illustrates well how sociocultural patterns are played out through linguistic choices. All speech communities offer similar resources, whether multilingual or monolingual.

Linguistic choice is always significant. Grandchildren in multilingual settings choose particular languages, as well as particular styles within those languages, to address their grandmothers. And teenagers in monolingual communities are equally skilled at choosing appropriate ways of talking to their grandparents

Where next?

In this chapter, we have explored the idea that language choice is typically a complex matter, motivated by a range of factors. The obvious constraint of what languages we have in common with those we are addressing is only a starting point in most social contexts. Other factors such as setting and topic are often relevant, as well as more subtle issues of social identity and social values. Language choice can be a means of conveying a political position or a means to a bargain; it can indicate ethnic identity or it can signal educational aspirations and social goals. Respect and solidarity are further dimensions which are always potentially relevant in interpreting language choices. The dynamic nature of such choices offers a challenging research programme for those interested in tracking the ways in which people draw on their linguistic repertoires to convey subtle social and affective meanings.

The other major issue raised in this chapter was the patterns of language shift which seem inevitably to typify communities whose language is in a minority position, whether politically, economically or demographically. In immigrant communities, proficiency in the home language almost always disappears over three, or at most four, generations. And many indigenous languages have completely disappeared under the onslaught of colonial 'killer languages' as discussed in Chapter 12. The (kind of) language your grandchildren will use to you is an issue well worth reflecting on.

Answer to question about features in example above which do not fit the description of Patois from Box 16.1:

Hortense uses a number of plural forms, although the description in Box 16.1 suggests Patois does not mark plurals with 's': e.g. *maybes, hours, windows, spectacles.*

SOME POINTS TO PONDER

▶ Talk to a friend whose family's 'first' language is a language other than English, but who also use English in the home. Ask the friend when they use English and when they use the other language in their everyday life. Then try to devise a table to capture the patterns your friend describes. What problems come up?

▶ Are you aware of any evidence of language shift or language loss among people you know? Does the pattern fit the description in this chapter or not? If not, why do you think it is different?

▶ Find a novel with characters who speak a non-standard variety of English or an English-based creole? Using Box 16.1 as a guide, identify two linguistic features which the novelist uses to characterise the speakers' language as non-standard?

▶ What features of your language alter when you talk to your mother vs. your school-teacher or tutor vs. your grandfather? Why do you think your language alters? Is topic a factor? If you were talking to each of them about a recent holiday would you still speak differently to each?

READING AND REFERENCES

Any good introduction to sociolinguistics will provide readable material to illustrate the ideas covered in this chapter. We especially recommend Holmes (2001) but there are many other good introductions, including Mesthrie et al. (2000), Thomas et al. (2003), Trudgill (2000) and Coupland and Jaworski (1997).

Bell, Allan (1984) 'Language Style as Audience Design', *Language in Society*, 13 (2): 145–204.

Chomsky, Noam (1965) *Aspects of the Theory of Syntax* (Cambridge, MA: MIT Press).

Coupland, Nikolas (1980) 'Style-shifting in a Cardiff Work Setting', *Language in Society*, 9 (1): 1–12.

Coupland, Nikolas and Adam Jaworski (eds) (1997) *Sociolinguistics: A Reader and Coursebook* (Basingstoke: Macmillan).

Holmes, Janet (2001) *Introduction to Sociolinguistics*, 2nd edn (London: Longman).

Hymes, Dell (1972) 'On Communicative Competence', in John B. Pride and Janet Holmes (eds), *Sociolinguistics* (Harmondsworth: Penguin), pp. 269–93.

Mesthrie, Rajend, Joan Swann, A. Deumert and William L. Leap (2000) *Introducing Sociolinguistics* (Edinburgh: Edinburgh University Press).

Romaine, Suzanne (1994) *Language in Society* (Oxford: Oxford University Press).

Smith, Zadie (2000) *White Teeth* (London: Penguin).

Thomas, Linda, Shân Wareing, Ishtla Singh, Jean Stilwell Peccei, Joanna Thornborrow and Jason Jones (2003) *Language, Society and Power: An Introduction*, 2nd edn (London: Routledge).

Trudgill, Peter (2000) *Sociolinguistics: An Introduction to Language and Society*, 4th edn (London: Penguin).

Why Can't People in Birmingham Talk Right?

17

What's the matter?

One of the authors was born in Liverpool and during her childhood and teenage years she spoke the Liverpool dialect, known locally as 'Scouse'. Scouse has many distinguishing features, including lexical items like *bevvied* for 'drunk', *jigger* for 'alley', and idiomatic phrases like *come 'ed, whack* for 'come along, mate/pal', and *ay up* for 'watch out'. At secondary school the elocution teacher worked hard at eradicating the evidence of pupils' regional background, focusing especially on their pronunciation. She provided pronunciation drills to get the students to alter their vowels to something closer to those used by news readers. For instance, she practised *Mary, the nurse, has fair hair*, since Liverpudlians tend to have the same vowel sound in *fair* and *nurse*, unlike news readers. Talking Scouse was only one notch up from talking Brummie (using a Birmingham accent), an accent considered the lowest of the low on any British accent evaluation table (Giles and Powesland 1975; Bishop et al. 2005).

But then along came the Beatles and the fabulous Liverpudlian four transformed this author's life in more ways than one. Most relevantly for this

---

TERMINOLOGY

Box 17.1   Accent vs. dialect

ACCENT is simply a matter of how we pronounce words. So, for example, some English speakers pronounce the word *cup* with the same vowel that they use in the word *book*, while others use different vowels in these two words.

If people have different DIALECTS, this involves differences not only in pronunciation, but also in grammatical features and vocabulary. So, for example, some of those who pronounce *cup* with the same vowel that they use in *book* also use the word *maiden* to refer to what others call a *clothes-horse* (for hanging clothes on to dry), and they may also use the expression *I ain't done nowt* where speakers of a different dialect would say *I haven't done anything*.

chapter, they transformed attitudes to a Scouse accent. It was suddenly not just acceptable, but positively fashionable. Ironically, having been drilled throughout her teenage years to learn new vowel distinctions such as *bare* vs. *burr* and *book* vs. *buck*, she now found that she was not always sure about how to pronounce certain words, especially rarer words with these sounds in them. This example illustrates the fickleness of attitudes to accents. Many people don't realize that fashion affects attitudes to accents, but a little reflection makes it clear that they are just as subject to social influence as more obvious areas such as dress and musical tastes. (See Box 17.1 for an explanation of the difference between accent and dialect.)

Attitudes to dialects are also subject to fashion, though the well-established status of the so-called 'standard' variety of a language provides something of a brake in this area. For example, African American Vernacular English (AAVE), earlier called Black English, is different enough from Standard American English to be practically unintelligible to many English speakers, especially those from outside the USA. But it has great prestige among many young people world-wide because of the glamour associated with anything American. Other non-standard dialects are also regarded differently by different groups and at different times. British Black English has increasing status among some groups of young Londoners, black and white, reflecting its increasing use on television, and in films and music videos. And Cajun French, once a despised variety, is increasingly fashionable as a marker of Cajun identity among young people from higher socio-professional backgrounds in Louisiana, USA.

The issue addressed by this chapter, then, is why do people prefer some accents and dialects to others? What is the basis for our attitudes to different varieties of language? And what are the implications of such attitudes? The answers take us deep into sociolinguistics, the exploration of the relationship between language and society.

Love me, love my accent

When you ask people about their attitudes to different accents of their mother tongue they are generally able and willing to provide an evaluation. People in Britain will provide evaluations of Cockney (London) vs. Edinburgh vs. Dublin accents, for instance, and Americans will share their views about the ways English is spoken in Los Angeles vs. New York vs. Austin, Texas. French speakers readily compare Canadian and European French, and speakers of Norwegian compare the various Norwegian accents. Interestingly, evaluations of different accents are often widely shared among large groups of people. So, for instance, most Scottish accents are rated highly in Britain, while New York, and especially Brooklyn, accents are typically regarded as unpleasant and even 'dumb' in the USA. (Many decades ago William Labov [1966: 499] described New York as 'a great sink of negative prestige', and it seems that not much has changed.) And RP (Received Pronunciation), the accent used by news readers on the most conservative

BBC radio and television stations, an accent associated with a high level of education, is generally agreed to be the 'best' English accent in England, even while it is considered a HYPERLECT and derided as 'real posh' by many British people from regions with very different pronunciations. What is the basis for such evaluations, and for such widespread agreement on ratings of particular accents? The answer is that attitudes to accents reflect social judgements, as we will show. In other words, we evaluate accents not on the basis of any intrinsic linguistic features, but rather on the basis of the associations that they trigger.

Let's consider, first, the fact that people are generally very willing to rate different accents in terms of their attractiveness or prestige. Sociolinguists have played a number of different accents to people, asking them to evaluate features such as the pleasantness of the voice, the status of the speaker, and even their intelligence, reliability and sense of humour (see Figure 17.1). By using a method known as the MATCHED GUISE technique, which involves one person producing a number of different accents (although, crucially, the listeners do not realize this), the researchers ensure that people are responding to different linguistic features and their associations, rather than to characteristics of the individual who is speaking. People are generally quite prepared to do this on the basis of listening to a voice on a tape. As the researchers point out, we do it all the time when we listen to the radio and answer the telephone. If someone asks us we can usually provide our impressions of a disembodied voice, including an impression of what they look like, even if we have never met them. Indeed people are often surprised when their mental image of their favourite radio broadcaster or DJ turns out to be very different from the reality.

Consider, next, the fact that there is often widespread agreement among people about the relative attractiveness or prestige of different accents. In

Speech rating scale

Listen to the tape and indicate with a tick where you would place the speakers on the following scales.

Speaker I	1	2	3	4	5	
competent	——	——	——	——	——	incompetent
pleasant	——	——	——	——	——	unpleasant
reliable	——	——	——	——	——	unreliable
sincere	——	——	——	——	——	insincere
friendly	——	——	——	——	——	unfriendly
intelligent	——	——	——	——	——	unintelligent
highly educated	——	——	——	——	——	uneducated
high status job	——	——	——	——	——	low-status job

Figure 17.1   Example of an accent evaluation scale

many places where English is spoken, for instance, the results often indicate that RP is widely admired as a prestige accent, even when those who are rating the accents do not speak RP. RP was rated very highly in New Zealand, for instance, until the mid-1990s when American English began to challenge its top status (Bayard 2000). In Britain, speakers with certain regional accents are often not rated highly on characteristics such as status and competence, though they get higher ratings on friendliness and sense of humour. Studies also show that the urban accents of industrial towns are generally not viewed very positively, and, in general, in all societies where these experiments have been conducted, speakers with socially lower class accents of any kind get very low ratings (Giles and Powesland 1975, Mugglestone 2003; Bishop et al. 2005).

All this provides good evidence that people are evaluating the social characteristics of the accents, rather than any intrinsic linguistic superiority, as they often think. A study which provided very interesting and even more convincing evidence in this respect was undertaken by some British sociolinguists, using a number of different languages and accents (Trudgill and Giles 1977). They wanted to demonstrate that even aesthetic judgements about accents are socially based rather than intrinsic features of a language. They first demonstrated that British listeners who were unfamiliar with the French language rated middle-class Canadian French and working-class Canadian French as equally pleasant; French Canadians, by contrast, rated the middle-class accent as much more pleasant than the working-class accent. Similarly, while Greek listeners agreed on evaluations of Athenian Greek as far superior to Cretan Greek, British listeners who knew no Greek did not agree at all about the relative merits of the two accents. Finally, they showed that even when listening to unfamiliar accents of their own language, American English listeners did not agree with each other on ratings of a range of British accents, for example, and they certainly did not show the uniformity of evaluative response of British listeners who recognized the accents.

Another interesting finding from such research is that people often do not recognize their own accents on tape. Many people think they do not have an accent of any kind – it is other people who have accents. Others do not recognize how non-standard their accent is compared to what they consider the prestige accent. In Britain, for example, two early researchers in this area reported that 'very many English people who have not heard their voices on tape imagine that they have RP whilst their neighbours have an "accent". Even when they have heard themselves, the prestige of RP is so high that they are often unwilling to admit to themselves that they deviate from it' (Giles and Powesland 1975: 31). Similarly, the American sociolinguist, William Labov, tells of the distress he unwittingly caused two of his New York interviewees when he played back their recorded speech to demonstrate that they did not in fact use the prestigious 'r' (in words such as *car* and *card*) that they were convinced characterized their accents (Labov 1966: 329). Ironically, of course, [r] pronunciation in such words is considered evidence of *lack* of education in Britain, where the prestige accent RP is [r]-less in such contexts. This is simply further evidence of the social basis of such value judgements, and the arbitrariness of the linguistic features which happen to be favoured in different places and at different times.

On the other hand, those who *are* aware of their accents often do not like them. Many sociolinguists report that people comment negatively on their own speech. 'I talk 'orrible' is a common remark in English surveys, probably reflecting the critical evaluations of schoolteachers, and even parents in some cases. This raises the issue of why people continue to use an accent which is socially disfavoured and which they claim to dislike. The next section provides some clues about a possible answer to this apparent conundrum.

Social and ethnic accents – components of identity construction

In every study undertaken world-wide, people with working-class or lower-class accents are negatively evaluated compared to those with educated, middle-class accents. And while regional accents may be considered attractive in some communities and on some features (e.g. friendliness, sense of humour), working-class accents are typically downgraded on almost every trait. Similar issues arise in relation to ethnic accents and dialects. The accents of speakers identified with an ethnic minority are often subject to the same kind of downgrading, especially if many members of the ethnic group are at the bottom of the social ladder. In New Zealand, 'broad' Maori accents of English are associated with low social class status and with an ethnic group which is overrepresented in the prison and unemployment statistics (Bayard et al. 2001). In Australia, Aboriginal English has little social status, a reflection of the social 'problems' associated with many of the dispossessed Aboriginal peoples. In the United States, Mexican-American English is downgraded in social evaluations of its status, especially in the school context (Giles and Powesland 1975). Why then do people maintain these distinctive ways of speaking?

One possible explanation is the importance of our accents to our identity and as a signal of our group membership. Sounding like Prince Harry or Hilary Clinton may lead people to evaluate your accent positively on a status scale, but it won't cut much ice in most local pubs or bars, or in soccer or netball changing rooms. Talking like a toff is all very well if you are a toff, with networks forged at posh schools, but for the vast majority of the population, social identity is linked to their local community, and the local community is typically characterized by pronunciation which differs from that of the prestige accent precisely in order to signal local rather than national identity (see Chapter 2).

Social context is crucial too. We all alter the way we speak in different contexts (see Chapter 16). When speaking to the school principal on the telephone, or requesting a job interview, or doing a reading at the local church, most people are able to shift their accents towards the locally recognized prestige accent, at least to some degree; but at home and with friends in relaxed contexts, local accents prevail. We signal that we belong by talking like our mates. And our evaluations of people's speech are similarly influenced by context. One interesting study, which demonstrated the complexities of the allegiances signalled by speech, asked people to rate a number of male speakers not only on what kind of job they might be able to get, but also on their chances of 'coming out on top' in a street fight (Labov 2001: 195). Not surprisingly the kind of accent that was considered to merit a job as a TV announcer was not the accent associated with the most likely victor in a street fight. The follow-up question was, 'How likely is this person to become a friend of yours if you got to know him?' The results clearly demonstrated the association between the status of an accent and the social background of the person assessing the accent, as well as the function of accents as markers of in-group membership. Interestingly, too, Labov found that the association of non-standard speech with 'toughness' was much stronger among middle-class people; for working-class people such speech was normal; it had no particular 'tough' connotations.

Asking listeners to evaluate accents on tape ensures that they are all responding to a measurable sound bite, but this method does not take account of the extent to which assessing people's speech is very much a contextual and dynamic affair. Nor does it allow for the extent to which talk is a continuous subtle balance of conveying aspects of our social identity (gender, age, social group) while simultaneously taking account of the on-going demands of the interaction (as described in Chapter 14). So, just as people draw on a wide linguistic repertoire in constructing their social identity in particular contexts, they may evaluate others' ways of speaking differently at different points in the on-going flux of a specific speech event. A standard accent evaluation scale could not elicit useful reactions, for example, to the kind of rapid conversational code-switching illustrated in example (5) in Chapter 16.

So attitudes to accents have a consistent social basis. They derive predominantly from our attitudes to the users, and to the contexts in which the varieties are typically used. We choose to maintain or change our accents, or to move up and down an accent scale, on the basis of the particular kind of social identity we want to convey in a particular context, and the allegiances we wish to signal. The same is true of dialect choice, though consideration of dialect brings another dimension into play, namely the relationship between the standard dialect or standard language and the written language, with obvious educational implications (Quirk 2003).

Attitudes to dialects

Attitudes to standard and non-standard dialects differ greatly from one country to another. In many European countries, such as Germany, Austria, Norway, Italy, Spain and Switzerland, for instance, widespread linguistic variation at all levels of language – vocabulary, grammar and pronunciation – is evident in the everyday speech of people from different regions, and this is regarded as normal. The local regional dialect is used in everyday conversation, while the standard language is used in school and for more formal encounters. There is no stigma in using the local dialect. Indeed visitors who do not know it signal their status as outsiders, and are at a decided disadvantage in many social interactions and community events. There is no implication that one variety is inferior to the other. Each is appropriate in its context, and citizens acquire the standard dialect or, as it is more usually labelled, the standard language, in the course of their schooling. Attitudes to the standard are matter-of-fact rather than admiring or respectful – it is simply the variety appropriate for formal contexts and writing.

For a range of reasons, attitudes to standard English are rather different. As with other standard varieties, it is generally recognized in countries such as Britain and the United States that the variety used in writing, in the national newspapers, for instance, and in speech by radio and TV news readers, for example, can be labelled STANDARD ENGLISH. But attitudes to varieties which differ from this standard are far less tolerant and matter-of-fact than those in Europe. In Britain, standard English is a uniform, socially sanctioned dialect which is taught in schools and used by those who have been well educated. There is very little lexical or grammatical variation in this standard dialect across the whole of Britain, though of course the way it is pronounced differs from region to region. (It is not, in other words, linked inextricably to RP.) So, although one author spoke with a strong Liverpool accent in her teens, and another author used a Yorkshire accent, while the third spoke with a southern English accent, we all used standard English. Similarly in the United States of America, most Americans would agree that Standard American English as a dialect (as opposed to an accent) is widely used in print and in the national broadcasting system, and generally acquired in school by those who don't speak it natively.

Non-standard dialects of English are typically stigmatized. People who use rural dialect forms, such as *thou* for 'you', or [t] for 'the', or who say *I walks to work every morning* rather than *I walk to work every morning* are widely regarded patronizingly as ignorant and uneducated. Non-standard dialect forms are unprestigious in the eyes of educated members of the majority group, simply because they are associated with lower-status social groups or minority ethnic groups.

Non-native varieties of English

Another issue which raises its rather ugly head in this debate is the question of who decides what counts as standard English. While there are still some who argue that British standard English is the benchmark, they are a dying breed. Features of American grammar (such as the use of *gotten,* or the use of *be* in a sentence such as *we insisted he be allowed to leave*) are regarded as features of a standard English by millions of native speakers. Spellings such as *humor, color,* and even *thru',* are standard in American dictionaries and being spread daily through the use of the internet and Microsoft spellcheckers. Those who don't regard American Standard English as *the* standard variety of English, cannot deny its status as *one* standard variety of English. Similarly New Zealand English, Australian English and South African English have developed their own standard varieties which share most features with British and American standard English, but which have some distinguishing features that are established as components of the standard variety of English in those countries.

The issue becomes considerably more complex when we consider the varieties of English spoken in places such as Hong Kong, Singapore, Malaysia, Nigeria and India. There has been a fierce debate between linguists who consider that English no longer 'belongs' to England, or even America, and those who consider that there can be no such thing as a non-native standard variety of a language. The first group attribute standard status to varieties such as Malaysian English and Indian English, while the second group point out that there is often no recognition or acceptance of such varieties within the relevant countries, nor agreement that the establishment of indigenous standard varieties of English is desirable. The former group are undoubtedly gaining ground as sociolinguists establish the distinctive features of varieties such as standard Singaporean English (e.g. Gupta 1999) and Hong Kong English (e.g. Bolton 2002), and young people grow up using such varieties from a very early age (as one variety among others in a multilingual verbal repertoire in many cases).

To sum up then, it is *who* uses an accent or dialect and *where* they use it that determine people's attitudes, regardless of linguistic features. Claims that an accent is ugly or unintelligible or uneducated simply reflect the fact that its users have low social status or mana. Social factors not linguistic features underlie the different attitudes to linguistic variation found in different communities. In many countries, linguistic variation is regarded as a fact of life. It is assumed that everyone will learn the local variety in the home and acquire the standard language at school. And while the metropolitan accent, where there is one, is generally admired, it is typically not regarded as essential for economic and social success.

Can your accent affect your life chances?

Attitudes are particularly complex in places where English is used. RP is regarded as a prestige accent by many, and though it is not a prerequisite for every job or for social success, it is still regarded as a distinct advantage by many employers in England. It is interesting to see that other accents are developing prestige, too, however. Certain regional accents are now an advantage if you want a job in one of the endemic call centres that deal with mail orders, airline reservations and railway ticket bookings, and especially if you are canvassing opinions or trying to sell goods by cold calling. Hence, companies are strategically selecting the 'call girls' (the vast majority are female) for their 'communication factories', as Deborah Cameron (2000) labels them, according to the audiences they are targeting. All this indicates that accents

Box 17.2   Scouse accent kills Lisa's Dublin dream

The Irish Post, 17 March 2001

A third-generation Irishwoman has been left devastated after her dream of working in Ireland was shattered – because she has a Liverpool accent.

Lisa Donnelly was rejected by a Dublin-based nanny agency because they said her accent meant it would be impossible to place her with a family in Ireland.

The rejection came despite Lisa being a qualified nursery nurse and having worked as a nanny for families in Switzerland and America. . . . Lisa had sent off her application and references after being given the address of the Executive Nannies agency by a friend. But when she telephoned to ask if they would give her an interview she was instantly rejected.

She said: 'As soon as they heard my accent they didn't want to know. I was born in Liverpool and am proud of that but I love Ireland. I have studied Irish history and it was my dream to live and work in Ireland. It knocked me sick that 150 years ago many of our ancestors came to Liverpool from Ireland and now a woman in Dublin is telling me that they don't like my accent.'

matter, and that social judgements of the way people talk continue to play a part in employment opportunities, even if the spectrum of acceptable accents has widened. Box 17.2 illustrates again the social basis for evaluations: in an ironical twist her Liverpool accent lost a young woman a job in Ireland, while 50 years earlier it was the Irish accent which was disparaged in Liverpool.

The implications of negative attitudes to certain accents and to non-standard dialects are also evident in school. There is abundant evidence that expectations influence the performance of pupils in schools. Children who start school with a stigmatized accent or dialect face the challenge of overcoming the teacher's negative expectations of their scholastic abilities, expectations based simply on their working-class or ethnically marked accents. And the same pattern is seen in reverse when New Zealand university students downgrade lecturers with Asian accents of English, claiming they are unintelligible and poor teachers. (Charming film stars from Eastern Europe and successful Polynesian sports giants do not face such complaints.) And a similar explanation underlies the fact that negative attitudes to Canadian French accents (based on the status of Canadian French people) may dampen the enthusiasm of Canadian English pupils for learning French. Prejudice is at the basis of most such responses; attitudes clearly influence people's judgements of intelligibility, and affect their language-learning motivation.

Where next?

The discussion in this chapter should make you suspicious when people use a person's accent as a basis for judgements about their intellectual abilities, personality or social skills. The material surveyed will have made you aware that attitudes to accents and dialects, whether positive or negative, can clearly have widespread repercussions in people's daily lives. Those with currently favoured accents and dialects have an in-built advantage in many social spheres. Those with unpopular accents and disparaged dialects frequently fight a battle with irrational prejudice in getting a good job and having their intellectual calibre recognized. Research in this area needs to be on-going because such attitudes are so much a matter of fashion. For those who want to challenge attitudes based on social prejudice, it is helpful to keep up to date with current research in this area.

SOME POINTS TO PONDER

▶ Do people in your community think that they speak a distinct dialect or with a distinctive accent? If so, what are their attitudes to this dialect or accent? Are they proud of it? If not, why not? How do their attitudes fit with those described in this chapter? Do they support or challenge the points made?

▶ When you overhear people on the phone can you deduce anything about the person they are talking to from the way they are speaking? If so, how would you explain this?

▶ Do you think attitudes to accents of English are changing? What do you think about the Queen of England's accent? What do you think of the accent used by the President of the USA? What do your father and grandmother think about these accents? Are their views the same as yours?

▶ What do you think about the vocabulary of the DJs on your favourite English-speaking music station? Is there any evidence of influence from other varieties of English? What do your mother and grandfather think about this language? Is there any evidence of change in attitudes?

▶ Some of our former students who are teaching English in Korea have been asked if they can speak with an American accent rather than a New Zealand accent. For young Koreans, learning English means learning American English. In China, on the other hand, New Zealand accents are generally welcomed. If you live in a non-English-speaking country, what kinds of accents are being promoted in English classes in your country? On the basis of the material in this chapter, can you suggest why?

READING AND REFERENCES

Among the most readable books on the issues raised in this chapter are Bonfiglio (2002), Cameron (1995), Lippi-Green (1997), Milroy and Milroy (1999) and Mugglestone (2003).

Bayard, Donn (2000) 'The Cultural Cringe Revisited: Changes through Time in Kiwi Attitudes toward Accents', in Allan Bell and Koenraad Kuiper (eds), *New Zealand English* (Amsterdam and Wellington: Benjamins and Victoria University Press), pp. 297–322.

Bayard, Donn, Ann Weatherall, Cynthia Gallois and Jeffery Pittam (2001) 'Pax Americana? Accent Attitudinal Evaluations in New Zealand, Australia and America', *Journal of Sociolinguistics* 5,1: 22–49.

Bishop, Hywel, Nikolas Coupland and Peter Garrett (2005) 'Conceptual Accent Evaluation: Thirty Years of Accent Prejudice in the UK', *Acta Linguistica Hafnien sia* 37: 131–54.

Bolton, Kingsley (ed.) (2002) *Hong Kong English: Autonomy and Creativity* (Hong Kong: Hong Kong University Press).

Bonfiglio, Thomas Paul (2002) *Race and the Rise of Standard American* (Berlin: Mouton de Gruyter).

Cameron, Deborah (1995) *Verbal Hygiene* (London: Routledge).

Cameron, Deborah (2000) *Good to Talk? Living and Working in a Communication Culture* (London: Sage).

Giles, Howard and Peter F. Powesland (1975) *Speech Style and Social Evaluation* (London: Academic Press).

Gupta, Anthea Fraser (1999) 'Standard Englishes, Contact Varieties and Singapore Englishes', in Claus Gnutzmann (ed.), *Teaching and Learning English as a Global Language* (Tübingen: Stauffenburg Verlag), pp. 59–72.

Labov, William (1966) *The Social Stratification of English in New York City* (Washington, DC: Center for Applied Linguistics).

Labov, William (2001) *Principles of Linguistic Change: Social Factors* (Oxford: Blackwell).

Lippi-Green, Rosina (1997) *English with an Accent: Language Ideology and Discrimination in the United States* (London: Routledge).

Milroy, James and Lesley Milroy (1999) *Authority in Language: Investigating Standard English*, 3rd edn (London: Routledge & Kegan Paul).

Mugglestone, Lynda (2003) *Talking Proper: The Rise of Accent as Social Symbol* (Oxford: Oxford University Press).

Quirk, Randolph (2003) 'Language Varieties and Standard Language', in Roxy Harris and Ben Rampton (eds), *The Language, Ethnicity and Race Reader* (London: Routledge), pp. 97–106.

Trudgill, Peter and Howard Giles (1977). 'Sociolinguistics and Linguistic Value Judgements: Correctness, Adequacy and Aesthetics', in F. Coppieters and Didier L. Goyvaerts (eds), *The Functions of Language and Literature Studies* (Ghent: Story-Scientia).

<http://www.otago.ac.nz/anthropology/Linguistic/Accents.html> – a site dealing with attitudes to accents

Part IV

Language, Brain and Mind

Why My Feets Hurted?

18

What's the matter?

Parents instinctively worry about their children. But should they be worried when little Sam says my *feets hurted when I runned* (other, that is, than to worry about the health of Sam's feet)? Or is there cause for concern when littler Sam says *allgone outside*? Or when even littler Sam says *dut* for duck or uses *dut* (which they thought meant duck in Sam-ese) when pointing to seagulls, sparrows and butterflies? If Sam is doing these things at an appropriate age, then the answer is that they should not be worried, because these sorts of phenomena are normal parts of language acquisition. In fact, these 'mistakes' should actually be taken as positive signs that Sam is discovering the patterns of language, an essential aspect of the language acquisition process.

In this chapter we highlight some of the significant discoveries in the study of language acquisition during early childhood. These are discoveries that relate to the acquisition of one's first or native language over the first five years or so. The scope of this chapter is therefore severely limited, since language learning is a life-long process. Most obviously, as we grow up many of us become involved in learning second and further languages, for which see Chapter 20. But we also continue to learn our native language throughout our lives, learning new modes of expression, accents, nuances, and so on. Yet despite these limitations in the scope of the chapter, we will only be able to scratch the surface of the incredibly complex yet amazingly painless process of first language acquisition.

Born international

Take Sam away from his English-speaking parents at birth and place him for adoption with a Finnish-speaking family, and he will learn Finnish as his first language and not English. That is, while our ability to learn a language is inherited from our biological parents, the specific language that we learn is not. Infants are born with the ability to learn *any* language; what and how they learn depends on what they are exposed to (Box 18.1).

BOX 18.1   Terminology of language acquisition

FIRST language and NATIVE language are terms that are used rather interchangeably to refer to the language that a child acquires during infancy. In some situations of BILINGUALISM (see Chapter 19), an infant will have more than one first language. SECOND language and FOREIGN language (see Chapter 20) are used to refer to a language learned after the first language has become established. Second-language learning is sometimes distinguished from foreign-language learning, with the latter taking place in a country where the language being learned is not spoken as a native language. A distinction is often but rather inconsistently made between language ACQUISITION (in infancy) and language LEARNING (later). A NATIVE SPEAKER of a language is someone who has acquired that language as their native language.

Consider, for example, the differences between the sounds used in languages. For instance, the difference between the consonant sounds at the beginning of [bi:] and [pi:] is important in English, distinguishing here the words *bee* and *pea*. But not all languages have different [b] and [p] sounds, and those that do distinguish them do not do so in exactly the same way (that is, the details in how the sounds are said differ across languages). Now, very young infants appear to be able to hear a lot more contrasts between sounds than they will need for the language they are learning. For instance, it has been shown that infants in Kenya, being brought up with the language Kikuyu, hear the difference between the English-like consonant sounds in [bi:] and [pi:] just like infants being brought up in an English-speaking environment. This is interesting, because Kikuyu does not make the same kind of distinction as English. It appears that at six weeks children – regardless of the language of their environment – can hear the differences between over 150 sounds, from all the world's languages. (Individual languages generally have far fewer sounds than this. English is relatively well endowed with 44 distinct sounds; Rotokas, spoken in Papua New Guinea, has just 11.) By six to eight months of age, however, infants have become 'fine-tuned' to differences actually made in their language, and are no longer sensitive to the differences *not* made in their language. So Kikuyu children will by this age no longer hear the 'English' difference between [b] and [p].

How do we know what very young children can hear? Clearly we cannot ask a two-month-old infant to point to a picture of a *pea* when hearing [pi:], and to one of a *bee* when hearing [bi:]. What researchers can do, however, is measure the amount of attention infants pay to a sound that is played to them. One way of doing this is to measure the rate at which an infant sucks on a dummy (this is done by connecting the dummy to a computer) while hearing a series of sounds. If the sounds are all the same, the infant gets used to them and the sucking rate slows down. Change the sound, and the infant starts sucking harder. By carefully controlling the differences between the sounds, experimenters can determine whether certain changes are more likely to be heard as different sounds than other changes.

Over the first year or so, infants' spoken output consists of sounds that become gradually refined and increasingly identifiable as speech. The earliest sounds are linked with grumbling and eating. Then sounds appear that indicate social interaction with parents and others, usually single speech sounds like vowels and nasals (e.g. [m] and [n] sounds). The range of language-like sounds subsequently increases, as children practise a greater range of vowels and consonants, including many not found in the adult language around them. It is not always obvious to the casual observer that this is speech, since many early attempts are clumsy and influenced not only by the limited exposure the infant has had to how speaking is done, but also by a lack of precise control of the speech organs. The infant's tongue is bulky compared with an adult's, and sounds that require the presence of teeth are obviously going to be tricky. One view given of the apparent chaos of early speech production is that infant babbling shows that they are trying out all the sounds of the world's languages before selecting the sounds of the language they are learning. It is certainly true that infants still have the potential to learn how to produce the sounds of any language, but it is unlikely that they are yet physiologically able to produce them all.

From about six months, infant output becomes more clearly representative of the sounds of their language, and starts to reflect its syllable structure, with 'reduplicative' babbling, such as *nanana*, *bababa*, etc. These changes reflect increasing control over the speech apparatus, as well as increasing perceptual discrimination of the sounds of their language, with children developing a more coherent idea of what the targets are that they need to achieve in order to use the same building blocks of communication as their parents.

Early words

Very young children are clearly going through a detailed learning process that prepares them for the move to more readily recognizable language. But the first major landmark that most parents will tell you about when discussing their child's language development is the 'first word'. Usually this is something that the parents recognize as the equivalent of a word in the adult language. There are no fixed criteria here, but generally this is a word that the child uses with some consistency of form to refer to a particular person, thing or activity. It is highly likely that an outside observer would not recognize the first word as a word, but parents can, because of their greater familiarity with the child's pronunciation patterns and ways of referring to objects and people. 'Mispronunciations' in early speech production typically include the simplification of consonant clusters (so saying something like [pe:] for *play* or [te:n] for *train*), using the same consonant before and after a vowel (e.g. *bub* for *tub*), and producing sounds with the blade of the tongue rather than the back (so, *dut* for *duck*). Although these features can make it difficult to recognize the words, children usually also indicate what they mean through non-verbal communication such as gaze and gesture (looking and pointing at objects, which are typical pre-linguistic methods of communicating).

Prior to the landmark first word, children will have started the complex task of discriminating words in the speech they hear. The text below makes clear how complex this is:

spokenlanguagedoesnothavethoseconvenientgapsbetweenwords

You can probably make sense of that text, because you have some words in your MENTAL LEXICON (the dictionary in your head) that you can spot in the string of letters. Once you have detected one (e.g. *spoken*), the beginning of the next one becomes clearer. But children will have some initial difficulty carrying out this task, because they have a very impoverished lexicon against which they can match the input (imagine doing the same task as above but for a language that you have not learned). Parents (and older siblings) tend to help out here, by using CHILD-DIRECTED SPEECH, a particular style of speaking also variously known as 'baby talk', 'motherese', 'parentese', 'care-giver-ese', or 'infant-directed speech'. This way of speaking, to an extent used also when talking to pets (i.e. generally used for small cuddly creatures), is slower, has exaggerated intonation and quite a lot of repetition. It is grammatically simpler than adult-directed language, and focuses on topics in the 'here and now', i.e. objects and events that the child can currently see. Not surprisingly, a considerable amount of early input that children receive is in response to their own gazes and gestures, e.g. pointing to objects that they want to have or that they want to be named – learning the names of objects is a great language game for young children.

The early words spoken by children are not only relatively poorly articulated, but they also tend to have a different range of referents from adult usage. Two phenomena have been identified here – UNDEREXTENSION and OVEREXTENSION. Underextension is quite common and is when children use a word to refer to an object in a very restricted context, e.g. using *dut* to refer to a specific yellow plastic duck in the bath (but not to any other duck, plastic or living, nor perhaps indeed to that same plastic duck when it is not in the bath). Underextension is not very obvious to the observer because when children use the word it is generally appropriate. It is the situations where they could but do *not* use the word that reveal the limitation. By contrast, overextension is less common but more obvious. It is when children use a word to refer not just to one specific object (or activity) but to a whole range of objects, including some for which that word is not appropriate in the adult language, so using *dut* not just for the plastic duck in the bath and other ducks, but also for other waterfowl, other birds in general, other flying things like butterflies or planes, and so on. A frequently cited example of overextension is the use of *doggie* to refer not just to the family pet (which might be the case in the earlier stage of underextension) and to other dogs (the adult-like norm), but also to any four-legged animal (cat, pig, sheep, horse, cow, etc.).

This pattern of under- and overextension shows how children learn to use words as labels. To start with, the tendency is to believe that every object has a unique label, leading to underextension. Then the labels become generalized to groups of objects with similar properties (which could be visual features, tastes, tactile features and so on). As children learn more labels, they are able to refer in a more discriminating way to sub-groups of objects, gradually refining their referent sets towards those of the adults. An example of this development of vocabulary is shown in Table 18.1 (data from Clark and Clark 1977).

Table 18.1   Development of child vocabulary

Stage	Word	Typical referents
1	bow-wow	a particular dog
2	bow-wow	dogs, cows, horses, sheep, cats
3	(a) bow-wow	dogs, cats, horses, sheep
	(b) moo	cows
4	(a) bow-wow	dogs, cats, sheep
	(b) moo	cows
	(c) gee-gee	horses
5	(a) bow-wow/doggie	dogs, cats
	(b) moo cow	cows
	(c) gee-gee/horsie	horses
	(d) baa	sheep
6	(a) doggie	dogs
	(b) cow	cows
	(c) horsie	horses
	(d) baa	sheep
	(e) kitty	cats

An important aspect of the process of refining vocabulary is learning more and more words. The increase in young children's productive vocabulary is astonishingly rapid, as illustrated in Figure 18.1 (based on an early diary study by Smith 1926). Most of the early words are nouns, i.e. words that are used as naming labels for the objects and people in the child's environment. One study (Nelson 1973) looked at the first 50 words produced by each of 18 children, and found that about two-thirds were nouns.

Putting words together

While children are still learning words, they start to show evidence of mastering another way of using language, namely putting two words together. This generally happens at around one and a half years of age, though as with all these landmarks of acquisition there is considerable variation in timing (but

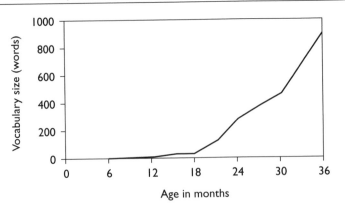

Figure 18.1   Vocabulary size over the first 36 months (data from Smith 1926).

not so much in the order in which they happen). Initial two-word strings are really closely linked single-word utterances (*mummy, read*), which get uttered more and more fluently, becoming single two-word utterances. The typical form of these structures is shown by *allgone milk* (when looking at an empty cup), *more read* (as a request, holding up a book), and *mummy sleep* (describing the mother lying down). Even with just two words, children can start to be creative, putting together sequences they almost certainly have not heard before, such as *allgone outside*, used to indicate that the door has been closed (and therefore that what was outside is no longer visible).

New examples of two-word utterances accumulate very rapidly. It has been argued that this is made possible by a sort of simple grammar for these utterances, known as PIVOT GRAMMAR, involving the combination of 'pivot' words from one, fairly small set (*allgone, more, no, up*, and so on), with words from a larger and rapidly expanding 'open' set of words (generally nouns and proper names, i.e. referring words). So typical utterances using this sort of frame would be *bandage on, blanket on, fixed on*, etc. Pivot and open class words tend to occur in relatively fixed order, suggesting that the grammar being developed at this stage is one with fixed slots for particular word types.

A way in which children show differences in meaning at this early stage is through using different patterns of stress on what are otherwise identical two-word strings. For instance, *Sam bed* could mean something like *this is Sam's bed* or *Sam is in bed*. The first meaning, indicating ownership, is likely to be expressed by stressing the first word. The second meaning (showing location) by stressing the second word. Stress – here in children's speech as also in adult speech – highlights the most important piece of information (*whose bed is this? – it is SAM's bed; where is Sam? – Sam is in BED*).

At around two years of age, three-word strings start to appear, and then longer and longer sequences, though it will be a while before children have the control required to produce adult-like utterances. At every stage, children can understand longer strings than they produce. It is not clear whether the limitation on their production is because (a) they don't have enough short-term memory for stringing together a long sequence; or (b) they simply don't realize a need for longer strings (after all, they generally manage to achieve what they want with shorter sequences); or (c) their understanding is limited to the most salient words of what they hear (i.e. the words that are stressed most in the adults' utterances). This last possibility is reflected in the forms of early sentences that are produced by children, which are often character-ized as TELEGRAPHIC SPEECH (see Chapter 11), i.e. similar to the forms of language used in old-fashioned telegrams, where 'grammatical' words are left out, and just the contentful words (nouns, verbs, adjectives, adverbs) are retained.

Emergence of grammar

Once children start producing sequences of words in a single utterance, some sort of organization is needed. At the two-word stage we saw patterns that have been characterized as 'pivot grammar'. But as we saw in Chapter 10 there is more to grammar than word order and the use of pivot and open class words. One important aspect is the use of word endings to indicate when something happened or is going to happen, or that more than one instance of an object is being referred to. One question that is asked of child language acquisition data is what evidence there is for how children go about the process of learning this aspect of grammar.

Typically, children learning English (parallel findings are reported for rele-vant features in other languages) go through stages in their use of endings for past tenses and plurals, as shown in Table 18.2.

Table 18.2   Acquisition stages for English past tenses and plurals

Stage	Past tense	Plural
(i)	walked, went	cats, feet
(ii)	walked, goed/wented	cats, foots/feets
(iii)	walked, went	cats, feet

At stage (i), the forms that are being used are the same as in the adult language. By stage (ii), however, something has happened that results in what seem like mistakes for certain words, when compared with the adult forms. The forms at stage (iii) are then correct again. The 'stages' shown in the table should not be thought of as discrete periods of time, as there is a lot of overlap as children gradually move from one way of doing things to another. The stage can also take different amounts of time for different children. So what is happening at stage (ii)? Well, if we look closely at the examples here (which are quite typical of young learners of English), we see that the 'mistakes' are regularized forms of irregular words. That is, the regular pattern for making past tenses is to add –*ed*, and that for making plurals is to add –*s*, but the verb *go* and the noun *foot* are irregular (cf. *went* and *feet*). (You can try a mind exercise to demonstrate the strength of the regularity: make up a new verb or a new name for something, e.g. *to froost* or *a splud*. Now try to use the verb in the past and the noun in a plural form. You will almost certainly get *yesterday I froosted both of the spluds*. You could also try this with young children to find out whether they are making the same generalizations.) The stage (ii) child is overgeneralizing the regular pattern to the irregular forms by adding regular endings either to the present and singular forms (*goed, foots*), or to the irregular forms that they had been using at stage (i) (giving *wented, feets*). This phenomenon (known both as OVERREGULARIZATION and OVERGENERALIZATION) is interesting and also very important, because it reveals that although children initially learn by copying the language that they hear (which is why they produce correct forms at stage (i)), while they are doing this they are also creating their own internal grammar. This grammar is built upon the recurring patterns that they detect in what they hear, which includes showing past by using –*ed* (or one of the three spoken equivalents of -*ed*, as in *walked, hummed, pointed*), and plural by using –*s* (also in three spoken forms, as in *cats, dogs, horses*). The linguist Noam Chomsky, using a term from child psychologist Jean Piaget, refers to children as 'little scientists' because of the way in which they discover the organizational principles of language by investigating the data for themselves. Nobody teaches children what past tenses or plurals are; each child discovers the patterns of language afresh.

As children produce longer and longer utterances, they move closer to adult-like usage of grammatical devices such as endings and word order. In addition, there is good evidence that young children make use of the differing patterns of intonation to show differences in meaning, even before they have good control of word order or the use of particular grammatical elements. Table 18.3, for instance, shows the typical development of wh-questions (questions using a *wh*-question word like *what, where, who*, etc.) At the first stage, the question is indicated by the use of the *wh*-word and rising

Table 18.3   Acquisition stages for English wh-questions

Stage	Example	Form
(i)	Where doggie? Where mummy go? Why my feets hurted?	Question intonation + fronted wh-word
(ii)	Where we was driving yesterday? Where the other one will go? What Sammy has done?	Question intonation + fronted wh-word + auxiliary
(iii)	What did you doed? Why was we going?	Question intonation + fronted wh-word + auxiliary + subject inversion

intonation (questions without a *wh*-word might be marked just by intonation, as in *sit chair?*). At the second stage, an auxiliary verb is used (*was, will, has* in the examples), and the form of the question is almost an echo of what the child might have heard from a parent in a context like *tell me what Sammy has done*. At the third stage, the child is also reversing the order of the subject and auxiliary verb, so giving *did you* instead of *you did*. The form is clearly much more adult-like now; the child has gained control of how these kinds of questions are formed, though some further polishing is needed.

Where next?

We opened this chapter with some questions about whether parents should worry about what appear to be mistakes in the speech of their children. We have seen that the examples given in those questions are in fact all instances of perfectly normal language development, and as such they are probably a cause for celebration rather than concern. We have also seen that these kinds of examples provide a rich source of evidence about the language acquisition process and the road of discovery (and creativity) that children are walking during the early years of their lives. Appreciation of the processes of language acquisition is a key aspect of understanding how the mind works, and is therefore a continuing productive area of research in psychology as well as in linguistics, as courses, textbooks and journals in this area testify.

SOME POINTS TO PONDER

▶ Why does Chomsky say that children are 'little scientists'?
▶ What evidence is there that children do not learn language simply by copying? Think here of what they say, what they hear and of the relationship between these two.
▶ Although over-regularization is powerful evidence for rule building, there are other examples that suggest that more is going on. What do verb forms like *thank* (instead of *thought*) and *hat* (as a past of *hit*) tell us about what a child is doing?
▶ Try asking friends to give you past tense forms for the nonsense verbs *grife* and *kring* (do this for instance by getting them to complete a sentence like *Today I am grifing my email, yesterday I also ___ my email*). Do they provide regular past tense forms for both (*grifed, kringed*) or do they give other forms (like *krang*)? How does this compare with what children do?

READINGS AND REFERENCES

The research showing that Kikuyu-language infants can hear the difference between [bi:] and [pi:] just like English-language infants was carried out by Streeter (1976), and is one of a large number of studies on early speech perception, many of which are reviewed by Gerken (1994). The idea that children try out all possible sounds is attributed to Jakobson (1968), but is found in other works on child language too.

For reviews of studies of early vocabulary growth see Clark (1993: Ch.2) and chapters in Aitchison (2003). The notion of pivot grammar was initially developed by Braine (1963). Notions of the child as a little scientist are explored in Piaget (1952) and Chomsky (1975).

Most introductory textbooks on the psychology of language discuss child language acquisition, as do any introductory linguistics texts. A highly readable example of the former is Aitchison (2000).

Aitchison, Jean (2000) *The Articulate Mammal*, 4th edn (London and New York: Routledge).

Aitchison, Jean (2003) *Words in the Mind: An Introduction to the Mental Lexicon*, 3rd edn (Oxford: Blackwell).

Braine, Martin D. S. (1963) 'The Ontogeny of English Phrase Structure: the First Phase', *Language*, 39: 1–13.

Chomsky, Noam A. (1975) *Reflections on Language* (New York: Pantheon).

Clark, Eve (1993) *The Lexicon in Acquisition* (Cambridge: Cambridge University Press).

Clark, Herbert H. and Eve V. Clark (1977) *Psychology and Language* (New York: Harcourt Brace Jovanovich).

Gerken, LouAnn (1994) 'Child Phonology', in Morton A. Gernsbacher (ed.), *The Handbook of Psycholinguistics* (San Diego, CA: Academic Press), pp. 781–820.

Jakobson, Roman (1968 [1941]) *Child Language, Aphasia and Phonological Universals* (original title *Kindersprache, Aphasie und allgemeine Lautgesetze*), trans. A. R. Keiler (The Hague: Mouton).

Nelson, K. (1973) 'Structure and Strategy in Learning to Talk', *Monographs of the Society of Research in Child Development*, 38: 149.

Piaget, Jean (1952) *The Origins of Intelligence in Children*, trans. Margaret Cook (New York: International Universities Press).

Smith, M. (1926) 'An Investigation of the Development of the Sentence and the Extent of Vocabulary in Young Children', *University of Iowa Studies in Child Welfare*, 3(5).

Streeter L. A. (1976) 'Language Perception of 2-month-old Infants Shows Effects of Both Innate Mechanisms and Experience', *Nature*, 259: 39–41.

Does Bilingualism Rot the Brain?

What's the matter?

Pat has two young boys who, like Pat, have been brought up speaking only English. Pat also owns a small film production company, and new filming possibilities mean that the family is now planning to move for a few years to a different country. This is a country where English is not widely spoken. Pat can see some obvious practical advantages of learning the language of this country – although the bulk of the film production work can continue in English, interaction with local clients, and visiting local supermarkets and restaurants will require at least some knowledge of the language. What about Pat's children? Should they be placed in a local school and encouraged to learn a new language by being thrown, as it were, in the deep end? They might make new friends more readily this way, but Pat is worried about the additional burden this is going to put on them at a time that they may already find emotionally quite difficult. Having to learn a new language in order to get by in school may also have a negative effect on other aspects of their learning. Perhaps it would be better to send them to an 'international' school, to continue learning (and playing) in English. After all, in a few years they'll be going back to their native country anyway. A well-meaning, but misinformed friend points Pat to something they once read on the topic:

> the brain effort required to master two languages instead of one certainly diminishes the child's power of learning other things which might and ought to be learnt.   (Jespersen 1922: 148)

So Pat opts for the international school. But then another expatriate Pat meets through work talks about their own positive experiences of learning languages at school, when they found it really exciting to learn that different languages have different ways of talking about the world. They belong to a bilingual support group, and tell Pat about other research they have come across. Now Pat reads that

> one can now put forth a very persuasive argument that there is a definite cognitive advantage for bilingual over monolingual children in the domain of cognitive flexibility.   (Lambert 1977: 30)

Pat might be forgiven for now feeling rather confused. Why is there this apparent clash of views? It turns out, as we show in this chapter, that there are different social and political contexts for these views, and that these can colour opinion as to whether bilingualism rots the brain or may actually be good for you. Worryingly, perhaps, this difference in opinion can have a marked effect not just on individual choice about education but on education policy itself. That is, if policy makers are convinced (or allow themselves to be persuaded) that bilingualism 'rots your brain', then this could lead to the shelving of bilingual education programmes.

Why worry about bilingualism?

It is perhaps curious that bilingualism is singled out for attention. After all, bilingualism is not that unusual as a linguistic phenomenon. It is found in all reaches of society, is not peculiar to any age group, and is evident in virtually every country in the world. More than half the world's population is bilingual, a statistic that is not at all surprising when you consider that there are roughly 30 times as many languages as countries in the world.

One reason why linguists (and others) are fascinated by bilingualism is that a large proportion of the researchers are themselves monolingual or work in predominantly monolingual speech communities, in which bilingualism is the exception rather than the norm. It is for this kind of reason that, as Romaine (1995) points out, a book called 'Monolingualism' would seem strange while one called 'Bilingualism' does not. It is often more interesting to study the curious ways in which other people do things. Some of the interesting aspects of bilingualism concern how people with two languages might think and reason, aspects which are closely linked to the question of whether bilingualism rots the brain. But what exactly do we mean by 'bilingualism'?

What is bilingualism?

There is probably no simple definition of bilingualism. Most researchers would agree that the 'bi-' in bilingualism does not have to restrict us to two languages, and so we will also be thinking here of multilingual situations. Of course, people can be bilingual, but so too can whole communities. If a community is referred to as bilingual, this could mean that all speakers in that community speak the same two languages, possibly using one of them in work or official contexts and the other one at home. Or it could be that the community as a whole uses two languages, but any individual speaker only uses one of them. 'Officially' bilingual countries could also fall between these two types – in Canada, for instance, there are groups that speak French only, others that speak only English, and others that use both French and English. There are lots of possible interpretations of 'bilingual community'.

In everyday terms we might think of a bilingual person as being someone who knows or uses two languages. But what does it mean to 'know' or to 'use' two languages? Is someone a bilingual if they can say 'hello' in two languages, even though they may not be able to use one of the languages in any other way? According to some definitions they are. But according to other definitions a bilingual has to have native-speaker abilities in each of their languages. Is this now too extreme? It would certainly rule out many people who have excellent command of two languages but speak one of them with a non-native accent and so might not pass convincingly as native speakers of that language.

Other definitions talk of bilinguals (or at least 'balanced' bilinguals) as being equally proficient in two languages, but it is not clear how easy it is to equate levels of proficiency in two languages, since the differences between languages mean that there will be different types of proficiency tests. On top of this, there are many different types of proficiency (e.g. in speaking, listening, reading, writing) – would we insist on equal proficiency in all language skills? Maybe it is enough to say that a bilingual is someone for whom two languages are interchangeable. But now we have come full circle, because this would exclude the many highly proficient speakers in bilingual communities where the two languages are used in different contexts. For these bilingual speakers the two languages are not interchangeable because it would be inappropriate to use one in contexts in which the other alone is normally expected.

Another angle on the definition of bilingualism involves consideration of the language systems involved. That is, it is sometimes argued that IDEAL or FULL BILINGUALS should be able to maintain two distinct linguistic systems, one for each language. But is this the usual pattern for bilingualism? In fact it is not, as bilinguals generally do a lot of language mixing, which is sometimes mistakenly taken as proof of confusion and that bilingualism rots the brain.

We can also distinguish between different bilinguals in terms of how they have become bilingual. Some are bilingual from birth (or at least from a very early age) and are sometimes referred to as SIMULTANEOUS bilinguals. Others have become bilingual later in life (e.g. at school age or later); these are known as SUCCESSIVE bilinguals. But not all successive bilinguals are the same. For some, a second language has been added to the first (ADDITIVE BILINGUALISM), while for others the second language ultimately replaces the first (SUBTRACTIVE BILINGUALISM). Similarly, bilingual acquisition during childhood, which constitutes simultaneous acquisition to the extent that the child is still learning their first language(s), can happen in a number of ways. This may depend in part on the language environment but also on any 'strategy' towards bilingualism that has been adopted by the parents (see Box 19.1). In most natural bilingual contexts (and since bilingualism is so widespread this effectively means in most language acquisition contexts), parents do not follow any explicit strategy for their children's language learning – bilingual acquisition is simply the norm. But in other contexts (such as the hypothetical situation described in the opening of this chapter) parents might carefully plan a language learning policy. But these have varied success – the most unnatural strategies (e.g. where one of the parents uses a language that is not the native language of either parent nor of the community in which the child is living) are more likely to break down. This is perhaps the most pervasive problem with such learning policies – maintaining a language that does not have community support (see Chapter 12).

ILLUSTRATION

BOX 19.1   Parental strategies

Examples of parental strategies frequently adopted in childhood bilingual acquisition (after Romaine 1995)

Type	Parents' languages	Dominant language in community	Parental strategy
1. One person – one language	Different	Language of one of the parents	Speak own language to child from birth
2. Non-dominant home language	Different	Language of one of the parents	Speak non-dominant language to child, who is otherwise exposed to dominant language outside the home
3. Non-dominant home language without community support	Same	Not that of parents	Speak own language to child
4. Double non-dominant home language without community support	Different	Not that of parents	Speak own language to child
5. Non-native parents	Same	Same as parents'	One parent always addresses child in non-native language
6. Mixed languages	Bilingual	May be bilingual	Code-switch and mix languages

Also: using different languages at specific times of day/days of week

Clearly 'bilingualism' has a large range of flavours. So it is perhaps understandable that there is also a mix of feelings about the effects of bilingualism on the individual. But what gives rise to views that are as strongly polarized as those expressed in the extracts cited earlier?

Level playing fields?

It is worth reflecting on where and when those extracts come from. The first dates from the early part of the twentieth century, and reflects some of the views being formed in Western Europe and the United States at a time when immigration was seen by many as a bad thing. It has been argued that to cope with migration into economies already under threat, tests of intelligence and of linguistic ability were frequently administered to would-be immigrants in a language they barely understood. These 'bilinguals' were usually adults, with little support in a new country, who were struggling to learn the language of the majority population. The second extract reflects the results of later research, largely in Canada, where bilingualism was being widely promoted among a relatively stable population. Families taking part in bilingual programmes were keen participants who shared the view that bilingualism has many advantages. The bilinguals in this case were mainly children who were still learning their first language and who were probably more open to language learning than the adults in many of the earlier studies. Given such a big difference between the two situations, it is not at all surprising to find different conclusions about the value of bilingualism, but it seems that these conclusions are determined by social and political factors as much as by linguistic and educational ones.

What is rotten in the state of bilingualism?

The most general negative view on bilingualism is that bilinguals are less intelligent than monolinguals. We have already seen that at least some of the results leading to this conclusion are based on intelligence tests conducted in a language in which the 'bilingual' has had only little experience. It also appears that some of the tests were frequently run in an environment (e.g. in an immigration office) which would have been quite uncomfortable for the participant. But not all intelligence tests on bilinguals have been carried out on older immigrant populations. For instance, one widely cited study carried out in Wales in the 1920s compared English-monolingual and Welsh/English-bilingual children. The children came from both urban and rural areas. Overall the bilinguals scored worse in intelligence tests, and this led to the same general claim that bilingualism impairs intelligence. In this case the effect was attributed to the emotional turmoil caused by having to cope with two languages. Interestingly, though, the difference between bilinguals and monolinguals in the intelligence test were only clear for the rural children – scores for the bilingual and monolingual urban children scarcely differed. This was taken to show that the urban bilinguals found it easier to get over the language conflict, and so performed as well as the monolinguals. It is just as likely, though, that the urban bilinguals had simply had more exposure to English than the rural children.

Claims have also been made that bilinguals are more prone to stuttering, possibly because of 'syntactic overload', that is, because the decisions about what sentence forms to use become more difficult the more languages you have to choose from. As pointed out by Romaine (1995), these claims, which spread rapidly amongst educators, appear to be based largely on a single case study, and are at odds with many other studies that show a range of advantages for bilinguals – with two grammatical systems at their disposal – over monolinguals.

A final area in which bilingualism gets a poor report involves CODE-SWITCHING, or the mixing of languages in single utterances (see Box 19.2). Code-switching is sometimes argued to show a lack of education or even bad manners. Not surprisingly, this type of comment comes largely from the monolingual communities who have to 'suffer' the indignities of not being able to understand words or phrases in the language. It must be said, though, that bilingual communities themselves often have a negative view of code-switching. In bilingual communities in Nigeria, for instance, code-switching is referred to as *adalu ade* or 'verbal salad'. More worryingly, perhaps, it has been argued that code-switching shows that the speaker does not have complete control of the two languages involved, leading to characterizations of bilinguals as 'semilingual'. This notion of semilingualism is found in many of the negative approaches to bilingualism, and is reflected in Jespersen's claim that a bilingual child

> hardly learns either of the two languages as perfectly as he would have done if he had limited himself to one. It may seem, on the surface, as if he talked just like a native, but he does not really command the fine points of the language.   (Jespersen 1922: 148)

In reality, switching between languages is an important and valued aspect of how bilinguals communicate, and can often provide them with a few tricks not available to monolinguals, such as changing language to show a change in characters or settings when telling a story. (Note, though, that monolinguals do code-switch between different varieties or registers of one language; see Chapter 16.) So a less negative view of code-switching is to see it as part of a legitimate stylistic tool. Switching is also a linguistic feature that is largely outside of conscious control, as exemplified in a television show in Senegal in West Africa, again referred to by Romaine (1995). In this show, participants from the Wolof/French bilingual community try to talk on a single topic for several minutes using only Wolof. They find this extremely difficult to do, particularly if the topic is on an issue or context that normally involves French, such as talking about school. This illustrates also the point made earlier about how many bilingual communities may use different languages in different contexts – here the distinction is between the language of the home (Wolof) and that of administration and education (French).

Ways in which being bilingual might be good for you

We have commented above that many of the negative claims made about bilingualism may be misplaced, and might reflect other issues, such as whether the bilingual has had much access to the language in which intelli-

BOX 19.2   Code-switching

Code-switching is the use of elements from more than one language in a single utterance. It is frequently and naturally found amongst bilinguals, and has a number of types, including the following:

Type	Description	Example (roman/italics indicates different languages)	Languages involved: English and . . .
Code-mixing	Insertion of single words from one language into sentences in the other	Have *agua* please	Spanish
Tag-switching	Inclusion of a 'tag' (e.g. 'you know') from one language into a sentence in the other	The proceedings went smoothly, *ba*	Tagalog
Inter-sentential switching	Swapping from one language to another at the end of a sentence or clause	Sometimes I'll start a sentence in English *y terminó in español*	Spanish
Intra-sentential switching	Swapping from one language to another within a sentence (includes also code-mixing)	*Won o* arrest a single person	Yoruba

Examples from Romaine (1995). Other sources given there.

gence tests are carried out. But can bilingualism actually be good for you? The passage from Lambert quoted earlier starts with the following claim:

> There is, then, an impressive array of evidence accumulating that argues plainly against the common sense notion that becoming bilingual, that is, having two strings to one's bow or two linguistic systems within one's brain, naturally divides a person's cognitive resources and reduces his efficiency of thought.   (Lambert 1977: 30)

What is this 'impressive array of evidence'? Most of it arises from carefully conducted studies comparing monolinguals and 'balanced' bilinguals. For instance, ten year-old English/French bilinguals were compared with French monolinguals in the French-based schooling system in Québec, Canada. The outcome was the claim that bilinguals have greater mental flexibility, as shown in tests where participants had to reorganize visual patterns such as tangrams to make stylized pictures of objects (Box 19.3). It was argued that this greater mental flexibility results from the fact that bilinguals have to work with two sets of labels for the same objects and so they are better able to separate form (the labels, e.g. French *chat* and English *cat*) from content (e.g. the cat being referred to).

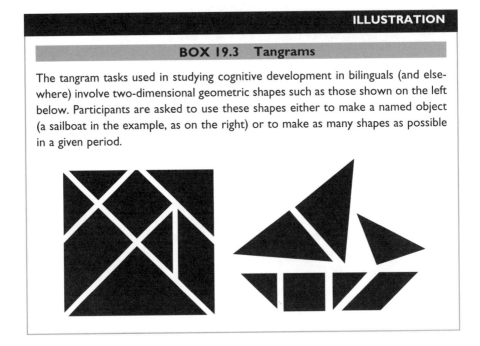

ILLUSTRATION

BOX 19.3   Tangrams

The tangram tasks used in studying cognitive development in bilinguals (and elsewhere) involve two-dimensional geometric shapes such as those shown on the left below. Participants are asked to use these shapes either to make a named object (a sailboat in the example, as on the right) or to make as many shapes as possible in a given period.

Similarly, bilinguals also seem to be better at divergent thinking (for instance, imagining all the things that can be done with a paper-clip). It is interesting to note that traditional intelligence tests – which were the basis for earlier claims relating bilingualism to low intelligence – tend to focus on convergent thinking, i.e. on finding one specific answer to a question. So perhaps the earlier claims were based on too narrow a view of intelligence. Further findings are that bilinguals are more creative, possibly because they have different networks of meaning in the different languages and have learned to view the world in different ways. There may well be an influence here of familiarity with more than one culture as well as with more than one language.

Finally, there is a growing body of evidence that bilinguals are more 'aware' of language. This 'metalinguistic' awareness has been shown in tests where children are asked to play certain language games, such as changing the names for objects and calling a cow a *table* and so on. Bilinguals are better at making these changes, and also find it easier to comment on what they are doing, interestingly saying that they are making the changes 'because it's our game'. Bilinguals have also been shown to have greater 'phonological' aware-ness, i.e. understanding of how spoken words are built up from constituent parts, for instance how the word *cat* is made up of three speech sounds [k – æ – t] or of an onset and rhyme [k – æt]. Phonological awareness has inde-pendently been correlated with progress in learning to read, which suggests at least one practical benefit to being bilingual.

Where next?

In this chapter we have contrasted two views of the relationship between bilingualism and other aspects of cognition. It is clear that these two views are heavily influenced by the sociopolitical climates surrounding the studies of bilingualism and the expectations that are made of bilinguals in these climates. It is also clear that the contrasting findings can provide powerful political and social weapons that might be used by those advocating for or against bilingual education programmes. Of course bilingual education can mean quite different things in different contexts. Some examples in an English-speaking country might include the enforced learning of English as a second language amongst immigrant children; teaching the whole school syllabus equally divided between English and the immigrant language; or teaching all subjects in the immigrant language, assuming that English will be picked up outside the school context. The choice between these kinds of approach may depend on educational philosophy, as well as on views about the importance of separating the two languages between two different contexts of use. More worryingly, perhaps, the choice often comes down to political views about the role that should be played by immigrant groups – obliging them to learn the majority language and (implicitly or explicitly) to turn their backs on their own community language may reflect a desire to force all communities into a single mould, or even to deny certain groupings equal access to resources and wealth.

Finally, though, we must not lose sight of the fact that bilingualism is not at all unusual, in global terms, and that for most bilinguals the question of whether bilingualism rots the brain or is good for you is not an issue.

SOME POINTS TO PONDER

Imagine that you have been asked by concerned parents whether they should bring up their child to be bilingual.

▶ What background information would you need to have about the situation before giving advice?
▶ What negative impacts of bilingualism would you warn them about?
▶ What positive effects of bilingualism might you highlight?
▶ What strategies for bilingual language acquisition could you suggest?

REFERENCES AND READING

Two detailed and engaging textbooks on bilingualism and the issues confronted by bilinguals are those by Romaine (1995) and Grosjean (1982), who both provide useful reviews of the literature.

Grosjean, Francois (1982) *Life with Two Languages* (London: Harvard University Press).

Jespersen, Otto (1922) *Language* (London: George Allen & Unwin).

Lambert, Wallace E. (1977) 'The Effects of Bilingualism on the Individual: Cognitive and Socio-cultural Consequences', in P. Hornby (ed.), *Bilingualism: Psychological, Social and Educational Implications* (New York: Academic Press), pp. 15–28.

Romaine, Suzanne (1995) *Bilingualism* (Oxford: Blackwell).

Saer, D. (1924) 'The Effects of Bilingualism on Intelligence', *British Journal of Psychology*, 14: 25–38.

Building Another Tongue

What's the matter?

If we could patent a foolproof quick and painless way of learning a second language, we'd be sure to make a lot of money. This is because one thing that we often get asked as linguists, especially when we reveal that we have taught courses on language learning, is whether there is such a thing as a fail-safe strategy for learning a second language. The simplest answer, but one which tends not to gain us a lot of credit and would certainly not bring in any cash, is 'no'. A more complex and ultimately more accurate answer is 'it depends', followed by a long list of the factors which have been shown to affect success in language learning. This chapter discusses some of these factors. It does not – indeed cannot – provide a recipe for success, but it does at least point to some of the issues that might be worth taking into consideration.

If I've done it once, why can't I do it again?

Children seem to soak up their first language like sponges. While they are not born with a particular language, children are certainly predisposed towards learning a first language. It seems that as long as they get language input, they will seek out the structures and regularities in that input and learn the language. As pointed out in Chapter 18, the process of learning a first language, although complex, is nevertheless painless. So it is tempting to believe that if we can reconstruct the process of learning a first language and apply it to learning a second language then we have a guaranteed recipe for success. This is – in part – the viewpoint that lay behind many 'natural' approaches to second language learning that were popular in the 1960s and 1970s. But it is a view that ignores the fact that the second and first language learning situations are different in ways that make such a strategy unlikely to succeed. So what has changed? It is sometimes said that children *acquire* a first language, but that we have to *learn* a second one. What has made learning a second language different from acquiring a first language? And are there any factors that have not changed?

One big difference is the nature of the input. When children are learning their first language they listen to people telling them about things in the 'here and now'. That is, when we talk to children we generally talk to them about things that they can see or hear or feel, rather than things in the room next door or that might happen tomorrow. In addition, we tend to use child-directed speech (see Chapter 18), a special way of talking that uses exaggerated intonation, and has clearer breaks between words and simpler vocabulary, and we tend to accompany our talk with a lot of gesture and animated expression. While there are many different kinds of second language learning contexts, it is not clear that any of them are quite like the first-language context in terms of having this type of input. In a formal learning context (classroom or lecture hall) the input might be in terms of grammar exercises, vocabulary lists, etc., which will be removed from the here-and-now. In less formal learning situations, such as when the learner is involved in role play, or is living in a country where the language is spoken, the language they hear is more likely to be relevant to the situation they are in, but it is also more likely to be more complicated or sophisticated than the learner is capable of dealing with. Proponents of a more 'natural' approach to language learning recommend that learners should be given input that not only has situational relevance, but that also is at a level that is just above their current ability – this is often referred to as 'comprehensible' input. It is argued that child directed speech is also geared towards providing 'comprehensible' input.

As well as differences in the input, there are different expectations concerning the types of output that learners should be producing. Parents don't expect their toddlers to be able to talk back to them at length about things that they have been discussing. But often this kind of expectation is made of learners, bolstered perhaps by the fact that second-language learners are generally older and from outward appearance seem to be mature enough to get involved in a 'proper' conversation. Also, when children learn their first language their perception and comprehension skills run ahead of their production skills (again, see Chapter 18). But when it comes to second language learners there is often a greater emphasis placed on production skills (sometimes this is for the practical reason that a student's output is easier to assess than their comprehension).

A further difference concerns practice. It has been pointed out that when children acquire their first language they seem to do a lot of repetition, perhaps using the same frame over and over with new elements in it. This is certainly part of language play between children and adults, and there is even evidence that toddlers practise the forms of language as they lie in their cots. But what appears to be more effective for second-language learning than simple repetition (as in rote learning of vocabulary or grammar) is learning in a context of meaningful communication.

Differences in feedback are also an issue. In the second language context, there are two main types of feedback that learners might receive. One is whether what they have said or written is correct according to the rules of grammar of the language they are learning (a kind of *cognitive* feedback), while the other is an indication that what they have produced is valued (or not) for its content (so a kind of *affective* feedback). Positive affective feedback is probably important in encouraging the learner to continue participation, while positive cognitive feedback contributes strongly to the reinforcement of the forms of language being used. Compare this with feedback that children get when learning their first language – very little of this deals with the form of their language output. In fact it has been observed that there is a paradox in first language learning. This is that parents give feedback to their children for the accuracy of the content of their language and not for the correctness of its form, yet children grow up being able to speak grammatically but untruthfully!

Does age matter?

If I try to learn a second language before I reach a certain age, will I be more likely to succeed? It has long been argued that perhaps the most crucial influence on the relative difficulty of second language learning compared to first language acquisition is the age factor. That is, there is something about the process of growing up that means that older learners approach the learning task in a different way to younger learners. Most often this has been debated in the context of whether there is a CRITICAL PERIOD for language learning, i.e. that learning a second language is more likely to be successful if it is done before a certain age.

Some support for the notion of a critical period comes from studies of people with brain damage (which can result from stroke or head injury). The parts of the brain that do most of the language work are mainly in the left hemisphere. If damage occurs to that side of an adult's brain, then it often affects language (see Chapter 23). However, research on brain-damaged children shows that infants sustaining significant left-hemisphere damage are still able to acquire language, and that the job of looking after language acquisition is taken over by the right hemisphere. But the ability to successfully acquire or re-acquire language diminishes for children whose brains are damaged at a later age, so that left-hemisphere brain damage at around 11 to 14 years of age is much less likely to result in full or even near-full recovery of language functions. It is said that by the age of puberty there has been lateralization of brain function, i.e. that the different portions of the brain responsible for different mental and physical tasks have been established. After lateralization, re-learning a language after brain damage is difficult. The critical period for learning a language (first or second) has been argued to be this period before lateralization of brain function.

What other evidence is there then for an influence of age on language learning ability? It turns out that there are plenty of apparently conflicting claims in this area, but that it all depends on what is meant by language learning ability. It has been maintained that:

• younger learners (pre-puberty) are better;

- older learners are better;
- younger learners are better at some things;
- older learners are more efficient, but younger learners are more successful.

The claims that younger learners are better are based on the observation mentioned earlier that language learning involves less effort for younger learners, especially in the so-called critical period. It is not entirely clear that this is solely because of the development of specialization within the brain, because there are other changes that are taking place through to adolescence that will also have an impact on language learning. These include general changes in learning style – older children and adults tend to take a more analytical approach to learning, mapping out the learning tasks and wanting to understand the way in which the material works, while younger children learn more intuitively. Also, younger children may feel less inhibited when it comes to using a different language, and inhibition has been shown to be a major barrier to successful communication and language learning.

The apparently contradictory claim that older learners are better is one that is focused on the speed of learning, and tends to come from short-term 'teach and test' studies, which ask students to learn some language material which they are then tested on shortly afterwards. Older learners do better in these kinds of tasks, but it has been argued that this is probably because they are better at developing strategies for doing the tests, rather than necessarily being better learners. When learners are compared over the longer term, then there is evidence that the learning 'sticks' better for the younger learners.

Many of the studies looking at age effects have tended to focus on the learning of vocabulary and grammar. Studies that also include the learning of pronunciation and oral communication skills have tended to show that young learners are particularly good at achieving closer to native-like competence in these areas. It is claimed that there may in fact be multiple 'critical periods', with that for pronunciation finishing earlier than those for vocabulary and grammar. And even within the area of pronunciation there may be earlier cut-off times for some skills than others – it has been suggested, for instance, that getting the intonation right becomes more difficult after as early an age as six years. A critical difference between pronunciation and other language skills is that the former involves the development of fine motor skills to distinguish the different sounds of languages, and this may be a crucial factor. At the same time, a reason for the 'fossilization' of non-native pronunciation in older speakers may be that they are more comfortable maintaining such foreign-accented pronunciation, considering it to be part of their identity.

If there is a consensus view coming out of the research on the role of age in language learning then it is probably that age is not per se an obstacle to learning a language, that older learners may show initial advantages in terms of speed of learning, but that younger learners are more likely to end up with native-like language skills. This is particularly clear for pronunciation skills, but even for grammar there is evidence that an early start is beneficial. The data shown in Figure 20.1 come from a study of Korean and Chinese immi-

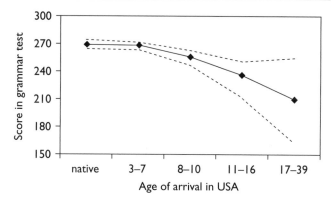

**Figure 20.1   Average grammar scores (solid line) in English for US immi-
grants from Korea and China, by age of arrival. Maximum score is 276 (all
were tested approximately ten years after arrival). Dotted lines indicate
the range of scores for each group. Based on data from Johnson and
Newport (1989).**

grants to the United States of America, who were given an English grammar
test after approximately ten years in the USA, but who had arrived at different ages (Johnson and Newport 1989). The youngest arrivals score at a
native-like level, and the scores gradually dip away for participants who
started learning English at a later age because they were older when they
arrived. The authors of this study also note that within the groups who
arrived between three and 16 years of age there is a strong correlation of age
of arrival with test scores, but that this is not the case within the older group.
That is, there is a gradual lowering of scores for people who started learning
up to the age of 16, but not beyond that age, suggesting that from late teens
onwards the age at which learning starts makes no difference to eventual
achievement.

It's the thought that counts

What motivates people to learn a language? For children learning their first
language, their motivation is going to include communicating needs (*feed me,
change me, put me to bed*) but also the desire for social interaction (*play with
me, talk to me, listen to me*) and the acquisition of knowledge (*what is that for?
tell me about that, why?*). For second language learners it has been argued that
there are two main types of motivational factor: integrative and instrumental. INTEGRATIVE MOTIVATION is when the learner does not just want to learn
the language for the sake of learning the language or for getting by in the
language, but because they want to identify with the speakers of that
language, and understand, or even adopt, their cultural values, and so on.
INSTRUMENTAL MOTIVATION has its focus on learning a language for a particular purpose – perhaps because the learner needs to get some credits towards

a qualification or because they have been seconded to work in a country where that language is spoken, or because they want to make themselves understood on a holiday there.

A series of studies looked at the role of these different types of motivation in language learning success. It was found, for instance, in both Canada and the USA that integrative motivation towards learning French was a much better predictor of success than instrumental motivation. In addition, a comparison of learning success in two areas of the USA where there are strong French-language communities – Louisiana in the south and Maine in the northeast – showed that stronger community support for French in Maine was reflected in better learning outcomes. In the Philippines it was found that attitudes towards American culture were reflected in success at learning English. Students in Manila who identified with American culture, and showed integrative types of motivation, were amongst the most success-ful learners. And of course it is not just the attitudes of the learner that are important – studies have also shown a major influence on learning outcomes of the attitudes expressed by parents, classmates, teachers and others towards the language being learned.

Where does the first language come in?

Clearly second language learners by definition already know a language, and they will bring their knowledge of that language to the task of learning a second language. But how available is this knowledge to them? When we ask students attending our courses on language learning processes whether they have learned a language, many of them will say that they haven't. This is because our learning experience and therefore also most of our knowledge of our first language is intuitive and not explicit (knowing how rather than knowing what), and so the students tend not to think of their first language as being one they have learned – they certainly have little memory of having learned it. The impact it may have on second language learning may there-fore be rather subtle, in particular in comparison with the impact that having learned a second language may have on approaches to learning subsequent languages.

Nevertheless, there is a great deal of discussion of the role of the first language in second language learning, and a great deal of controversy. On the one hand, it is argued that knowledge of a first language can transfer to the second language learning process. Therefore it is necessary to make a compar-ison of the two languages concerned, so that we can make predictions about what knowledge is going to help and what will hinder the process of learning the second language. On the other hand, it is argued that the first language is largely irrelevant, and that learning a second language follows a develop-mental sequence, just as first language acquisition does. The term associated with the first of these approaches is CONTRASTIVE ANALYSIS, that associated with the second is INTERLANGUAGE.

Contrastive Analysis was a popular approach to second language learning in the 1960s and 1970s, and was particularly favoured in the area of language curriculum development. As the name implies, this approach involved comparison of the properties of two languages (e.g. what sounds they use, what vocabulary and grammatical structures they have), in order to determine the differences between the languages. There were two versions of what is known as the Contrastive Analysis Hypothesis – the stronger version maintained that the result of the comparison would be a prediction of areas of difficulty, which would help to prioritize teaching/learning goals. The weaker version claimed that at best the comparison could be used to come to some understanding of why learners with a background in one language (L1) made certain mistakes when learning the other language (L2). Contrastive Analysis frequently produced scales of difficulty for L1 learners of L2. One such scale is presented in Table 20.1. The examples, from a comparison of English and German, are our own, but the framework is taken from the work of Prator in the 1960s (see, for example, Ellis, 1985).

Aside from the practical difficulties involved in developing a complete and coherent contrastive analysis of two languages, researchers in this area found that types of difference were not always a good predictor of levels of difficulty. Support for the strong version of the Contrastive Analysis Hypothesis was short-lived, but the weaker version still proves useful in considering possible interference errors in second language learners' output.

Table 20.1   Scales of difficulty in learning a second language, as developed in the Contrastive Analysis approach

Level of difficulty	Learner process	Explanation	Example
0	Transfer	No difference	Many sounds ([s, p, n], etc.) are found in both languages
1	Coalescence	Two forms in L1 but one in L2	lens / lentil → Linse
2	Underdifferentiation	Item found in L1 but absent in L2	She is **a** journalist – Sie is Journalistin
3	Reinterpretation	Item in L1 given new shape or used differently in L2	Glottal stop for [t] in English [bʌʔə] (*butter*); used in word onset in German [ʔabent] (*Abend* 'evening')
4	Overdifferentiation	Item absent in L1 but found in L2	Nouns have grammatical gender in German (*der Tisch* 'the table'; *das Messer* 'the knife'; **die** Flasche 'the bottle')
5	Split	One form in L1 but two in L2	know < *wissen* (facts) / *kennen* (people)

Table 20.2   Developmental sequence of L2 question formation

Stage	Example
1. Rising intonation	*You like sushi?*
2. Wh-questions without inversion	*Where you want coffee?*
3. Inversion	*Are you my teacher?*
4. Embedded questions, with inappropriate inversion	*I don't know what do you want*
5. Embedded questions without inversion	*They asked what you said*

Contrastive Analysis implied that second language learning involved picking up aspects of the second language that are different from the first language. The Interlanguage approach, however, focuses on the fact that language learning involves building a system for the language and that as we do this we continually assess what we have built by checking it against new input. This is no less true for second language learning than it is for first language acquisition. It is argued that all learners do this in the same way, regardless of their first language experience. Therefore, there should be common patterns to, say, the structures produced by learners of English as a second language, no matter what their first language is. One such pattern is seen in a 'developmental sequence' of how such learners produce question forms, as in Table 20.2.

More thorough research has shown, however, that there are differences between learners with regard to developmental sequences such as this, and that at least some of those differences may be attributed to the particular first language involved (for instance, German speakers learning English tend to go through a stage where they invert the subject and the main verb, as in *Like you sushi?*). It would seem then, that to understand the process of building a second language, we need to consider aspects of both the first and the second language, as well as the characteristics of the learner and the learning situation.

Where next?

Having looked at some of the issues involved in second language learning, are we able to provide a recipe for successful language learning? As we have just indicated, we probably need to think about the first and second language and the differences between them as well as any natural order for learning the second language. We have also seen that the learner's motivation to learn is a key factor, and that age can play a role too. Finally, there are many further individual factors that have been examined for their role in language learning, and that we have not had space to detail here. These include getting on well in group learning situations; being prepared to make mistakes, even if it makes you look foolish; making good use of all available learning opportunities; being able to make use of learning that is focused on meaning (through interactions, etc.), as well as learning that is focused on form (through drills and vocabulary lists). These factors in turn will have different relevance in different learning situations. In short, there is no easy answer as to how to build another tongue.

SOME POINTS TO PONDER

▶ Why might it be an advantage to keep a foreign accent?
▶ Why is there no simple answer to the question of how age influences second language learning?
▶ Make a list of the similarities and differences you think there may be between the first and second language learning contexts. Discuss how important these similarities and differences might be in predicting the success or otherwise of second language learning.
▶ An important issue that has not been discussed in any detail in this chapter concerns the personality traits of the second language learner. How do you think personality differences might affect second language learning?

READING AND REFERENCES

A good selection of textbooks on second language learning is available. Most, such as those by Ellis (1985) and by Lightbown and Spada (1999) listed below give a historical perspective that includes discussion of Contrastive Analysis, Interlanguage and other approaches, as well as investigating social and psychological issues involved in language learning.

Probably the best known and most significant work on the impact of attitudes and motivation on language learning is reported in Gardner and Lambert (1972), and further developed in Gardner (1985).

Prator's hierarchy of difficulty derived from contrastive analysis of two languages was originally presented as a lecture in 1967, but has subsequently been widely reported in textbooks on second language learning and teaching, e.g. Ellis (1985).

Ellis, Rod (1985) *Understanding Second Language Acquisition* (Oxford: Oxford University Press).
Gardner, R. C. (1985) *Social Psychology and Second Language Learning: The Role of Attitudes and Motivation* (London: Edward Arnold).
Gardner, R. C. and W. Lambert (1972) *Attitudes and Motivation in Second-Language Learning* (Rowley, MA: Newbury House).
Johnson, Jacqueline S. and Elissa L. Newport (1989) 'Critical Period Effects in Second Language Learning: the Influence of Maturational State on the Acquisition of English as a Second Language', *Cognitive Psychology*, 21(1): 60–99.
Lightbown, Patsy and Nina Spada (1999) *How Languages are Learned* (Oxford: Oxford University Press).

You've Tasted the Whole Worm

What's the matter?

Have you ever stumbled over words or mixed them up when speaking? Have you ever committed a tip of the slongue as you watched a *patterkiller* turn into a *flutterby*? Why is it that we sometimes stumble over our words? And why do some types of slip happen more than others? There are two types of answer to these last two questions. One focuses on possible causes, and includes claims that errors reveal what we are really thinking. This is implied when people talk about making 'Freudian slips'. For instance, when one of the authors was talking about a sale of produce at their child's school, they said *it's a fund raiding exercise* (instead of *fund raising*) – did this reveal that they really felt the exercise was making a raid on their wallet? We hope not, but the example gives you an idea of the kind of interpretation that is sometimes given for speech errors.

The other type of answer is more interesting for linguists, especially *psycho*linguists. It focuses on the mechanisms of speech errors, rather than their underlying causes. So, what kinds of representations do we have in our heads for words and for other bits of language? What processes are involved in finding those representations when we want to talk or when we listen to others? How do we build utterances from these representations? In this chapter we look at psycholinguistic answers to some of these questions. We start by looking at what speech errors can tell us about how language works. Then we turn from the speaker to the listener, and think about how we recognize words in the stream of speech that we hear. Finally we look at how readers and listeners build up their understanding of sentences.

Tips of the slongue

What are speech errors? Essentially, they are lapses in the language production of native speakers. They are different from the errors made by learners who don't yet know the language fully. The two types of error generally provide evidence about different sorts of processes – general language production processes in the case of native speaker errors, and language learning processes in the case of learner errors. This is not to say that native speakers do not make learning errors, or that learners do not experience slips of the tongue. But the study of speech errors is largely focused on the kinds of error made by normal adult native speakers.

Speech errors are a wonderful source of data about how language works. They are wonderful because many of them are also entertaining – partly because of the kinds of Freudian interpretation mentioned earlier. They are wonderful also because they are relatively easy to observe. Except under special circumstances (see below), scientists do not need to bring speakers into the laboratory in order to collect speech error data. In fact, many collections of speech errors have been made by researchers taking their notebooks or tape recorders to lectures, conferences, staff rooms, and pretty much anywhere else they go, so that they can note down the errors that people make. Finally, for psycholinguists speech errors are wonderful mainly because they are not totally random, but seem to fit certain patterns. If speech errors were random and unpredictable, then it would be hard to learn anything from them, other than to say that from time to time something goes wrong. But because of their patterns, speech errors can tell us quite a bit about the normal language production processes, processes that have – for whatever reason – been disrupted.

The relative ease with which we can collect speech error data does have its costs. The main cost is concern over how comprehensive and reliable the data are. That is, many errors may go unnoticed simply because we usually expect speakers to make sense, and so we may unconsciously filter out or repair the errors that they make. In other cases, a speaker may choose the wrong word, but the word still fits the context in which it was said, and so the error may go unnoticed and uncorrected. This might be the case, for instance, if you are sitting in an office and ask someone to put something on the *table* when really you meant *desk*. In addition, even when we think we have spotted an error, we might not be able to determine what it is that the speaker meant to say, which makes interpreting the error more difficult. Better evidence about the intended utterance is available when the speaker notices the error and self-corrects, or when the researcher notes an error in their own speech production.

Like all listeners, the gatherer of speech errors is also open to 'slips of the ear', which can also make collections of errors unreliable. These errors include things like mishearing *She'll officially* … as *Sheila Fishley* …, or *a Coke and a Danish* as *a coconut Danish*. Slips of the ear are sometimes called MONDEGREENS, a term coined by Sylvia Wright in an article in *Atlantic Monthly* in 1954. As a child, Wright had heard a Scottish folk song that she thought included the lines *They had slain the Earl of Moray / And Lady Mondegreen*. In fact, as she realized much later, there was no Lady Mondegreen at all – the lyrics actually read *They had slain the Earl of Moray / And laid him on the green*.

Despite these potential shortcomings in data collection, speech errors can provide insights into how language is put together during speaking. Typically, speech errors are described in terms of the unit of language involved, and the type of the error. In the description of speech errors in English, the units are mostly words or sounds. The type of error includes choosing the wrong unit (SELECTION errors) or putting words or sounds together in the wrong order (ORDERING errors). At the word level, for instance, one word can substitute for another intended word, as in *white Anglo-Saxon prostitute* (where this last word was substituted for *Protestant*), or two words can compete so vigorously for the same utterance slot that they become blended, as in *He left it hangling there* (a blend of *hanging* and *dangling*). Ordering errors include ANTICIPATING an element later in the sentence, as in the sound error *We'll put your trash bans back*, where the [b] in *bans* anticipates the [b] in *back*, or the self-corrected word error *I suggest we kill all stone – all birds with one stone*. Or the error may show PERSEVERA-TION of an element, effectively the reverse of ANTICIPATION, as in *a phonological fool* for *a phonological rule*. Another ordering error is where two sounds or words swap places, as in spoonerisms (see below) and in word exchanges like *Seymour sliced the knife with a salami*.

The examples above are typical of the main types of error. What they show is that when we speak we marshal together linguistic units, finding words to make phrases and sounds to make words, and that sometimes something goes wrong at the point where we make a selection from our linguistic inventory. At other times, though we have selected the right elements, an error arises when they are inserted into the utterance, so that they end up in the wrong place.

How is the dictionary in your head organized? Is this MENTAL LEXICON like a written dictionary, sorted according to the forms of the words, but based perhaps on pronunciation rather than spelling? Or is it like a thesaurus, organized into areas of meaning? Looking at word selection errors can tell us about the probable organization of the mental lexicon. For instance, word substitutions generally involve inserting the opposite of what the speaker intended, as in *Must you leave? It's still so late!* (for *early*). So there is similarity of meaning. But there are also substitutions with similarity of form, such as . . . *a professional wrestler who was caused severe industry* (for *injury*). These form-based word selection errors are known as MALAPROPISMS after the character Mrs Malaprop from Sheridan's 1775 play *The Rivals*. Mrs Malaprop's examples include *I have since laid Sir Anthony's preposition before her* (for *proposition*). More recent celebrity examples come from US President George W. Bush: *We cannot let terrorists and rogue nations hold this nation hostile* (for *hostage*), and former Vice-President Dan Quayle: *Republicans understand the importance of bondage between a mother and child* (for *bonding*). With blends, we find that the words involved tend to be similar in both form and meaning, with a meaning relationship of (near-) equivalence rather than oppositeness. It is claimed that blends arise because two words compete for the same output slot, as in *baggage* and *luggage* producing *buggage*, or *slick* and *slippery* making *slickery*. Taken together, these word selection errors suggest that the mental lexicon is organized on the basis of meaning and form at the same time. Psycholinguists argue that words in the mental dictionary have all kinds of links to other words, creating a complex spider's web or network of connections.

Sound errors tell us how the sounds that make up words are organized and put together. Typically, sounds involved in misorderings occupy a similar slot in the structure of the word. Speakers make a plan for articulating what they want to say, and this plan includes the structure of the words that are going to be needed, with positions for where the consonants are going to be and where the vowels will fit in. When an ordering error arises, then vowels swap with other vowels and beginning consonants with other beginning consonants, and so on. Errors where beginning consonants get swapped are known as SPOONERISMS, named after William Spooner (1844–1930), who was Warden of New College Oxford. Whether by accident or design (some claim he did this for effect), Spooner became known for errors in which the beginning sounds of words were transposed, such as *You have hissed all my mystery lessons, and in fact tasted the whole worm. I must insist that you leave by the next town drain* and *the Lord is a shoving leopard.*

Not all speech error data come from observations of speakers going about their normal business of speaking. One group of psycholinguists devised an experimental method for inducing spoonerisms, largely because they were interested in what kinds of monitoring we do of our own speech output. In this experiment, participants saw series of word pairs. Within the series, the first word in a pair would almost always begin with one sound (let's call it sound A), and the second word with another sound (i.e. sound B, giving an AB order for the pair). After a long series of AB pairs like this, a pair appears where the first word starts with sound B and the second with sound A (a BA order). Normally the participants just had to read the words to themselves, but for some, notably for the BA pairs, they got an additional cue which told them to say the pair out loud as soon as possible. The experimenters were interested in how often the participants would be induced by the repeating AB pattern to produce an AB reading of the BA pair, and what kinds of things affected the participants' likelihood to do this. Table 21.1 gives some examples. The first three word pairs in each column illustrate the AB pattern that the experimenters were using, and the fourth pair is the BA order for which they were trying to induce a spoonerism, together with the result of the spoonerism, in italics. The number below that indicates the percentage of presentations of each type that resulted in spoonerisms.

Participants were much more likely to produce a spoonerism if the result was a sequence of two actual words of English (*shot hurt*, type 1) than if it

Table 21.1   **Example stimuli from spoonerism experiments**

Type 1	Type 2	Type 3
ship hull	ship hull	ship hull
short haul	short haul	short haul
sheet hem	sheet hem	sheet hem
hot shirt > *shot hurt*	heel shelf > *sheel helf*	hit shed > *shit head*
c. 20% slips	c. 6% slips	c. 4% slips

was two nonsense words (*sheel helf*, type 2). This indicates that speakers have a monitoring system that tries to ensure that our output is made up of real words – this finding matches the discovery that spontaneous slips of the tongue are much more likely to produce real words than nonsense words. What is of additional interest is that items in lists like type 3 resulted in fewer spoonerisms even than those in type 2. This indicates that the monitoring system not only makes sure that the output is real words, but also that these are not rude, potentially taboo words or phrases like *shit head*. Other pairs that resisted spoonerism were *bird tins, smart fell, tool kits, fits tall, duck sick*.

These studies of spontaneous and induced speech errors are just one source of data about language production. Others include tongue-twisters and patterns of hesitation and speech pauses, as well as the speech patterns of brain-damaged patients (see Chapter 23).

Finding the right words

Do you know the word *splundle*? It shouldn't take you too long to say that you don't. Now imagine that you had to look through the dictionary in your head to check whether *splundle* was there. Let us guess that your mental lexicon contains some 30,000 words. (As is pointed out in Chapter 7, estimating the size of someone's vocabulary is not straightforward, so this must remain a guess.) Even at an astonishing rate of 100 words per second, which is 20 times as fast as a good reading pace of 300 words per minute, it would take you five minutes to search all the way through and decide that *splundle* is not there. Clearly, then, we don't find the words that we hear (or not find the non-words that we hear) by simply looking one-by-one through the list of words that we know. So just how do we locate a word in our mental lexicon so that we can find out what it means and work out how it contributes to the message that the speaker is trying to get across?

There are a number of views of this. Psycholinguists like to build these views into 'models' of the processes involved, and one of the most popular is the 'cohort' model. This model suggests that when we hear the first few sounds of a word we get hold of a group (or cohort) of words in our mental lexicon that begin with these sounds. For instance, if you are listening to the word *catapult* and you have heard the first two sounds ([kæ]) then you can access all words that you know that begin with these sounds (which include *cap, can, Canberra, carry, catch,* and many others – in one on-line resource, the MRC Psycholinguistic Database, there are 781 words listed as beginning with [kæ]). Of course, this happens very quickly and without us usually being aware of it. Once we have a cohort of words we can use two types of information to change the levels of 'activation' of each candidate. First, we continue to hear more sounds of the word. For instance, hearing [t] as the next sound increases the activation of *catapult, caterpillar* etc., and makes *cap, can, carry* less likely candidates. This effect of the actual sounds being heard is sometimes referred to as 'bottom-up' processing. At the same time, 'top-down' analysis can affect the likelihood of cohort members depending on whether or not they fit the current context. So if you are hearing [kæ] in the context *They fired the [kæ]*, then the information that you have retrieved from your mental lexicon about the verb *cancel* would mean that the activation level of this word would be greatly reduced because the word does not match the context. That is, it is grammatically very odd to have a verb following the article *the*, and so it does not make much sense to speak of *firing the cancel*. Other cohort members may be differentiated according to plausibility – for example, *caterpillar* will lose activation, since caterpillars tend not to be fired (Figure 21.1).

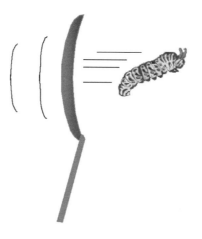

Figure 21.1   'They fired the caterpillar'

Usually the combination of bottom-up and top-down analysis will ensure that the appropriate word is rapidly recognized and interpreted. Researchers have run large numbers of experiments exploring the details of this kind of process. Because they are mainly exploring fast involuntary activities that listeners are involved in, the experiments have to be very sophisticated. Their results tell us a lot about how the mental lexicon organized, as well as about how we get words from that lexicon. For instance, just as we saw with the evidence from speech errors above, results of research on word recognition suggest two types of link between words – those that involve similarity of form (pronunciation) and those that involve similarity in meaning. It also turns out that words that we use often are easier to recognize – one metaphor that is used to describe how this might happen says that commonly used words have a higher 'resting' level of activation than infrequent words, and therefore get recognized more easily. And we get words from the dictionary not by checking against one word at a time, but by looking at clusters of words in parallel. So we are able to determine that *splundle* is not a word because all of the initially activated words lose most of their activation once we get to the [n]. This is much faster than checking against each of the 30,000 or so words in our dictionaries.

On being led up the garden path

As we start to recognize the words in a sentence, we build an interpretation of the sentence itself. This depends on knowing what kinds of words we are dealing with (nouns, verbs, articles, etc.) as well as what they might mean, i.e. on the kinds of information that become available from our mental lexicon as we recognize words. But how do we piece all this information together to understand a sentence? When they run experiments to try to answer this question, psycholinguists seem to delight in giving people particularly difficult sentences to work with. A relatively famous example in the psycholinguistic literature is *The horse raced past the barn fell.* You will probably find that you need to look at this sentence a few times before it makes sense. It is argued that this sentence is difficult because readers (and listeners) prefer to interpret *raced* as a main verb (with *the horse* as its subject, as in *The horse raced away from the rest of the field*). To understand the sentence as intended, we have to realize that it is a shortened form of *The horse which was raced past the barn fell,* just like *The boy given the lollies left* is a shortened form of *The boy who was given the lollies left.*

Sentences like *The horse raced past the barn fell* are called GARDEN PATH sentences, because the reader is 'led up the garden path', making an analysis which turns out to be wrong. Consider also your preferred interpretation of *The spy saw the man with the binoculars* – who has the binoculars, the spy or the man? It has been claimed that we process sentences using a preferred grammatical analysis, regardless of whether it makes sense. The preference for *The spy saw the man with the binoculars* is to assume that the phrase *with the binoculars* tells us about the verb *saw*, so that it is the spy who has the binoculars. Logically, then, if we read *The boy wrote to his friend with the broken tooth*, then the initially preferred analysis would be that the boy used the broken tooth to write to his friend. It is argued that we may not always be aware of having made the wrong analysis with this type of sentence, because we revise it so rapidly. Evidence showing that we do make a wrong analysis comes from measurements of where someone's eyes are looking while they read sentences like this – readers go back and reread earlier sections of sentences on which they have 'garden-pathed' even if they may not be conscious of having made the wrong interpretation. It is further argued that the cost of this type of revision (in terms of processing time or memory load) is small compared with the gains to be had from following a relatively automatic sentence analysis which works most of the time.

Other studies argue that our initial interpretation of sentences is determined not just by their grammatical structure, but also by other considerations, such as preferences for certain structures with certain words. For instance, you are less likely to think that *the driver* is the object of the verb *stopped* in *When the truck stopped the driver . . .* than in *When the police stopped the driver . . .*, and this is because the inanimate subject *truck* is not likely to stop a driver. Other features of sentences that are important for our understanding include the use of punctuation (*When the truck stopped, the driver . . .*) and prosody as an equivalent of punctuation in speech.

Where next?

Not everyone has a psycholinguistic laboratory where they can conduct the kinds of controlled listening and reading, speaking and writing experiments that are often needed to reveal more detail concerning how we produce and process language. But we can observe language users around us, and think about why they produce speech errors of certain types more than others, why they pause in certain places, or why they produce the writing or typing errors that they do. We can also think about why it is that certain sentences and phrases lead us to misunderstanding, albeit temporarily, or why we are entertained by certain headlines, such as *Sisters Reunited after 18 Years in Checkout Queue*, or *Hospitals Sued by 7 Foot Doctors*.

SOME POINTS TO PONDER

▶ What does speech error data tell us about how the dictionary in our heads might be organized?

▶ Using speech synthesis we can make a sound that is ambiguous between [g] (the first sound in *get*) and [k] (the first sound in *kit*). Let's call this sound X. Why do listeners interpret this as [g] in *leX* but as [k] in *fliX*?

▶ The word *dog* is more frequently used than the word *dock*, and *clock* is more frequent than *clog*. If listeners heard stimuli with the ambiguous consonant described in the previous question, which of the [g] and [k] sounds do you think they would be more likely to hear at the end of *doX* and *cloX*?

▶ Ask a group of friends to give you completions for the sentence *The man killed the bear with a ___*, and another group to do the same for the sentence *The man shot the bear with a ___*. In each of the responses, do the phrases from *with* to the end of the sentence tell you about the man or about the bear? Is this the same in both cases? If not, can you explain why not?

READING AND REFERENCES

A very accessible general introduction to psycholinguistics is Aitchison's *The Articulate Mammal* (2000), and a more detailed one can be found in Harley (2001). Aitchison (2003) also provides a good introduction to the organization of the mental lexicon.

The analysis of speech errors is given extensive coverage by Fromkin (1973, 1980) and Cutler (1982). The Appendix to Fromkin (1973) gives a long list of errors from her collection. The experimental work inducing spoonerisms is by Motley, Camden and Baars (1982). The most comprehensive review and collection of slips of the ear is Bond's (1999) book on this subject. A web search for *mondegreens* will turn up many interesting examples of mishearings, particularly of the lyrics of well-known songs.

Many of the issues involved in sentence processing are reviewed by Mitchell (1994) and by Pickering (1999).

Aitchison, Jean (2000) *The Articulate Mammal: An Introduction to Psycholinguistics*, 4th edn (London: Routledge).

Aitchison, Jean (2003) *Words in the Mind: An Introduction to the Mental Lexicon*, 3rd edn (Oxford: Blackwell).

Bond, Zinny S. (1999) *Slips of the Ear: Errors in the Perception of Casual Conversation* (San Diego, CA: Academic Press).

Cutler, Anne (ed.) (1982) *Slips of the Tongue and Language Production* (Berlin: Mouton).

Fromkin, Victoria A. (1973) *Speech Errors as Linguistic Evidence* (The Hague: Mouton).

Fromkin, Victoria A. (ed.) (1980) *Errors in Linguistic Performance: Slips of the Tongue, Ear, Pen, and Hand* (London: Academic Press).

Harley, Trevor (2001) *The Psychology of Language: From Data to Theory*, 2nd edn (Hove: Psychology Press).

Mitchell, Don C. (1994) 'Sentence Parsing', in Morton Ann Gernsbacher (ed.), *Handbook of Psycholinguistics* (San Diego, CA: Academic Press) pp. 375–409.

Motley, Michael T., Carl Camden and Bernard Baars (1982) 'Covert Formulation and Editing of Anomalies in Speech Production', *Journal of Verbal Learning and Verbal Behavior*, 21: 578–94.

Pickering, Martin J. (1999) 'Sentence Comprehension', in Simon C. Garrod and Martin J. Pickering (eds), *Language Processing* (Hove: Psychology Press) pp. 123–53.

<http://www.psy.uwa.edu.au/mrcdatabase/uwa_mrc.htm> – on-line version of the Medical Research Council Psycholinguistic Database; accessed 14 November 2004.

Is Language a Strait-jacket?

What's the matter?

When learning a second language you may have been struck by a word that captures quite neatly some idea for which you had not previously had an expression. This experience of finding that there is a single word for an idea or concept is quite satisfying, but at the same time you might find yourself wondering whether coming across the word somehow made the idea more real, that it perhaps didn't really exist as a concept until you had a word for it. An example encountered by one of the authors is the German word *Schadenfreude*, which roughly means 'malicious pleasure at other people's misfortunes'. Did the author take such pleasure before encountering the German word, or did the experience only really become crystallized by knowing there was a word for it? This chapter looks at some of the issues concerning this relationship between language and thought. This is a real chicken-and-egg problem – which came first, and which one makes the other possible?

A vision of the future?

George Orwell's novel *Nineteen Eighty-Four* contains some changes to the English language that reflect changes to society as portrayed in the novel, which he discusses in an appendix called 'The Principles of Newspeak'. The discussion highlights some of the views that might be taken on the relationship between how we use language and the way we (are able to) think.

> The purpose of Newspeak was not only to provide a medium of expression for the world-view and mental habits proper to the devotees of IngSoc [English Socialism], but *to make all other modes of thought impossible*. It was intended that when Newspeak had been adopted once and for all and Oldspeak forgotten, a heretical thought – that is, a thought diverging from the principles of IngSoc – should be literally unthinkable, *at least so far as thought is dependent on words*.   (Orwell 1949: Appendix; italics added)

Orwell discusses the word *free*. Under the circumstances portrayed in the novel, this could only be used with meanings as in *This dog is free from lice*, and not in the sense of politically or intellectually free, 'since political and intellectual freedom no longer existed even as concepts, and were therefore of necessity nameless' (ibid.). He also writes of how certain crimes would be impossible to commit, because 'they were nameless and therefore unimaginable' (ibid.). Before you say how neat it would be if crime control was that easy, think about what other kinds of control could be exercised, e.g. by banning expressions like *ice-cream*, *football*, *holiday*, etc. The picture that Orwell paints is one where language change is politically motivated, with the intention of increasing control over people's behaviour and belief systems. But the relationship between language and thought is complex, and Orwell is not alone in having contemplated whether thought influences language (concepts that do not exist are 'of necessity nameless') or vice versa (the absence of words for certain ideas makes them 'unimaginable'). One of the most widely discussed theories that supports the notion that thought is dependent on language is known as the Sapir–Whorf hypothesis.

The Sapir–Whorf Hypothesis

Edward Sapir (see Box 22.1) made a number of interesting observations on Native American languages that relate to the language-and-thought discussion. For instance, he noted that when speakers of Wintu (in the Penutian family of languages, and spoken in California) want to spread a piece of news they need to pay attention to whether the news is something they learned through direct observation or whether they heard it from someone else. This would be like the difference between seeing Pat scoring the winning goal yourself, and telling people about this, and hearing from someone else that Pat scored the winning goal, and then passing this information on. This is an important distinction for Wintu speakers, and is shown in endings on their verbs, much as English uses -*ed* to mark past tense. The implication is that the way in which Wintu marks things on its verbs compels Wintu speakers to adopt a certain way of thinking about the world. However, another way of looking at this is to argue that the Wintu language originally developed this marking because it was once culturally important for speakers of Wintu to indicate whether they knew something for a fact rather than on the basis of reports (so thought has influenced language). Subsequently, the language–thought relationship may have been reversed, so that later generations find that they have to choose between different verb forms and this makes them sensitive to the distinction between what they know to be true for themselves and what they have heard from others. Sapir's studies led him to the conclusion that 'the "real world" is to a large extent unconsciously built up on the language habits of the group' (1929: 209).

One of Sapir's students, Benjamin Whorf (see Box 22.2) was somewhat more explicit:

BOX 22.1   Edward Sapir

Edward Sapir (1884–1939), American anthropologist and linguist, was one of the leaders of structural linguistics. Trained at Columbia, Sapir taught at Chicago and Yale. He is perhaps best remembered in connection with the so-called Sapir–Whorf hypothesis, but was productive in many other areas of linguistics and produced linguistic descriptions of a range of Native American languages. His exploration of the relationships between language and culture, between linguistics and anthropology, led him to a view that language influences the ways in which people think.

'We dissect nature along lines laid down by our native languages. The categories and types that we isolate from the world of phenomena we do not find there because they stare every observer in the face; on the contrary, the world is presented in a kaleidoscopic flux of impressions which has to be organized by our minds – and this means largely by the linguistic system in our minds'.   (Whorf 1956: 213)

The views of Sapir and Whorf have been captured in what is referred to as the SAPIR-WHORF HYPOTHESIS, though it should be noted that the term was not coined by them. The hypothesis is often broken down into two basic ideas, known as LINGUISTIC RELATIVITY and LINGUISTIC DETERMINISM. Both deal with the questions of whether and how language influences thought.

BOX 22.2   Benjamin Lee Whorf

Benjamin Lee Whorf (1897–1941) had trained as a chemical engineer at the Massachusetts Institute of Technology, before working as a fire prevention inspector. He developed an interest in linguistics and anthropology, and in 1931 began studying linguistics at Yale University under Edward Sapir. Whorf's main linguistic interest was the study of Native American and Mesoamerican languages. He studied the Hopi language in great detail, and his observations of this language, as well as his experiences as a fire prevention inspector, were influential in his development of the notion of linguistic relativity.

LINGUISTIC RELATIVITY champions the differences between languages, and claims that because of these differences each language is likely to categorize the world in a unique fashion. So in the quotation above, Whorf talks about the 'kaleidoscopic flux of impressions' that needs to be categorized through language. An example that is often discussed in this context (and to which we return later in the chapter) is how languages refer to colours. The colour spectrum is effectively a continuum of different frequencies of light, but languages do not have an infinite range of colour terms to refer to all those different colours. Instead, each language has its own set of colour words, and each language puts boundaries between colour categories in different places. Whorf's work on Hopi (an Uto-Aztecan language from Arizona) resulted in a number of observations about the different ways in which languages carve up the perceived world. For instance, Hopi has one word for everything that flies but is not a bird. So Hopi speakers would group together planes, pilots, hot-air balloons, toy kites, etc. and use one word to refer to these as a category, distinct from birds. This seems odd to English speakers, because their language doesn't have the same category of non-bird flying-things (but see also Chapter 7).

LINGUISTIC DETERMINISM, as its label implies, is the idea that language can determine how we think about the world. There are strong and weak flavours of linguistic determinism. Strong linguistic determinism claims that language really does determine thought, so that language and thought are effectively one and the same. This strong version is not widely supported. Opponents argue that if language completely and utterly determines thought then thought should not be possible without language, and so how, for example, would pre-linguistic children be capable of logical deduction? And if language determines thought, then how and why would language have evolved in the first place (if early humans had no language and therefore no thought, it is unclear what they would need to communicate through language)? And how could children learn a language if they have no concepts for which they are trying to find verbal labels (see Chapter 18)?

Some of the examples given by Whorf of language determining thought and therefore behaviour have been vigorously challenged. On the basis of his experience as a fire prevention inspector, Whorf famously used the example of the word *empty* in *an empty gasoline drum*, and argued that the meaning of the word determines people's thought and behaviour, so that they treat the drum as safe. In reality, an empty gasoline drum is far from safe, Whorf points out, since it contains highly flammable fumes. A criticism of Whorf's view is that the danger results not from language determining thought, but from an inappropriate understanding of the situation, i.e. from not actually knowing that a drum that is empty of gasoline nevertheless can contain fumes. In another example, an employee who did not speak English as their first language placed drums of liquid labelled as 'highly inflammable' near a heater. They mistakenly thought that because a 'flammable' liquid is one that burns, then a 'highly inflammable' liquid must be one that does not burn. Again, critics point out that the issue here is inappropriate understanding, in this case of what the words mean.

The weak version of linguistic determinism maintains that language influences thought, but not that it determines it completely. In other words, the way in which language *encodes* reality might influence how we think about the world. Think again about those situations where learning a second language introduces us to new words like *Schadenfreude*. We might argue that because other languages encode things in different ways, the speakers of those languages get used to a different perspective on life. Of course, English can encode something of what is meant by *Schadenfreude*, but it takes several more words to do so than the one succinct word of German. This is why the German word has entered English dictionaries, indicating that *Schadenfreude* is now an accepted word of English, alongside hundreds of other loanwords like *cuisine, taboo, pyjamas*, etc.

What colour is that coffee pot?

A long-running (but amicable) dispute between one of the authors and his mother concerns the green coffee pot that she insists is brown. As indicated above, one of the areas where there has been frequent discussion of the relationship between language and thought is the use of colour terms. Physicists tell us that colours are spread out over a continuous dimension of wavelengths of light, but when we look at how languages refer to colours it seems that they have quite different inventories of colour terms. The question that arises is whether the availability of different colour terms influences our perception of colour? For example, ancient Greek did not distinguish *black* and *blue*, so were *black* and *blue* therefore not perceptually distinct for the citizens of ancient Greece?

Some of the early studies of colour terms suggested that the colours that people find easiest to describe and that are best remembered do depend on the language spoken. Researchers did experiments with coloured counters, asking people to look at a set of such counters, and then after some time to look at counters in a larger set and say which counters in this second set they had previously seen. They found that participants remembered best the colours that had the simplest or most basic colour terms in their language, and that these best-remembered colours depended on the language of the participant. For instance, if their language does not have separate words for 'yellow' and 'orange' (as is the case in Zuni, an Aztec-Tanoan language of New Mexico), then participants are not very good at remembering whether the yellow and orange counters were in the first set shown to them (compared for example with speakers of English). This seems to support the position of weak determinism – the availability of linguistic forms (basic colour words) for the colours has influenced the participants' memory for the counters they saw. It does not provide support for the strong version of determinism, since there is no sign that differences between the languages have affected participants' ability to actually perceive the differences between colours.

Another important issue that is frequently overlooked in these discussions is what physiologists and biological psychologists can tell us, namely that the eyes do not in fact register colours as though on a continuum, but rather that there are centres of perceptual salience and somewhat fuzzy boundaries between colours. So the results with coloured counters are at best weak evidence for determinism, since what they might really show is that if you have *both* a word for something *and* a strong visual image for it (e.g. an image for a perceptually central version of 'red') then these together aid recall.

Experiments with speakers of a language that only has two colour terms (Dani in Papua New Guinea) show that speakers are quicker to learn a new colour (i.e. have a better memory for it when asked to pick it out again) if it corresponds to a 'basic' colour like fire-engine red than if it is a more peripheral version of the colour (Heider 1972). Again, such a result could easily be explained in terms of perceptual salience of certain colours, irrespective of linguistic encoding of colours.

Further evidence for the role of perceptual salience in the use of colour terms comes from studies that show remarkable similarities across languages. In a range of languages from both industrialized and non-industrialized societies (the inclusion of the latter is important because earlier studies failed to control for the fact that speakers of different languages converse with one another in the global economy), it has been found that words for colours cluster at certain privileged points in perceptual space. These tend to be near (but not always at) the colours named *red, yellow, green, blue, purple, brown, orange, pink, black, white* and *grey* in English (Kay and Regier 2003). Earlier, Berlin and Kay (1969) suggested that variation between languages in their use of basic colour terms is constrained by a sort of pecking order, shown in Table 22.1. The table should be interpreted as follows: if a language has just two colour terms, then these will be for 'black' and 'white'. If it has a third term, it will be for 'red'; a fourth will be for either 'green' or 'yellow'; if it has five, these will be 'black', 'white', 'red', 'green' *and* 'yellow', and so on. Alternatively, if it is discovered that a language has a term for 'brown', then there is a good chance that it will also have terms for all the colours above 'brown' in the table. The relative perceptual salience of colours on this hierarchy is also reflected in the fact that children start to discriminate colours in roughly the order indicated. These various observations about colour terms suggest that perception influences language and not vice versa.

Table 22.1 Berlin and Kay's hierarchy of colour terms

Number of colour terms in a language	Colour terms included
2	'black' & 'white'
3	& 'red'
4, 5	& 'green' ∧ 'yellow'
6	& 'blue'
7	& 'brown'
8–11	& 'grey' ∧ 'orange' ∧ 'pink' ∧ 'purple'

Language and cognitive processes

A further aspect of the relationship between language and thought concerns whether the (type of) language we speak affects our ability in certain types of cognitive processes. Take basic number skills. Languages differ in the words that are available for counting. Do the differences between languages affect number skills? At the most basic level, there are languages that have a very limited set of counting words (equivalent perhaps to *one*, *two* and *many*). But there are other differences, such as precisely *how* numbers are encoded. One study compared English, French, Japanese and Korean. The words for the numbers 1–20 in those languages are shown in Table 22.2. Notice that Japanese and Korean are consistent in indicating place value (i.e. base 10) explicitly through the number words (so the words for *eleven* in these languages are 'ten-and-one' and so on), whereas English and French are less consistent. The researchers looked at the understanding of place value in children of around six years of age in the United States, France, Japan and Korea. They found that children in Japan and Korea, where the languages make place value most explicit, understood it earliest. It is of course possible that there are other differences between the children (e.g. in the educational systems and the emphasis placed on learning mathematical skills at an early age), but the implication taken from such data is that because place value is

Table 22.2   The numbers 1–20 in four languages

Number	English	French	Japanese	Korean
1	one	un	ichi	il
2	two	deux	ni	ee
3	three	trois	san	sam
4	four	quatre	shi	sah
5	five	cinq	go	oh
6	six	six	roku	yook
7	seven	sept	shichi	chil
8	eight	huit	hachi	pal
9	nine	neuf	kyu	goo
10	ten	dix	juu	shib
11	eleven	onze	juu-ichi	shib-il
12	twelve	douze	juu-ni	shib-ee
13	thirteen	treize	juu-san	shib-sam
14	fourteen	quatorze	juu-shi	shib-sah
15	fifteen	quinze	juu-go	shib-oh
16	sixteen	seize	juu-roku	shib-yook
17	seventeen	dix-sept	juu-shichi	shib-chil
18	eighteen	dix-huit	juu-hachi	shib-pal
19	nineteen	dix-neuf	juu-kyu	shib-goo
20	twenty	vingt	ni-juu	ee-shib

explicitly encoded in their languages, Japanese and Korean children have an advantage when it comes to conceptualizing place value.

Another neat set of examples exploring whether language is a strait-jacket involves eyewitness testimony. Eyewitness recall of events seems to be influenced by the way in which questions are put to them. One study showed participants a video of a traffic accident, and then asked them one of the two questions in (1).

(1a)   How fast were the cars going when they hit?
(1b)   How fast were the cars going when they smashed into each other?

As you might be able to predict, a higher estimate of speed was given by participants who were asked question (1b). In a related study, participants again saw a video of an accident and were asked one of the questions in (2). The second question, in which a definite article (*the*) is used, resulted in more 'yes' answers, even though the video showed no broken headlight.

(2a)   Did you see a broken headlight?
(2b)   Did you see the broken headlight?

We have given these examples because it has been argued that they show how language (the language of cross-examination) can influence memory for an event. But the use of this as evidence for linguistic determinism has been questioned, not least because it is not clear whether the language of the question has altered the participant's memory, or whether it has resulted in confusion between the actual remembered event and a reconstructed event based on the misinformation in the question. And in any case, other studies have shown that 'false memories' can be induced by non-linguistic means too (e.g. by photographs purporting to be of some event from the participant's past).

Finally, think about the language of advertising – are you more likely to buy a product that is 95 per cent fat free, or one that contains 5 per cent fat?

Where next?

The examples we have discussed have all been relatively controversial, which probably reflects the circular relationship between language and thought. The issue of whether colour terms determine colour perception or vice versa has still not been resolved, and is probably unlikely to be settled.

A crucial factor in the discussion of linguistic determinism is the notion of *codability*, or how easy it is to describe a concept using language. The closer something is to a central shade of a colour, then the easier it will be for speakers to describe that colour (compare a stop light and a fox). Historically, of course, the development of a term for that colour may have resulted from the fact that the colour had to be encoded ('coined') to meet some communicative need in the first place.

Tasks that explicitly ask participants to go through an encoding process (naming a colour) are perhaps asking them to raise a concept from unconscious to conscious thought. The psychoanalyst Sigmund Freud asks how a concept becomes conscious, and answers, 'By coming into connection with the verbal images that correspond to it' (1937: 248). So maybe language determines conscious thought, since thought is made conscious through language. But on this argument, we would conclude that language does not completely determine thought, because most thought is unconscious. And presumably we have a much richer range of concepts than can be brought to consciousness, if bringing thought to consciousness is limited by language. Encountering new encodings when learning a second language might just be unlocking some of those concepts.

To get a better understanding of this complex relationship between language and thought, the reader is encouraged to consult texts in semantics (the study of meaning) but also in linguistic anthropology and the philosophy of language.

SOME POINTS TO PONDER

▶ A variable message system used to indicate traffic conditions on New Zealand's motorways uses the words *incident ahead* rather than *accident ahead*, on the argument that it is not always at first clear whether a road block has been caused by an accident. Considering the various arguments raised in this chapter, discuss reasons for and against this policy.

▶ In the research on place value reported in this chapter, Korean children scored better than Japanese children, and English-speaking children scored better than French-speaking children. Is there any evidence in Table 22.2 for why either of these differences should be observed?

▶ Do you think that looking at how bilinguals use their two languages might be relevant to the issues discussed in this chapter?

▶ Look through a magazine or newspaper and consider the language used in advertising. Can you see how the choice of language is trying to influence thought, e.g. by 'sexing-up' the products advertised?

READING AND REFERENCES

The first detailed study on colour terms, which has spawned a huge number of further investigations, was conducted by Berlin and Kay (1969). This study and related works are of interest also to linguists who address the question of whether there are universal properties of language, i.e. features that can be found in all languages.

The relationship between language and number place value is explored by Miura et al. (1993). The work on eyewitness testimony by Elizabeth Loftus (Loftus and Palmer 1974; Loftus and Zanni 1975; see also Loftus 1996) has had a strong impact on how questions are asked of eyewitnesses, and has contributed to sensitivity to and reduction of leading questions in legal contexts.

Berlin, Brent and Paul Kay (1969) *Basic Color Terms: Their Universality and Evolution* (Berkeley, CA: University of California Press).

Freud, Sigmund (1937) 'The Ego and the Id', in John Rickman (ed.), *A General Selection from the Works of Sigmund Freud* (London: Hogarth Press).

Heider, Elinor (1972) 'Universals in Color Naming and Memory', *Journal of Experimental Psychology*, 93: 10–20.

Kay, Paul and Terry Regier (2003) 'Resolving the Question of Color Naming Universals', *Proceedings of the National Academy of Sciences of the United States of America*, 100 (15): 9085–9. (Available on-line at http://www.pubmedcentral. nih.gov/articlerender.fcgi?artid=166442; accessed 28 October 2004.)

Loftus, Elizabeth F. (1996) *Eyewitness Testimony* (Cambridge, MA: Harvard University Press).

Loftus, Elizabeth F. and John C. Palmer (1974) 'Reconstruction of Automobile Destruction', *Journal of Verbal Learning and Verbal Behavior*, 13: 585–9.

Loftus, Elizabeth F. and G. Zanni (1975) 'Eyewitness Testimony: The Influence of the Wording of a Question', *Bulletin of the Psychonomic Society*, 5: 86–8.

Miura, Irene T., Y. Okamoto, C. C. Kim, M. Steere and M. Fayol (1993) 'First Graders' Cognitive Representation of Number and Understanding of Place Value: Cross-national Comparisons – France, Japan, Korea, Sweden, and the United States', *Journal of Educational Psychology*, 85: 24–30.

Orwell, George (1949) *Nineteen Eighty-four: A Novel* (London: Secker & Warburg).

Sapir, Edward (1929) 'The Status of Linguistics as a Science', *Language*, 5: 207–14.

Whorf, Benjamin L. (1956) *Language, Thought and Reality: Selected Writings of Benjamin Lee Whorf'*, ed. John B. Carroll (New York: John Wiley).

When Language Breaks Down

What's the matter?

An elderly relative of one of the authors was once in hospital after having suffered a stroke, and asked his wife if on her next visit she could bring him some more socks. Since he was still confined to bed, she found it difficult to grasp why he wanted socks, and asked whether that was what he really wanted. His reply was 'Yes, I want socks, socks ... for my nose', which caused some (rather unkind) chuckling around the bed. While this may be amusing to the bystander, to the person experiencing this kind of difficulty with words it can be very distressing. The elderly relative – showing signs here of a PARALEXIA (using one word for another) – certainly had no inkling that he had said anything unusual. He genuinely believed he was talking about handkerchiefs and found the chuckles confusing and irritating.

Linguists and psychologists find language breakdown interesting and informative, since it can tell us about the workings of the 'normal' system in the same way that inspecting a broken piece of machinery (a car, say) might be able to tell us something about how that machinery normally works. (See similar comments in the discussion of speech errors in Chapter 21.) There are, however, very many different types of breakdown, and a major concern for the theorist (which may turn into a practical concern for the therapist) is to determine patterns of abnormal behaviour and relate these to different types of damage.

Why does language break down?

Most research in the area of language breakdown focuses on brain damage rather than chemical imbalance such as you might find in Parkinson's disease or in cases of severe depression. With brain damage, the loss of (parts of) language usually means loss of use of parts of the brain.

There are various causes of brain damage, but the main ones are head injury (quite frequently as a result of road accidents) and stroke. In strokes, a blood vessel in the brain becomes blocked or bursts, causing damage to nearby cells. Stroke damage tends to be more localized than damage from head injury, but both can result in impairment in one or more of a range of skills, many of which have an impact on an individual's ability to use language. Generally, though, if the patient's language abilities have been affected, then there will almost certainly be damage to the 'language areas' of the brain. Depending on where precisely the damage is, it will result in one or more types of impairment to the patient's ability to produce or understand spoken and/or written language.

The language areas of the brain are mainly in the LEFT HEMISPHERE (left half of the brain) with subparts having special responsibility for different language-related tasks. Recovery of language abilities after damage to these parts of the brain is variable, and depends on the age of the patient as well as on the type of damage. One of the main findings, as noted in Chapter 20, is that children up to the ages of 11–14 are able to learn or relearn language quite successfully. Often this involves using parts of the right hemisphere of the brain (if that has not also been damaged) for tasks that they would not otherwise have been used for. If the brain damage occurs after puberty, then it is generally more difficult to train other parts of the brain to take on responsibility for language. This finding is related to the idea that there is a critical period for language, which is before brain areas become relatively fixed in their specializations for certain skills.

Finding out what has happened to a brain-damaged patient can be something of a puzzle, since what we see on the surface, in terms of the patient's behaviour, could be due to one or more of a number of factors. For instance, a patient may be unable to say the word *pineapple* when asked to name that piece of fruit. This inability could have a number of causes, not all of which need involve components of the language faculty; and those that do involve language skills could involve different aspects of language. It could be that the patient no longer recognizes pineapples, in which case this is not specifically a language impairment. Or it may be that the patient cannot retrieve the word *pineapple* from their mental lexicon. This may in turn involve a break in some link between the concept of a pineapple and the word that expresses that concept, or it may mean that the word itself has been 'deleted'. Or perhaps the patient can find the word *pineapple* in their mental lexicon but cannot put together a plan for the sounds that make the word. Or the patient may no longer have sufficient physical control over their articulators (tongue, etc.) to make the sounds. What researchers and therapists look for is a bundle of things that the patient can and can not do, which may lead to the identification of a particular syndrome. And when patients with different bundles of symptoms are compared, then we can start to say some interesting things about how language works.

Types of language breakdown are broadly grouped into those that affect spoken language, which are usually referred to as types of APHASIA, and those that affect written language, or DYSLEXIAS. A range of language skills are affected by each of these kinds of impairment (and a patient can of course suffer from both at the same time). Here we are going to explore a few aspects of how the use of words and sentences is disrupted.

Lost for words

A patient's control of words can be affected in a number of ways – the example at the beginning of this chapter illustrated how one patient was able to use words, but did not always find the right one. A general term for this is ANOMIA (i.e. the loss of the ability to name things). Using the right kinds of tests, a therapist can show that although the patient is able to recognize some object that they have to name, they just can't say the right word for it. The therapist will also check that the patient has no difficulties with saying the sounds in the word, and that the problem really is that the patient can no longer find the right word. In a way, anomia is an extreme version of the tip-of-the-tongue phenomenon that we all experience when we know that there is word for something but we just can't find it – we know the thing or idea that we want to name, we have no difficulty with pronunciation, we just infuriatingly can't find the name (although research shows that we can remember some aspects of its name, like roughly how long it is, what sounds it starts with, etc.). Anomic patients will generally either say nothing at all when asked to name an object or they will give a wrong word. If they give a wrong word, it will often be related in meaning, like *sock* for *handkerchief, dog* for *cat, chair* for *table, knee* for *elbow*. Sometimes, patients will produce a word that has a similar form, such as *sympathy* for *symphony, leasing* for *ceiling,* or even a nonsense form that is similar to the intended word, such as *plick* for *clip, tubber* for *butter.* It is interesting to note that these difficulties are similar to the confusions evident in speech errors when non-impaired language users get words mixed up (see Chapter 21). Also, the nonsense forms are similar to nonsense words that might result from slips of the tongue when sounds are misplaced – typically these involve sounds from similar positions (e.g. the beginnings of syllables, like in *tubber* for *butter* and *leasing* for *ceiling*). That is, the anomic data and the speech error data together reflect the same basic patterns of organization of the mental lexicon, involving both meaning and form, as well as telling us something about how words are put together prior to articulation. The organization of the mental lexicon in terms of areas of meaning is reflected also in examples of selective anomia, where rather specific areas of meaning are affected, for instance just household objects or animals. Again, word substitutions in speech errors frequently involve words from the same semantic field. The fact that there are these common patterns in the results of brain damage and in speech error data is not surprising given that the intact language system would have been very similar in both cases.

One interesting example shows how anomia can be temporary, resulting from a short-term problem with blood flow through part of the brain, and with full recovery possible. The example involves the cognitive psychologist Mark Ashcraft, who was afterwards able to reflect on his experiences in a scientific article (Ashcraft 1993). While at work one day, Ashcraft suddenly found himself unable to use certain words which, although they were not ordinary everyday words, were nevertheless part of his everyday professional vocabulary, e.g. *data, experiment* and *printout.* Though he was still aware of the concepts they stood for, he just could not find these words when he wanted to talk about the day's work. Other word types were not affected, and he had no impression that his thinking was otherwise impaired. He was aware of what was going on, and was otherwise able to function (sit, walk, talk, etc.) quite normally. When he telephoned his wife, she noticed that something was not quite right, and that he sounded confused. She insisted that he be taken to hospital, but as he was about to leave – about 45 minutes after he first noticed that something was wrong – he suddenly found that he could recall the words that had previously been lost to him. He went to hospital anyway and learned that a small defect in his brain had diverted blood from some of the brain tissue, and that this very localized damage had resulted in the temporary anomia. Note that the anomia affected a very specific area of Ashcraft's vocabulary, and had no apparent effect on other linguistic skills such as grammar and pronunciation. This indicates how localized, biologically speaking, aspects of language ability can be.

Ashcraft and other people experiencing anomia have trouble finding words that they previously knew. Other effects of brain damage on word skills include word deafness and word blindness. It is worth looking briefly at these because they too can tell us something about how the language system normally works. WORD DEAFNESS is rare. The patient can't understand spoken words, but can read, write and speak normally. When they hear someone speaking their own language it frequently just sounds like a language they do not know. In some cases they can repeat back a word that they have heard, and even write it down, but without understanding it. Sometimes if they write the word down and then look at what they have written, they can understand it from the written form. Some of these patients are able to say accurately whether what they are hearing is a real word of the language (*smart, school, frost*) or a non-word (*slart, frool, smost*), despite not understanding the word, and even though the non-word may be very similar to a real word of the language.

We can try to make sense of this rather puzzling situation by thinking about what is involved in using words. Imagine that a simplified dictionary entry in our head is something like the parts of Figure 23.1 that are enclosed by the dotted line. There is a set of word meanings, represented by the picture of a cat, and some information about the word's written and spoken forms (*cat* and [kæt] respectively). Normally, we might expect to find the meaning of a word that we hear and that we already know by following the route marked with an A. Similarly, the route for finding the meaning of a word that we read would be via D. In the case of word deafness, it appears that the patient still has the word (they can find the meaning when they read it, and they are able to find the word in unprompted speaking or writing), and that they do not have any difficulty hearing sounds (as shown by their ability to accurately tell whether a word is a real word or a non-word). It seems that something is blocking the route marked as A. If they can tell whether [kæt] is a word, then the blockage is probably somewhere between the representation for the spoken form of the word and the stored meanings of the word, i.e. it affects the second arrow in route A. The strategy that works for the patient, in terms of finding the meaning of a spoken word, is to avoid the A route, and find the D route, via B (writing the word down) and C (reading the written form).

Our sketch is also useful when we look at WORD BLINDNESS, which is when a patient is unable to understand written words, but can read them aloud. Usually the patient can also tell you which written forms are real words even though they cannot understand them. We imagine that you will be able to add the appropriate routes to the sketch to show this, and that you would predict that such patients can often understand written words when they read them out loud.

Figure 23.1 is something of a simplification of the processes involved. For instance, what a patient with word deafness is most likely able to do is to 'translate' the heard form of the word ([kæt]) to a written form using correspondences between sounds and letters (so [k] to <c> or <k>, [æ] to <a>, [t] to <t>). Similarly the patient with word blindness may be able to read the letters of the written word and translate these to sounds in order to speak and then hear the word. The ways in which we get from the written form of words to the spoken form is one aspect of studying various types of DYSLEXIA. Just as looking at different types of word-finding difficulty can fill in some of the details of the sketch above, so looking at different dyslexias tells us about the normal processes of reading. In one type, known as SURFACE DYSLEXIA, patients perform poorly when reading real words aloud, particularly words with irregular spellings, i.e. words where the spelling does not follow some general convention for how the word should sound, like *love* and *steak*

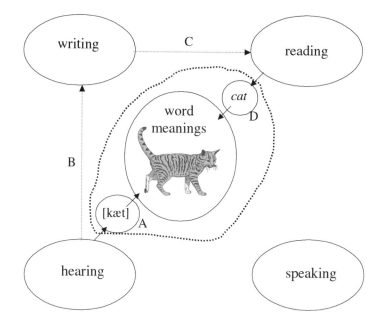

Figure 23.1   A sketch of the relationship between a dictionary entry and language skills

(which, if regular, would rhyme with *stove* and *leak*). However, these patients are very good at reading aloud nonsense words (*flane, yed*). These two behaviours suggest that surface dyslexics are using a rule system for converting letters to sounds, and aren't able to get hold of information that tells them about the exceptions like *love* and *steak*. Since information about the exceptions is almost certainly stored with those words in the mental dictionary, it appears that surface dyslexics are unable to use lexical knowledge in determining pronunciation.

Contrasting with surface dyslexics are patients with PHONOLOGICAL DYSLEXIA. They show good performance with real words, but poor performance with nonsense words. It appears that these patients have lost the rule system for converting letters to sounds, but are able to use lexical information to get a pronunciation for a word.

Taken together, these dyslexias suggest that reading aloud uses two different mechanisms – one is outside the dictionary, and involves rules for converting letters to sounds, and the other is inside the dictionary, where information about pronunciation is stored alongside other information associated with a word. This is known as a 'dual route' model of reading aloud. Normally we have access to both routes, as and when required; patients may not be so lucky.

Beyond words

As well as having consequences for finding words, brain damage can affect a patient's ability to manage the sentence structures of language. Generally, aphasic patients, i.e. those with problems affecting their spoken language, speak rather hesitantly and may also have problems understanding other people's speech. However, some interesting differences between patients with damage in different brain areas have been identified, an important one being between damage in BROCA'S AREA and damage in WERNICKE'S AREA (see Figure 23.2).

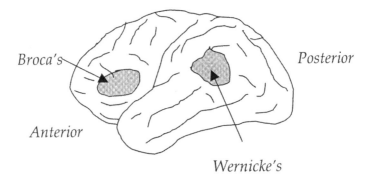

Figure 23.2   Sketch of the left hemisphere of the human brain

So-called BROCA'S APHASICS (i.e. those with damage in Broca's area) produce non-fluent speech, which is striking for its almost total lack of grammatical words, such as articles (*the, a*), prepositions (*in, on, at*), etc., as well as of grammatical endings like plural *–s* or the *–s* that marks the third person singular present tense of a verb, or the *–ed* that marks past tense. These patients can locate the words for things they want to talk about, but find it difficult to put the words together into well-formed sentences. Their speech is AGRAMMATIC, i.e. lacking grammar. Obler and Gjerlow (1999) cite the following example of a patient describing a (dated and sexist) picture that is often used in diagnosis of aphasia, the 'Cookie Theft' Picture (see Figure 23.3).

(1) kid . . . kk . . . can . . . candy . . . cookie . . . caandy . . . well I don't know but it's writ . . . easy does it . . . slam . . . early . . . fall . . . men . . . many . . . no . . . girl. dishes . . . soap . . . soap . . . water . . . water . . . falling pah that's all . . . dish . . . that's all.

The only really fluent phrases in such examples are rather formulaic stretches like *well I don't know.* As far as comprehension is concerned, Broca's aphasics can usually understand everyday conversations very well, but might find more complex sentences rather difficult to work out. For instance, when confronted with the sentences in (2) to (4), they may be more likely to say that (4) rather than (3) is equivalent to (2), basing their decision on the surface order of words (following a subject-verb-object preference) rather than the grammatical structures.

(2) The dog bit the boy
(3) The boy was bitten by the dog
(4) The dog was bitten by the boy

Figure 23.3 The 'Cookie Theft' picture from the Boston Diagnostic Aphasia Exam (reprinted from Goodglass and Kaplan, 1983)

WERNICKE'S APHASICS produce quite different forms of language to those seen in Broca's aphasics, as shown by the example in (5), also a description of the scene in Figure 23.3. Here, the description is grammatically well-formed, and there appears to be no problem finding the grammatical words that were absent in passage (1). There are problems, however, with finding content words, i.e. the names for objects, etc.

(5)   First of all this is falling down, just about, and is gonna fall down and they're both getting something to eat . . . but the trouble is this is gonna let go and they're both gonna fall down . . . I can't see well enough but I believe that either she or will have some food that's not good for you and she's to get some for her, too . . . and that you get it there because they shouldn't go up there and get it unless you tell them that they could have it. And so this is falling down and for sure there's one they're going to have for food and, and this didn't come out right, the, uh, the stuff that's uh, good for, it's not good for you but it, but you love, um mum mum [smacks lips] . . . and that so they've . . . see that, I can't see whether it's in there or not . . .

Wernicke's patients use their fluency to paraphrase, as a strategy to get around problems with word-finding, such as *some food that's not good for you* for *cookies*. They also produce a lot of what are called NEOLOGISMS, i.e. nonsense words that don't actually exist as words of the language they are speaking (sometimes called *Jabberwocky* in psycholinguistics, after the poem by Lewis Carroll in *Through the Looking-Glass and What Alice found There*). These patients also have severe problems with language comprehension, and so are usually unaware of what they have themselves said.

The output of Wernicke's aphasia is typically a stream of relatively fluent but largely content-less speech, while Broca's aphasics produce disfluent speech but with good access to content words. Since the different patterns of language output from these aphasic types are linked to damage in different areas of the brain's left hemisphere, it can be concluded that different brain structures take primary responsibility for different language skills – structures in Broca's area handle grammar, while those in Wernicke's area are more closely associated with the storage and retrieval of contentful words.

Where next?

The kinds of language impairment that can result from brain damage are diverse, and there are many more types of aphasia and dyslexia than those described above. As one author puts it, 'almost anything that one can imagine going wrong with language *can* go wrong. And some things one would not imagine could go wrong *do*' (Altmann 1997: 204, italics in original).

It is clear that studying damage to language abilities can be highly informative for linguists and psychologists, who are interested in the mechanisms by which we are able to use language, which we usually do with no apparent effort. But we must not lose sight of the fact that the study of language damage is one of the main diagnostic tools of clinicians whose job is to help recovery in patients with brain damage, and that while the effects of such damage are fascinating for us as linguists, they can be debilitating for the patients themselves.

Language breakdown in aphasia and dyslexia is studied in greater depth in psychology than in linguistics, and readers interested in finding out more about the phenomena discussed in this chapter should turn to courses and textbooks in clinical psychology and the psychology of language.

SOME POINTS TO PONDER

▶ Using Figure 23.1, describe the blockage suffered by patients with word blindness. What route through this figure shows a strategy that such patients might take when they are reading for meaning?

▶ When they are asked to decide if something is a real word or a nonsense word, people usually find nonsense words like *brane* and *heet* more difficult to judge than nonsense words like *splud* or *maist*. Why is this (think about what the nonsense words would sound like)? Does this finding support any aspect of the dual route model of reading described in this chapter?

▶ This chapter has given examples of the speech of a Broca's aphasic and of a Wernicke's aphasic. How do these examples indicate that different aspects of language are located in different parts of the brain?

▶ What are the similarities between the word-finding difficulties shown by stroke patients and those found in speech errors, as described in Chapter 21? Why are these patterns of similarity interesting?

READING AND REFERENCES

An accessible introduction to some of the issues revealed by the study of brain-damaged patients can be found in chapter 12 of Altmann (1997), and in relevant chapters in most textbooks on the psychology of language. Obler and Gjerlow (1999) give a more detailed introductory description of neurological evidence concerning language skills and impairment. The experience of temporary word loss outlined earlier in the chapter is recounted by Ashcraft (1993). Sheila Hale (2003) provides a fascinating and moving memoir of her husband's experience of language loss through stroke.

Altmann, Gerry T. M. (1997) *The Ascent of Babel* (Oxford: Oxford University Press).

Ashcraft, Mark H. (1993) 'A Personal Case History of Transient Anomia', *Brain and Language*, 44(1): 47–57.

Goodglass, Harold, and Edith Kaplan (1983) *The Assessment of Aphasia and Related Disorders*, 2nd edn (Philadelphia, PA: Lea & Febiger).

Hale, Sheila (2003) *The Man Who Lost His Language* (London: Penguin Books).

Obler, Loraine K. and Kris Gjerlow (1999) *Language and the Brain* (Cambridge: Cambridge University Press).

Conclusion:
Who Cares about Language?

What's the matter?

We seem to be faced with two conflicting notions when we ask who cares about language. On the one hand, it seems that not enough people care: millionaires, politicians, pop stars and demagogues of all kinds will say (apparently) anything at all, whether it sounds elegant or not, whether it even makes sense or not. They are never stopped and asked to explain precisely what they mean or to clarify an expression which was expressed in impenetrable gobbledygook. Consider, for instance, the following examples of 'Bushisms' (things said by George W. Bush, President of the USA) for which he does not appear to have been held to account and which do not appear to cause him any practical or political disadvantage:

> We need to counter the shockwave of the evildoer by having individual rate cuts accelerated and by thinking about tax rebates.
> (http://politicalhumor.about.com/library/blbushisms2001.htm)

> Rarely is the question asked: Is our children learning?

> Families is where our nation finds hope, where wings take dream.
> (Cited in Weisberg 2001)

On the other hand, we seem to be surrounded by people who do care, but they are all people who are irrelevant to our own social goals. It does not matter whether it is our own parents who tell us to 'Talk nicely, dear' or people who write letters to the editor of the newspaper or fulminate on public-access radio, most of the things they are complaining about are either things which are simply incomprehensible to us or things which seem to have lost relevance in the current period. In neither case do we have any strong reason to stop and re-evaluate our own linguistic output.

Here are two pieces of writing which show something of the range. The first, from the Wellington, New Zealand, daily broadsheet *The Dominion*, of 16 March 1998 (though it might have come from almost anywhere in the world at almost any date were it not for mention of the Maori people of New Zealand). It points out that while some Maori people have been arguing in the press over whether they should be called *Maori* or *Maoris* (the Maori language has no plural marker on this word), others are amongst the most disadvantaged in New Zealand society on a number of measures. The writer concludes:

250

I would have thought that the best brains in Maoridom might apply their undoubted talents to things more important than grammar.

In other words, while people keep coming back to the importance of language, surely there are more important issues facing us today. That is a point of view with which it is difficult to argue.

The second piece of writing comes from the reviews section of a learned journal (Drazin 1999: 376).

Now the conventions of modern scientific publication are based on accumulated experience, as well as technological development . . ., and we break them at our peril. Originality in science is to be welcomed in general, but originality in spelling, punctuation and grammar is not. . . . [such originality] will make many points hard for students to follow.

In other words, if your language use is too far from what is expected (in any direction) it makes things difficult for current users. Although the writer does not say so expressly, we know from our own experience that it is just as difficult to read nineteenth-century science (or linguistics) as it is to read poorly expressed science (or linguistics) today. The books the authors of this work were given as textbooks when they were starting in tertiary education would be unreadable for many students today (and no, it was not all that long ago!).

So there are two apparently conflicting messages. The first is that language is a tool, and should function in the background as a means of allowing us to solve whatever problems we might have. It should not itself be the focus of attention. The second is that language is so important in the presentation of ourselves and our messages that it is vital to pay attention to it. Indeed, some writers would say, it is so vital that if we cannot get the language right, the chances are we will not be able to get anything else right either.

The two are perhaps not as much in conflict as they first appear. We could perhaps rephrase the ideas as follows: good presentation of self and message is a fundamental skill which has to be taught, but once it is taught should then become a basic tool rather than a focus of everyone's attention. With such a formulation, we can see that the two may be compatible, but may apply to different stages in our education. Unfortunately, this is not the choice we are usually faced with. It is much more normal to meet the either/or decision: talk about language and demand perfection or ignore language completely.

Who focuses on language?

Another way of looking at this is to consider who the people are who focus on language and why they should do so. Even though we know that all generalizations are wrong, including this one, we can see the relevant people as falling basically into four groups: the old, the extracters, the professionals and the annoyed.

The old

The old may literally be old or they may just be conservative in this regard, possibly as a result of having been educated in a conservative institution. It is hard for us to remember that there are still people around who were 'taught' 'good English' with the tip of a cane. It was, in many cases, literally beaten into them. Learning to write or talk 'properly' (as defined by the school authorities) was a painful process. The reason that it was so painful was, of course, that this form of English did not come naturally to the people concerned. Their native variety of English was different from the expected form perhaps only in a few details, but these were seen as being crucial details. Breaking the rules that were propounded within the educational system was met with immediate sanction. Having had to learn the rules so painfully (and with such difficulty), these people find it very unjust when younger people break these same rules with impunity, without any sanctions being imposed whatsoever. Not only are no sanctions imposed, these people may even appear to succeed and gain prestige by using a variety of English in which these rules are not maintained (see the examples from Bush cited earlier). This seems doubly unjust, and it is understandable that the people concerned should feel aggrieved. Telling them that the rules that were imposed so fiercely were simply attempts to maintain the superiority of an earlier elite and had no particular value in themselves is not going to help in this kind of instance, even if we believe this to be the case. Telling someone they suffered in vain will not endear you to them.

Even if the sanctions imposed were not as draconian as corporal punishment, social sanctions may have felt just as important, and may have just the same effect. We are certainly subject to similar social sanctions today, even if not for the same linguistic errors. There are so many words meaning 'really good' among children in different parts of the world and at different times that we cannot possibly guess what it was you said when you were 14. But we are quite sure that if you had come out with *swinging* (which was used when two of the authors were about that age) or *random* (which was used recently by a group of 14-year-olds we know) your peers would have laughed you out of court.

The extracters

By extracters we mean here people who are attempting to extract information from texts, usually written texts, though the possibility of spoken texts cannot be ignored, without any interaction with the person who produced the text. In conversation, if you say something your listener doesn't immediately understand, they may signal (verbally, or by their expression) that they do not follow, and you can clarify your intention. In a fixed text you cannot do this; the text has to explain itself. So you are extracters, trying to extract meaning from our text, this book. But you are not the types of extracters we have in mind here.

A scarier kind of extracter is the human resource manager who tries to extract from a letter of application enough information to decide whether or not you should be offered a job interview. It is quite interesting to see what some of these people say. One, interviewed in *Metro* magazine (no. 104) for February 1990 said:

> As a consultant, you'd think twice before recommending someone, *no matter how well qualified otherwise*, who speaks badly, uses poor grammar and spells badly. You'd be surprised how many people submit a curriculum vitae which mentions a batchelor's degree. [Our italics; can you see the point of the last sentence in this comment?]

Such people wield tremendous power, and the only way to get past them is to play their own game, whether or not you believe that it is a fair game or a meaningful one.

The professionals

By 'professional' here we do not mean 'linguists', although they are in many ways the ideal professionals for dealing with language matters. We mean writers, lawyers, literary scholars, critics and others whose employment forces them to deal with texts and to judge texts on a daily basis. There is no doubt that such people develop a feeling for an effective text, a feeling which in most cases would be shared by others in a similar profession. Their comments tend to be based on what is the best, polished use of language for particular rhetorical purposes rather than on what is perfectly normal usage for everyday matters. Furthermore, such people tend to be rather conservative in their use, and to think in terms of written language not spoken language. In all of these ways they tend to differ from linguists who are trained to think about normal language use, spoken as well as written, and what is current usage as well as how that usage arose.

The annoyed

Everyone is familiar with the experience of saying a word like *hospital* ten times, and finding that it sounds really stupid. Because language works best when we are not thinking about precisely how we say individual words, the moment we start thinking about the mechanics of speech or the details of language, they start to feel really odd. We can be forced into this by having something drawn to our attention, either through the comments of some observer or through hearing it very frequently in a short period of time.

Sometimes the things we get annoyed about in this way are perfectly normal things that everyone says or uses. Using *you know* is a perfectly ordinary thing to do in conversation, but it becomes intrusive when someone does it very frequently and with no variation. Some of the things we get annoyed about are things which would not be normal in the most polished writing, but are perfectly normal in speech or informal writing.

Prescriptivists

From these last two groups in particular come the PRESCRIPTIVISTS, those who feel that they know how we should all speak and write and are willing to say so in public. Very often the things they have to say belong in the category of what Bauer and Trudgill (1998) call 'language myths', that is, things which many people believe to be true about language, but which are not demonstrably true. Examples of such myths are:

- children cannot read or write well any more;
- people in the media cannot write well any more;
- the language of people from one city (or one part of a city) is not as beautiful as the language of people from another city (or another part of the same city) (See Chapter 17.)

(See Bauer and Trudgill 1998 for these and other myths.) In particular, one of the recurrent themes in such complaints is that the speech of certain people (either individuals or groups) is not very good because it does not completely follow formal written language conventions. Rather than being a matter of complaint, this should be simply expected. The differences between the ways we speak (face to face with our interlocutor, having to produce a message under time pressure, subject to interruption and clarification) and the way we write (away from our audience, with relatively generous time to think about the formulation of the message and without interruptions from our audience) are themselves enough to guarantee that the two will be different, even before we start worrying about writing belonging in a literary tradition, being seen as a more prestigious activity, and so on. The argument that speech is not like writing (however well camouflaged) should never be suitable grounds for a complaint.

The view from linguistics

Linguists have four major points that they make again and again in response to the prescriptivist tradition. Since these points are frequently misunderstood, we will look at the misunderstanding once we have considered the individual points.

Lack of an independent arbiter

The prescriptive view is that there is an external measure of what is good in English (or any other language), a standard to which appeal can be made. Linguists, by contrast, see a language like English as being something extremely difficult to define; it is something which exists only in the outputs of people who are agreed to be using English. Since the evidence for English is in the output of millions of users of English, the only place we can look to see what English is like is in this output (of which we can only ever consider a very small portion). Any attempt to summarize and come up with a simple statement which will cover all of this output is inevitably flawed (a) because of the small sample considered, (b) because we are inevitably imperfect at stating generalizations about linguistic data and (c) because what we include in our sample is inevitably a subjective choice. So there is no external standard of what is English, and there is a fortiori no external standard of what is good English. Even where people agree about what is 'good' and what is 'bad' in English usage, these judgements tend to be made on the basis of a sample of very formal written English, which cannot be generalized to all of English in all possible environments. For all practical purposes, therefore, an appeal to an independent model of what is good English is an appeal to a fiction. English exists in its actual use.

The use of appropriateness as a guideline

Linguists point out that while it may be perfectly reasonable to talk to a baby using coos, gurgles, exaggerated intonation patterns, and a very small vocabulary, it would not be reasonable to address the audience at the university's graduation ceremony in the same way. On the other hand, it is probably not appropriate to address a baby in the same way that you would address a graduation ceremony. It is not that one is 'wrong' and the other is 'right'; it is that each is appropriate in a different environment. The same is true of the use of 'four-letter words', prepositions at the end of sentences, using *like* as a word introducing a speech act (*I was like, 'I'm not doing that!'*) and a host of other matters. Seeing them as right and wrong is less useful than seeing them as appropriate in different environments.

The ignorance of many commentators

A lot of prescription is based on the ignorance of the person making it. Some examples from our files should illustrate the point.

One commentator remarks that when the word *sophisticated* is used of competitors in beauty competitions it means that they are 'corrupted' because that is the real meaning of the word. A look in the *Oxford English Dictionary* (and look in the full edition, not the *Shorter* or the *Concise*) shows that one of the oldest meanings of *sophisticated* is, indeed, 'corrupted' or 'impure', especially when applied to fluids such as water and oils. The modern meaning used of people does not arise until the nineteenth century. But when we use *sophisticated* of a competitor in a beauty pageant, we are quite clearly not discussing water or oil, but a person, and the meaning is not at all ambiguous.

Another complains that 'we hear "meet with" instead of "meet", in disregard of the rule that transitive verbs are not followed by a preposition' (*New Zealand Listener*, 18–24 October 1986). The whole point is that *meet* can be used either transitively or intransitively; the speaker who uses *meet with* is not breaking any fundamental principle of transitivity. Rather the speaker is extending the pattern found in *have a meeting with*, which makes a perfectly logical analogy, and even allows us to say subtly whether the meeting was accidental or arranged.

Sometimes the errors are minor, like these two, sometimes they are quite crucial, but we see complaints about things which are perfectly in order so often that linguists are chary of making pronouncements about matters of language use without a little research.

The importance of language change

We have already seen that the only language which does not change is a dead language, and that the language of even five years ago is different from the language of today. By the time someone has noted that people are no longer making a distinction between the singular and plural of *criteria* or that *media* is being used as a singular noun, it is usually too late to stop the change. Many of the complaints about language usage are complaints that we should not have made the most recent change. Whatever one's personal feelings about this, making a fuss about it is as useful as making a fuss about the tide coming in or hemlines being a bit lower this year.

How this is interpreted and what it really means

Non-linguists find linguists totally wishy-washy when it comes to keeping up standards. Linguists, they feel, will accept anything, will say everything is perfectly in order, and will not help support the barricades against barbarisms in language and the decline of civilization (complaints are frequently expressed in this kind of emotional language).

Linguists say that people are trying to push them to accept and support norms which are not only artificial, but are already out of date. They see the value of a complaint tradition (Milroy and Milroy 1985) in stabilizing a standard language, but they feel that their function is not to take sides in these wars, which they see as being fundamentally misguided, but to describe the situation as it appears as objectively as possible.

This is what linguists are trained for. While not all linguists want to work among the people of Papua New Guinea or Vanuatu, writing down endangered languages, providing descriptions, grammars and writing systems for languages which have never known any of these things, nevertheless this is the kind of work which they are basically trained to do. They are trained to observe the patterns that are found in the speech of people, and determine what generalizations can be made about those patterns, so as to produce an economical, accurate and useful picture of the way in which language is spoken. How people feel about some of these patterns may be a useful piece of data; but it is not more important than what people actually say. Being asked to argue on behalf of or against some individual's subjective preference is thus not what linguists feel comfortable doing. Though there is a movement among some linguists to make their work more relevant to the communities they serve and less restricted to the ivory tower, nevertheless the more objectivist stance remains a dominant view within linguistics.

Where next?

People feel strongly about language, and some care passionately about it. So do linguists. But their passion tends to show itself in ways which are different from those shown by prescriptivists. You are now learning a little about being a consumer in the real world where these various attitudes are common currency. As wise consumers you need to know what to believe, where to find accurate information, and how to exploit what you know for your own ends.

There are times, such as in job interviews, when it is going to be to your benefit to play along with the normative view of being someone who is careful about language. As one reviewer said recently, 'Grammar is important if you want people to get the impression that you are paying attention to what you are saying or treating your audience with respect' (Lezard 2002). It is part of politeness. But there are times when you neither want to be polite nor need to be polite, and your language reflects that. Nobody is superpolite 100 per cent of the time. Learn how to read from people's language how they are reacting, rather than just judging their language as 'good' or 'bad'.

SOME POINTS TO PONDER

▶ There is an expression that somebody 'talks like a book'. Is that a positive or a negative judgement of the person concerned? Why is it worthy of comment? If people do not normally talk like books, why is that the case?

▶ One common prescriptive comment is that speakers today are losing useful distinctions between words like *uninterested* and *disinterested*, *imply* and *infer*, *less* and *fewer*, and so on. Try to find some sentences or contexts where the distinction between such words would be crucial to someone's understanding of what was said. What can you conclude? If losing useful distinctions is really what is at stake here, why are new distinctions like *meet* versus *meet with* rarely met with approbation?

▶ You may, like many young people all round the world, use 'quotative *like*' or 'quotative *all*' (as in *I was like, 'You can't do that!'*, or *I was all, 'Yeah, sure!'*). If you do, there are probably occasions on which you are more likely to use such expressions, and occasions on which you are less likely to use them. Think about when you are likely to use them, and then listen to your own or your friends' use over the next couple of days to see whether you were right. You may use these phrases more when talking to girls or when talking to boys; when talking to young people; when relating a series of events; when talking of your own reactions rather than someone else's; when speaking rather than when writing. How would you answer someone who claimed that such uses were simply 'wrong'?

▶ To find out what linguistic points people object to, you can read the Letters to the Editor column in newspapers or magazines. Some journals are a better source of such points than others. See if you can find some such letters. If you do, analyse them to see what point they are trying to make. It may be difficult to sort out exactly what is intended (it is hard to express yourself coherently in the few words you are allowed in a Letter to the Editor), but you should check in dictionaries and other reference works to see what the point is and whether it is correct. You should also ask yourself whether the matter is really one of right or wrong or one of appropriate or inappropriate.

READING AND REFERENCES

Bauer and Trudgill (1998) provide a relatively painless introduction to many of the misinformed ideas people have about language. Crystal (1984) shows that there are people who do care, and they tend to care about similar things. You need to consider why that might be. Part of the answer is given by Milroy and Milroy (1985), who talk about prescriptivism in the context of standardization. For some thought about what constitutes 'good English', see chapter 1 of Greenbaum (1988). Blamires (1994) is an example of an overtly prescriptive work. Some of the points made there are matters of good style or of logic; others are simply reactions to recent changes in English. The difficulty is to distinguish between these two types of observation.

Bauer, Laurie and Peter Trudgill (eds) (1998) *Language Myths* (Harmondsworth: Penguin).

Blamires, Harry (1994) *The Queen's English* (London: Bloomsbury).

Crystal, David (1984) *Who Cares about English Usage?* (Harmondsworth: Pelican).

Drazin, P. G. (1999) 'Review of J. Green, *Atmosphere Dynamics* (Cambridge University Press, 1999)', *Journal of Fluid Mechanics*, 400: 375–6.

Greenbaum, Sidney (1988) *Good English and the Grammarian* (London and New York: Longman).

Lezard, Nicholas (2002) 'Review of L. Trask, *Mind the Gaffe* (Penguin)', *Guardian Weekly*, 5–11 September.

Milroy, James and Lesley Milroy (1985) *Authority in Language* (London: Routledge and Kegan Paul).

Weisberg, Jacob (ed.) (2001) *Bushisms* (New York: Fireside).

Language Index

Afrikaans   42
Albanian   42, 43
American Sign Language (ASL)   53
Arabic   39, 93, 117
Aranda (Arunta)   92, 97, 100
Archi   77, 80
Armenian   42

Basque   43
Bengali   42, 143
Bislama   170
Breton   42, 43
Bulgarian   42

Catalan   42, 43
Common Scandinavian   27
Cornish   42, 43, 125
Czech   42

Dani   236
Danish   27, 42, 43
    compared with German   36, 44, 46–7
    similarity to Swedish   41
    vocabulary   73
Diyari   93, 94
Dutch   39, 42, 43, 45, 46, 75
Dyirbal   93

Enga   96
English
    Aboriginal   184
    acquisition of   199–200
    address in   137, 141
    African American Vernacular   181
    American   137, 141, 166, 187
    as a Germanic language   42, 43, 45
    as a 'killer' language   125, 128
    Australasian   159
    Australian   20, 67, 140, 187
    avoidance of   97, 100
    Belfast   20
    Birmingham   180
    British   137
    British Black   181
    changes in   70
    compounds in   31, 74–5, 76
    French influence on   46
    language of education   170
    Latin influence on   102
    Liverpool   180–1, 188
    loans in   95, 235
    loss of endings   27
    loss of number distinction   23
    Maori English   177, 184
    Mexican–American   184
    New York   181, 183
    New Zealand   137, 141, 158, 187
    nicknames   140
    non-native varieties   186–7
    number of sounds in   93, 194
    numbers in   237
    Old English   27, 30
    origins of suffixes   29–30
    pronunciation   31, 70
    RP (Received Pronunciation)   181,
        183, 186, 187
    Scottish   181
    Scouse   180–1, 188
    Singaporean   171
    source of creole   174
    source of loans   95
    South African   187
    spelling   61–71
    standard   175, 186
    syntax   94, 106
    Tyneside   148
    variability in   41
    verbs   8, 22, 31–2, 75–6, 94, 199,
        255
    vocabulary   73, 97, 161
    vocabulary change   31, 32
    word length in   86–8
Erromangan   76–7
Eskimoan languages   72–9, 89

Faroese   42

Farsi *see* Persian
Fijian 43
Finnish 43, 45, 70, 76
French
   as a Romance language 22, 42, 43,
     92
   Canadian 142, 163, 188
   colonial language 170, 208
   compared with Germanic languages
     36, 89
   gender in 8
   homophones in 96
   loans in 39
   numbers in 237
   paradigms in 76
   pronouns in 137
   sexism in 163
   source of loans 45, 46, 70, 95
   syntax of 28–9
   text messaging in 116–17
   variation in 148
Frisian 42, 43

Gaelic, Scottish 42
Gallego 43
Georgian 137
German
   compared with Danish 36, 44, 46–7
   compounds in 75, 88
   gender in 8
   Germanic language 42, 43, 45
   pronouns in 137
   syntax of 94, 105–6
   vocabulary of 2
Germanic languages 27, 39, 75
Gothic 42
Greek 42, 126
   Athenian versus Cretan 183
   Classical/Ancient Greek 42, 75, 235
   in New Zealand 127–8
   source of loans 70, 95
Gujarati 42

Hausa 45
Hawai'ian 44
Hebrew 12, 43, 106, 126, 131
Hindi 42, 177
Hittite 15
Hixkaryana 83, 129
Hopi 234
Hungarian 30

Icelandic 40, 42, 43, 95
   Old Icelandic 40
Indonesian 44
Inuit 72
Irish 42, 43
Italian
   as a Romance language 22, 39, 42,
     43, 92
   compared with Latin 27–8, 40
   patterns of sound 94
   pronouns in 137
   similarity to Spanish 41

Jamaican Creole (Patois) 169, 174
Japanese 10, 83, 94, 95, 106, 149, 176,
   237
Java 92
Javanese 176

Karelian 30
Kikuyu 194
Korean 237
Kunwinjku 97

Latin
   ancestor of the Romance
     languages 22, 23, 27, 39, 40,
     42, 43, 92
   infinitive in 102
   language of science 97
   number of vowels in 93
   paradigm size 94
   prestige of 102
   source of English words 30, 67, 70,
     95
   syntax of 94
   Vulgar Latin 39
Latvian 42
Lithuanian 42
Lwidakho 171

Malagasy 44
Maltese 43
Manx 125, 126, 127
Maori
   as a Polynesian language 43, 44, 45,
     130
   compared with Samoan 44, 45, 46
   decline and revitalization 128–9,
     131–3
   number of sounds 93

Maori – *continued*
    structures of   83, 94, 106, 130, 250
    vocabulary   94–5, 97
Marquesan   44
Menomini   127

Naman   131
Navajo   96
Nez Perce   96
Niuean   44
Norwegian   40, 42

Panjabi   42
Patois *see* Jamaican Creole
Persian   42, 106
Phrygian   12
Polish   42
Portuguese   22, 23, 42, 43, 92
Proto-Indo-European   15
Proto-World   45

Rapanui (Easter Island)   44
Romance languages   27, 39, 92
Romanian   23, 42, 43
Rotokas   194
Russian   9, 42, 43, 137

Samoan   43, 44, 45, 46, 176
Sanskrit   42
Sardinian   42
Serbian   42
Slovak   42
Slovenian   42
Spanish
    agreement in   9
    as a Romance language   22, 39, 42,
        43

change in   21
loans in   39
similarity to Italian   41
spelling of   70
vowels in   93
Swahili   9, 29, 43, 106, 148, 171–2
Swedish   41, 42, 43

Tagalog (Pilipino)   44
Tahitian   44
Tape   131
Thai   75
Tiwi   94
Tokelauan   44
Tongan   43, 44
Turkish   43, 45, 106
Tuyuca   130

Ubykh   129
Ukrainian   42
Ura   131
Urdu   42

Warlpiri   94, 97
Welsh   42, 43, 106, 126
West Greenlandic   43, 77–8
Wintu   232
Wolof   208

Yiddish 42
Yup'ik 78

Zulu   30
Zuni   235

!Xũ   93

General Index

accent   20, 62, 180
acceptability   103
accommodation   150
adjective   9
advertising   238
agrammatism   247
ambiguity   109
anomalist   14
anomia   243
anticipation   224
aphasia   242, 246
apostrophe   68–9
appropriateness   255
arbitrariness   14–15
Artificial Intelligence, first law of
   107
attitudes   127, 164, 166, 175
Austen, Jane   11, 34, 139
awareness, metalinguistic   210–11

babbling   195
baby-talk   98, 196
bees   51
Bible   7, 34, 159
bilingualism   170, 194, 203–11
   additive   205
   community   204
   country   204
   defined   204–6
   full or ideal   205
   personal   204–5
   simultaneous   205
   strategy for   205–6
   subtractive   205
   successive   205
blend   224
bonobo   54, 82
bottom-up processing   226
bow-wow theory   8–9
brain damage   241–2
Broca's aphasia   247
Broca's area   14, 246
Bush, George W.   224, 250

care-giver-ese   196
case-marking   28, 94, 106, 107
catastrophe   11, 14
category, grammatical   28
change
   intergenerational   21
   speed of   40, 256
   syntactic   27–9
Chaucer, Geoffrey   26
child-directed speech   196, 214
child language   112
chimpanzee   13, 38, 52–4
   pygmy see bonobo
Chomsky, Noam   53, 103, 200
citation   87
Clark, Helen   153
Clarke, Arthur C.   1
codability   238
code-mixing   171, 209
code-switching   171, 172, 208, 209
cognitive processes   237–8
cohort model   226
co-hyponym   74
colonization   127
colour terms   234, 235–6
communication, non-verbal   195
competence   171, 173
compound   75, 77
conservative language users   252, 253
consonant clusters   66, 195
consonant doubling   65
contact between languages   45
context, social   147, 148, 152, 170, 176,
   184–5
contrast   52, 165
contrastive analysis   218–20
core vocabulary   40
correctness   147–9
court of law   139–40
creole   55, 98, 99
Crichton, Michael   54
critical period   215
cultural transmission   54

Darwin, Charles   9, 10
daughter language   39
decision making   108–9
deep structure   103
design features   50–4
diachronic linguistics *see* historical
   linguistics
dialect   180
dialectology   23
ding-dong theory   10
discontinuity problem   11, 15–16, 49,
   55
discreteness   52
displacement   51
dog   49, 82
domain *see* context, social
dual articulation or duality of patterning
   51–2, 89
dual route model of reading   246
Dylan, Bob   63
dyslexia   242, 245
   phonological   246
   surface   245–6

economic reasons for language extinction
   128, 129, 173, 177
Elizabeth II   20
etymology   33
euphemism   162–3
eyewitness testimony   238

false memory   238
farewells   87
first language *see* language acquisition
flexibility, mental   210
foreigner-talk   98
formality   135, 147, 150, 152
Frederick II of Hohenstaufen   12
freedom from stimulus *see* displacement
Freudian slip   222

garden path sentence   228
gaze   195
gender   28, 141, 146–55
   gender identity   153–4
gene, FOXP2   14
generalization, supposed lack of   96
generic   157–8
gesture   15, 195, 214
gloss, inter-linear   28
gorilla   38, 53

grammar   46, 102–11
   descriptive   102
   emergence of   199–201
   internal   200
   learning of   216–17
   pivot   198
   prescriptive   102
   supposed lack of   95
   universal   103
   see also morphology, syntax
grammaticality   103
grammaticalization   30
greetings   87
Guinness Book of Records   88, 92

hedge   151, 154
hemisphere, left   242
Herodotus   11–12
historical linguistics   23
homophone   68, 96
hyperlect   182
hyponym and hyponymy   74

identity   130, 184–5
idiom   77, 87
imagery   161
incorporation   77
infant-directed speech   196
infinitive, split   102
infinity of language   82–9, 108
input, comprehensible   214
insult   141
interlanguage   218, 220
interruption   152–3

Jabberwocky   248
James IV of Scotland   12
Johnson, Samuel   26
Jones, Daniel   62
Joyce, James   86

keyboard see typewriter

la-la theory   10–11
language
   areas of the brain   242
   breakdown   241–9
   computer   107
   death   125–30
   first   194
   flowers, 'language' of   50

language – *continued*
  foreign   194
  myth   1, 254
  native   194
  natural   107
  nest   132
  processing   108
  related to thought   231
  second   194
language acquisition
  copying in   200
  first   193–201, 213
  grammatical development in
    199–200
  Language Acquisition Device (LAD)
    103
language family   41
  Afro-Asiatic   45
  Altaic   45
  Austronesian   41, 44
  Indo-European   41, 42
  Nostratic   45
  Uralic   45
language learning
  age in   215–17
  effect of first language in   218–20
  feedback in   214–15
  foreign   194
  motivation in   217–18
  natural approaches to   213
  practice in   214
  pronunciation in   216
  second   194, 213–21
language loss   126, 173, 241–9
language revitalization   126
language revival   126, 131–3
language shift   126, 172, 177
lateralization of brain function   215
letter   64–5, 66, 119
lexeme   77, 95
lexical item   77
lexicology   23
lexicon, mental   196, 224, 226, 243
lingua franca   171–2
linguistic determinism   233–5
linguistic relativity   233–5
listeme *see* lexical item
localization of brain function   244
logic   96–7

magic <e>   65

malapropism   224
matched guise   182
media   22, 129, 132, 186
memory   85, 87, 108–9
metaphor   161, 177
mondegreen   223
Monty Python   140
morphology   23, 33
Morse, Samuel   112
motherese   196
motivation, instrumental and integrative
  217–18
Mowgli   12
'Ms'   164
multilingualism   170
mutual comprehension   41

native speaker   125, 194
Neanderthal   13
neologism   248
Newspeak   231
Newton, Isaac   97
nickname   140
Norman Conquest   23
notation
  angle brackets   61
  asterisk   63
  decimal point   29
  italics   3
  square brackets   10, 61
noun   8, 77, 197
  phrase   105
number   23, 28

object   104, 105, 117–18
  indirect   105
onomatopoeia   8
ordering   224
original language, the   11–12
orthography   75, 131; *see also* spelling
Orwell, George   231
overextension   196–7
overgeneralization   199–200
overregularization   199–200

paradigm   76, 78, 100
paralexia   241
parent-ese   196
parrots   52
part of speech *see* word-class
pejoration   161

perseveration   224
person   23
phonetics   16, 33, 46, 70
phonology   46, 70
Piaget, Jean   200
pidgin   45, 55, 98, 99
pitch   153
plural *see* number
politeness   147, 149–51, 162, 257
polysynthetic language   77
pooh-pooh theory   9
postposition   107
predictability   112–17
predictive texting   114–16
preposition   106
prescriptivism   102, 254
prestige   23, 46, 183
productivity   51, 89
program, computer   107
pronoun   69
    address   and   137
    personal   69, 117–18, 174
    possessive   69, 174
    reflexive   69
protolanguage   55
proverb   87, 151
Psamtik I   12
pseudo-generic   159
psycholinguistics   113

Quayle, Dan   224
quotation   87

rate of change   40
rate of speech   2
reconstruction   39
redundancy   112–17
relatedness of languages   36–45
repertoire, linguistic   175, 177, 187
respect   143, 177
rules   89, 102
    transformational   103
Russell, Bertrand   49

Sapir, Edward   232, 233
Sapir–Whorf hypothesis   232–5
Saussure, Ferdinand de   14–15
school, bilingual   132
schwa   67
Scrabble   119
second language *see* language learning

selection   224
semanticity   50
semantics   23, 46
semilingualism   208
semiotics   15
sentence processing   228
setting, social *see* context, social
Seuss, Dr.   88
sexism   157–66
Shakespeare, William   50, 79, 95, 137
Shaw, George Bernard   61, 62
sign language   53
singular *see* number
slip of the ear   223
slip of the tongue   222–6
Société Linguistique de Paris (Paris
    Linguistic Society)   7
sociolinguistics   23
solidarity   136, 143, 177
song   10–11
sound symbolism   10; *see also*
    onomatopoeia
sounds, number of   93, 129, 194
speech error   222–6
    of anticipation, ordering,
        perseveration and selection   224
speech perception in infants   194–5
speech production in infants   195–201
spelling   61–71
    reform of   64
    see also orthography
spelling pronunciation   31
spoken language *see* written and spoken
    language
spoonerism   224, 225
standard
    external   255
    form   149, 254
    variety   23, 148, 186, 256
status   138, 152, 162, 163, 185, 186,
    187
    status-marked setting   140
stereotype   155, 165
stigmatization   186; *see also* prestige
stress   198
structure   117–19
surface structure   103
style   175–6, 176–7, 208; *see also*
    formality
subject   104, 105, 117–18
superordinate   74

swearing 150
Sweet, Henry 62
syntax 23, 33, 89, 90
  change in 27–9
  in ape communication 53, 54

Tannen, Deborah 146
telegram 112
telegraphic speech 112, 199
tense 28
term
  of abuse 142
  of address 135–43
  of endearment 141
text messaging 66, 112–17
  see also predictive texting
Thatcher, Margaret 153
title 137
T forms and V forms 137
tongue twister 226
top-down processing 226
translation 2, 3, 18
Turing, Alan 4
two-word utterance 197–9
typewriter 118

under-exploitation 114
under-extension 196–7
Universal Grammar 103
universals of language 80

verb 8, 75, 77, 104
  modal 8
  phrasal 77
vernacular 147

V form *see* T forms and V forms
vocabulary
  active vs. passive 79
  size 75, 79–80, 94–5, 226
vowel 117

Weinreich, Max 47
Wernicke's aphasia 248
Wernicke's area 246
wild children 12
Whorf, Benjamin 232, 233
Williams, Venus and Serena 139
wolf children *see* wild children
word 72–7, 80
  blindness 245
  content 114
  deafness 244
  exchange 224
  first 195–7
  frequency 113–14
  grammatical 114
  length 113–14
  recognition 226–7
  see also lexeme, word-form
word-class 8, 108
word endings 106, 107; *see also* case
  marking
word-form 77, 95
word-order 28, 94, 104–7, 117, 129
writing 8
written and spoken language 253, 254

yo-he-ho theory 10

Zipf's Law 113–14